ROUTLEDGE LIBRAI
LABOUR ECOI

CW00486806

Volume 5

TAXATION AND
LABOUR SUPPLY

TAXATION AND LABOUR SUPPLY

Edited by
C. V. BROWN

Routledge
Taylor & Francis Group
LONDON AND NEW YORK

First published in 1981 by George Allen & Unwin Ltd

This edition first published in 2019
by Routledge
2 Park Square, Milton Park, Abingdon, Oxon OX14 4RN

and by Routledge
52 Vanderbilt Avenue, New York, NY 10017

Routledge is an imprint of the Taylor & Francis Group, an informa business

British Library Cataloguing in Publication Data
A catalogue record for this book is available from the British Library

ISBN: 978-0-367-02458-1 (Set)
ISBN: 978-0-429-02526-6 (Set) (ebk)
ISBN: 978-0-367-11149-6 (Volume 5) (hbk)
ISBN: 978-0-367-11153-3 (Volume 5) (pbk)
ISBN: 978-0-429-02509-9 (Volume 5) (ebk)

Publisher's Note
The publisher has gone to great lengths to ensure the quality of this reprint but points out that some imperfections in the original copies may be apparent.

Disclaimer
The publisher has made every effort to trace copyright holders and would welcome correspondence from those they have been unable to trace.

Taxation and Labour Supply

Edited by C. V. BROWN

Contributions by

J. S. Ashworth
C. V. Brown
E. Levin
K. W. Glaister

A. McGlone
R. J. Ruffell
A. M. Ulph
D. T. Ulph

London
GEORGE ALLEN & UNWIN
Boston   Sydney

First published in 1981

GEORGE ALLEN & UNWIN LTD
40 Museum Street, London WC1A 1LU

British Library Cataloguing in Publication Data

Taxation and labour supply.
   1. Labour supply — Great Britain
   2. Taxation — Great Britain
   I. Brown, C. V.
   331.12′0941

   ISBN 0-04-336073-4

Set in 10 on 12 point Press Roman by Gilbert Composing Services, Leighton Buzzard,
and printed in Great Britain
by Biddles Ltd., Guildford, Surrey.

Contents

List of Documents*

*   To save printing costs the documents are contained on microfiche in a pocket at
    the end of this volume.
†   By BMRB.
‡   Other piloting was done in Glasgow — see Chapter 2

Acknowledgements

We are indebted to thousands of people. The largest number are those people we interviewed and who have been promised anonymity. We are grateful to them for providing data. We are also grateful for advice received from a number of individuals in various government departments including the Department of Social Security, Inland Revenue and the Treasury. We have learned a great deal from colleagues both in our own and other universities, including T. Atkinson, R. Barlow, A. J. Culyer, G. Break, W. A. Eltis, D. H. Greenberg, R. Hall, H. Hanusch, P. Hare, J. Heckman, D. Holland, M. Killingsworth, M. Kosters, R. Layard, J. Mirrlees, H. Rosen, T. Stevers, H. Watts, T. Wilson.

We have benefited from comments at seminars held in the following universities: Edinburgh, Glasgow, London, St Andrews, Stirling, Warwick, University of California (Berkeley), University of Wisconsin; and at the following conferences: International Institute of Public Finance, Nice, Belgian Institute of Public Finance, Colston Symposium on Income Distribution, Cambridge Conference on Econometric Studies and Public Finance. We have used computers in the following locations and are grateful for the assistance of their staff and to the sponsoring institutions for the use of heavily subsidized facilities: The Atlas Computer Laboratory and the universities of Edinburgh, Manchester, Newcastle and Stirling. We also owe a general debt to the literature which is only partially acknowledged.

We have benefited from talking to many individuals, and we have learned from editors and referees of journals that have published some of our papers. We are grateful to G. Kalton for advice on sample design, to J. Brand and his team at Strathclyde for assistance with fieldwork at the pilot stage, to the British Market Research Bureau for carrying out the main stage fieldwork. We have had secretarial and graphical assistance from a number of patient people including Miss C. MacSwan, Mrs A. Rocks, Mrs M. Smith and from Mrs C. McIntosh, Mrs E. Bruce and Mrs A. Cowie in producing the typescript for this book. Mrs S. Hewitt has assisted with the editing.

We are grateful to the following for permission to make use of materials:

Economic Journal, for an earlier version of Chapter 4, which was originally published as C. V. Brown and E. Levin (1974), 'The effects of income taxation on overtime: the results of a national survey', *Economic Journal*, vol. 34.

Editor, *Scottish Journal of Political Economy*, for parts of Chapter 5, which originally appeared as C. V. Brown, E. Levin and D. T. Ulph (1976), 'Estimates of labour hours supplied by married male workers in Great Britain', *Scottish Journal of Political Economy*, vol. 23.

Martin Robertson, publisher, for Chapter 14, which appeared originally in slightly different form as the Appendix to Chapter 13 of C. V. Brown and P. M. Jackson (1978), *Public Sector Economics*.

V. Halberstadt and A. J. Culyer, for Chapter 16, which was first published as C. V. Brown, E. Levin and D. T. Ulph (1977), 'Inflation, taxation and income distribution', in V. Halberstadt and A. J. Culyer (eds), *Public Economics and Human Resources* (Paris: Editions Cujas).

Our most important acknowledgement must go to the Social Science Research Council which not only funded the project over a decade but also provided advice from the Economics Committee and its secretary as well as from the Survey unit.

None of the organizations or individuals mentioned is responsible for any of the opinions or facts in the book.

Stirling
September, 1980   C. V. BROWN

Chapter 1

Introduction

This book reports on more than a decade of SSRC sponsored research on the effects of taxation on the supply of labour. The data is from a national survey in which over 2,000 weekly-paid workers were interviewed. Parts One and Two of the book discuss the data and provide our labour supply estimates. Part Three discusses some of the implications of labour supply estimates.

The importance of labour supply estimates hardly needs stressing: they are obviously important to an understanding of (1) the effects of the tax/ transfer system on the amounts of work done by various groups of individuals, (2) the distribution of income both before and after tax, (3) the size of the work force and the level of unemployment, (4) the level of national income and (5) the level of welfare.[1]

ORIGIN OF THE PROJECT

My own interest in the effects of taxation on incentives started accidentally soon after my arrival in Britain in the mid-1960s. Driving home one evening I decided to work out the net income I would receive for some extra-mural lecturing. While I knew that the standard rate of tax was 8s 3d and that earned income relief was two-ninths, the resulting sum was not an easy one to do in my head. It occurred to me that some people might ignore earned income relief and assume that their marginal tax rate was 8s 3d (41.25 per cent) rather than 6s 5d (32.08 per cent). This led to an interest in misconceptions. It was fairly easy to establish that there were widespread misconceptions about tax (Brown, 1968) and this raised the question of whether these misconceptions might affect behaviour.

Work on the project has evolved in a series of stages. The first was in a mini survey on misconceptions which was supported by the Carnegie Foundation and confined to the Glasgow area. Second was a pilot/ feasibility study for the present project, which was supported by the SSRC and was again confined to the Glasgow area. The third (main) stage is the subject of this book and was again supported by the SSRC. For this stage a national survey was conducted in 1971 in which over 2,000 weekly-paid workers were interviewed.

RESEARCH STRATEGY

This section outlines our initial strategy and compares it with what we have done. Research on labour supply has changed dramatically since the strategy for this project was initially formulated in the late 1960s. In the 1960s econometric work on labour supply was in its infancy and many of the problems discussed in subsequent chapters were not known. The initial research strategy involved the use of two largely independent methods of analysis. One, the most common at the time (following Break, 1957), was to start from people's perceptions of their behaviour and then to examine these statements for plausibility. The other approach that we planned (which has in the event become the dominant one, both in terms of our work and in the work of others) has been to examine behaviour directly using econometric techniques. It was hoped that if the approaches gave consistent results this would increase confidence in the findings.

This decision to use two approaches has had a significant effect on our work. In the interview approach it is important to have ways of checking people's statements about the effects of taxation on their behaviour. This meant that certain information had to be collected before questions about the effects of taxation could be asked. This in turn meant that (in general) only one interview could be attempted per household. The obvious cost of this approach is that we have inadequate data for household models. While the two approaches have not led to noticeably inconsistent results, the difficulties of comparison were not fully recognized which explains why we have said very little about it.

While in very broad plan this strategy has been followed through, there have been many changes. These have in part resulted from the rapid progress in the subject already referred to. A number of early ideas have not worked out. An attempt to improve the accuracy of our data by checking income data with employers was abandoned (see Chapter 2). Most disappointing to me personally is that we have made no significant progress in the study of misconceptions. On the other hand we have achieved a number of things beyond our original intentions. The detailed econometric developments outlined in Part Two were not envisaged and our initial plans did not include the discussion of the implications of the work that is the subject of Part Three.

PLAN OF THE BOOK

Part One – The Data

One respect in which my own view has not changed is the importance of good data. While there are econometric techniques that can correct for some kinds of data deficiencies these techniques are limited in their effectiveness. A great deal of the effort within the project has gone into collection and handling of data. Despite this effort the data has serious deficiencies and we try to make the reader fully aware of the problems. We believe that one of our most important findings is that estimates (particularly of the elasticity of substitution) are very sensitive to model specification and to data quality. Even though our data falls short of the ideal by a large margin, it is very much better than many of the data sets used for labour supply estimates (many of which were collected for other purposes). In particular our data is sufficiently rich that we have been able to experiment with a number of alternative ways of defining budget constraints. Chapter 2 discusses the sample design and the questionnaire, and Chapter 3 contains a general discussion of data quality. For the benefit of readers who may wish to examine our data base more closely we have included on microfiche copies of the questionnaire, full details of the sample design and copies of the fieldwork documents.

Part Two – The Results
Part Two contains our labour supply estimates. The chapters within this part appear in the order in which the work was done (except for Chapter 9 which was written about the same time as Chapter 6). While the chapters are largely self-contained, Chapters 6 – 9 are to some extent dependent on Chapter 5 and do not repeat many definitional matters discussed there.

We hope that these chapters make a useful contribution to the analysis of the labour supply of British workers. However, all of the findings should be treated as provisional. There are a variety of reasons (discussed in detail below) for this including truncation bias, small cell and incomplete response bias; numbers which are small relative to the techniques employed, lack of adequate household data, and measurement problems – particularly for non-employment income. It is likely to be some years until firmly established labour supply estimates are available for British workers.[2]

Part Three – Implications
Part Three of the book consists of six almost wholly independent chapters which explore several implications of labour supply elasticities. While some of these chapters make reference to the findings in Part Two, they are not dependent on these findings. Taken together they not only suggest the importance of labour supply estimates, but also the large amount of work that remains to be done in theoretical model building before the implications of labour supply estimates can be fully understood.

NOTES: CHAPTER 1

1 It is perhaps worth reminding those readers who are not professional economists that an increase in labour supply and an increase in welfare are not the same thing – most importantly because welfare includes leisure.
2 Since the autumn of 1979 we have been working on a new labour supply study, financed by HM Treasury, in which the Office of Population Censuses and Surveys will collect on our behalf a larger data set which we hope will overcome the deficiencies of our 1971 data set.

PART ONE   THE DATA

Chapter 2

Sample Selection and Questionnaire Design

This chapter contains summary information about sample selection and fieldwork, together with a discussion of the design of the questionnaire. The Appendix (documents on microfiche) contains a full description of the sample design, of the fieldwork procedures and a copy of the questionnaire. Where possible a distribution of responses is given for each question for both men and women. It is hoped that this will give the interested reader a feel for the data. Preparation for all the matters discussed in this chapter occurred more or less simultaneously but most of our time in the early stages was spent on the development of the questionnaire, which is discussed at the end of the chapter.

It was recognised at the start of the project that different groups of workers such as managers, professional people and self-employed business-men may respond in rather different ways to changes in taxes to the response of 'ordinary' workers. 'Ordinary' workers are more likely to be paid by the hour and frequently there is a premium hourly wage if more than a certain number of hours are worked. One of our earliest decisions was that it would be impractical to study all groups of workers simultaneously. We decided to concentrate on workers rather than managers because we thought it would be easier to measure both their wage rates and their labour supply. We also decided to concentrate on people who were at work. We recognized at the time that this decision meant ignoring the participation decision but we did not realize it would potentially cause truncation bias (see Chapter 3).

Having decided to study workers our next problem was to define what we meant by the term 'worker'. We required a definition that was arbitrary rather than judgmental as the decision about eligibility had to be made quickly on the doorstep by a large number of professional interviewers.

We noted that managers tended to be paid monthly and workers weekly. This was a simple, clear criteria which in the event worked well. It avoids the truncation bias which would have occurred if we had used income as our criteria for inclusion. However it excludes workers who happen to be paid fortnightly or monthly.

We also had to decide what we meant by at work. We wanted to include both full-time and part-time workers but wanted to exclude retired and other people who perhaps worked only for the occasional hour. The definition we adopted was people who usually work eight or more hours a week and who had been to work sometime in the seven days prior to interview. This decision leads to truncation bias. To reduce costs we decided not to interview in Northern Ireland or North of the Caledonian Canal in Scotland.

Our sample population is therefore weekly-paid employees in Great Britain South of the Caledonian Canal who usually work at least eight hours a week and who had been employed in the last seven days.

BRITISH MARKET RESEARCH BUREAU

The number of interviews contemplated required the use of professional interviewers. Given that the services of Government Social Survey (as the Office of Population Censuses and Surveys was then called) were not available to us, this meant making use of a market research agency. Extensive enquiries revealed a consensus that there were two agencies which could be expected to reach satisfactory standards on the complex fieldwork required. The two agencies were asked to estimate for the work and, after consultation with the SSRC, the British Market Research Bureau (BMRB) was awarded the contract. BMRB's contract included sample design, drawing of the sample, production of all necessary documents[1] (based on a fully piloted draft questionnaire that we provided), the fieldwork staff, coding, punching and the production of the data set on cards. There was extensive consultations at all stages of these procedures.

SAMPLE DESIGN

After advice from Professor G. Kalton, the following self-weighting sample design was produced. Two hundred constituencies were sampled. This was the BMRB master sample which was selected with probability proportional to size (PPS) after ranking constituencies within standard regions by the proportion of labour vote. Two areas in each constituency were selected by PPS and twenty-four addresses in areas were selected again by PPS.

The names of all electors at each selected address were then listed and two numbers were assigned to that address. The first number, called the interval number, was equal to the number of electors at the address and the second number, the starting number, was a random number between 1 and the interval number.

This information was then used to establish which people should be interviewed. This sift procedure was carried out by the interviewer and any responsible adult at the address. She first listed all the people at the address and then eliminated all those not in the population. Next all those in the population were listed in strict alphabetical order. The interviewers then attempted to interview the person whose name appeared against the starting number. The interval number was then added to the starting number and in the few cases where a name appeared against this number a second (or third) interview was attempted. On cases where multiple interviews were required these were conducted simultaneously.

FIELDWORK

After final piloting of the questionnaire five briefing sessions – lasting six hours each – were held between 29 September and 6 October 1971. The main fieldwork was undertaken between 4 October and 6 November 1971. The resulting response rate was regarded as unsatisfactory (see Chapter 3) and a second fieldwork period was held from 6 December to 24 December 1971. A detailed discussion of the response rate and of the quality of the data is contained in Chapter 3.

STRATEGY FOR ANALYSIS AND QUESTIONNAIRE DESIGN

The important strategic decision that affected questionnaire design was that we wished to use two largely independent techniques of analysis. The technique that was most commonly used at the time was the interview approach in which respondents are asked how they believe they are affected by tax. Following the example of Break (1957) it seemed important not to take claimed effects of tax at their face value. We therefore needed information against which to check the plausibility of claims. The reliability of this check information would be higher if we collected it before taxation was mentioned. This meant that taxation could not be mentioned until well into the interview. It also had the important effect (see Chapter 4) of restricting us to one interview per household, because if we took more than one interview (other than simultaneously) it could be clear to all but the first respondent that taxation was our main interest.

When the broad guidelines for the project were determined a decade ago, the econometric study of labour supply was in its infancy. It seems worth trying to reconstruct the way we saw the problem at that time. The simple theory of labour supply was of course well known, but the full implications of non-linearities in budget constraint were not well known – at least to us! Nevertheless it did seem obvious to us[2] even at that time that full knowledge of individual budget constraints was important. The original motivation for the project had arisen from a concern about the possibility that misconceptions about taxation reduced work effort (Brown, 1968). Because of this concern we wished to try to construct both perceived budget constraints and actual budget constraints. This concern over perceptions sensitized us to the possibility that people – even when they were being frank and honest – would provide us with incorrect data. Consequently we built a large number of checks into our procedures. Some of these were simple such as asking for all three of gross income, deductions and net income when any two would determine the third. We also asked for data on wage rates in a variety of ways. Thus all of the following questions were designed to provide alternative definitions of perceived or objective net wage rates: the basic wage rate (Q49b); the overtime premia (Q20); second job income, deductions and hours (Q42-44); bonus earnings (Q58); the marginal wage rate before (Q61a) and after (Q61b) deductions; the perceived marginal rate of income tax (Q75a) and of other taxes (Q76 and 77). We asked a number of questions on the related issue of knowledge and perceptions of the tax system.[3]

We wanted to have very accurate income data to help us to construct objective budget constraints and this led us to attempt to collect income data from employers. We asked respondents to sign a letter (reproduced in the Appendix, p.64) authorizing their employers to release certain specified information to us. Seventy-two per cent of respondents did sign the letter which was a higher proportion than many people thought we could achieve. Despite this relative success we abandoned the attempt to use this information. The exercise failed in our view because in a number of cases the information from the employer was clearly wrong. For example, in some cases net income exceeded gross income even though various deductions were shown. There were other less glaring arithmetical errors. In other cases the information *appeared* implausible and we *guessed* the respondent gave us correct information and the employer gave us incorrect information. We started from the assumption that the employers would give us more accurate information than the employee. We ended believing that the reverse was often the case. We might have used the employer's information in selected cases but this would have meant our making judgements which could have introduced a bias.

It is perhaps worth recording the impression that our respondents rarely deliberately misled us. We believe that apparently inconsistent and/or wrong information is due either to people not understanding particular questions or to fallible memories. When people did not want us to know something they usually refused to answer the question. A related impression is that given the complexity of the questionnaire it would have been difficult to consistently mislead even if there had been a wish to do so. If people understand that there is a good reason for asking questions they are remarkably co-operative.

We were also particularly interested in influences on preferences many of which are not narrowly economic in character. We recognized the importance of needs and put in questions about household composition and fixed financial commitments such as mortgages and HP. Similar considerations led to the insertion of questions about industry, region, social class, education, etc.[4]

It seemed plausible to hypothesize that people who enjoyed their work would work longer than those that did not. A review[5] of the literature of job satisfaction led us to two conclusions: first that job satisfaction was a multi-dimensional concept and second we accepted the view of Robinson, Athanasious and Head (1969, p.101) that –

> the instrument which appears to us to have the best credentials is the *Job Description Index*. Lengthy extensive and competent research went into the construction of this instrument . . .

The Job Description Index (JDI) is fully described in Smith *et al.* (1965). It measures job satisfaction on five scales that relate to work (the job itself), pay, promotion, people (at work) and supervisors. Each scale measures the relevant aspect of job satisfaction by asking people to agree or disagree with a variety of statements about their work. For example, in the work scale respondents are asked to agree or disagree with statements such as their work is 'fascinating, routine, satisfying, boring'. The full scales are reproduced in the Appendix.

The remaining questions were designed to test various hypotheses such as preferences for work being formed by peer group pressure at work or at home ('keeping up with the Joneses'). We even put in a question about whether the mothers/women in the household had previously worked because we were told that had proved to be the most important determinant of how much work married women did outside the home.

A great deal of effort went into the construction of the questionnaire – some fourteen versions of it were produced in total. Almost all of these were informally pretested by ourselves and/or by professional interviewers and one version was formally pretested for us by the Survey Research Unit at Strathclyde University. We found some difficulty 'translating' the concepts we wished to know into terms people could understand. We recognized at the outset that words such as marginal would not be understood. But we had to learn that even terms such as average and percentage presented difficulties. We gave a lot of thought to question sequence but were constrained by having to ask questions about taxation after asking check questions. We also wanted to ask 'threat' questions such as income questions towards the end of the interview. We found that people enjoyed being asked attitudinal questions more than factual questions, and so we tried to produce a question order that had variety in it. This appeared to work well. Despite our very long questionnaire – about 1¼ hours on average – it seemed to be well received. We think this is the result of the very considerable effort that went into its development. It is very easy to underestimate the difficulties in questionnaire design.

NOTES: CHAPTER 2

1   The documentation comprised address lists, contact sheets, the questionnaire, including five self-completion sections, prompt cards, appointment cards (for respondents), a letter explaining the purpose of the survey, a thankyou letter, a letter to employers (see later in text), University of Stirling pens (as gifts to respondents) and detailed interviewer instructions. Samples of these documents are in the appendices.
2   Judging from some of the questions asked in some of the negative income tax experiments in the USA at about the same time these points were not particularly obvious.
3   See Brown and Levin (1972) and Brown and Jackson (1978) for findings on knowledge of the tax system.
4   It is worth noting that 84 per cent of the sample left school before they were 16 and only 2 per cent remained at school after they were 18. Given this small variation it is implausible to expect that years of formal schooling can explain a large proportion of the variations in wage rates. This may appear to be inconsistent with the findings (e.g. of Layard and Zabalza, 1979) that education is important in explaining earnings. A possible reconciliation is that our population is confined to workers whereas other studies include salaried occupations. It may be that education influences earnings through choice of occupations. It should be recognized that typically salaried workers do not have hourly wage rates. This implies that attempts to explain wage rates as a function of education may be inappropriate.
5   By E. Levin.

Chapter 3

Data Quality

This chapter looks at the evidence on the quality of the data. The main question that is explored is the extent to which the data is representative of the population studied (weekly-paid workers). There are clear reasons why the data can be expected *not* to be representative of the *general* population. Neverthless it is of interest to compare briefly the characteristics of the sample with the characteristics of the general population.

SMALL CELL BIAS

The major part of this chapter is taken up with a discussion of non-response bias. While there is some limited evidence of bias it does not appear particularly strong. Nevertheless we cannot pretend that our results can be assumed to be representative of weekly paid workers. This is because there are two related, but conceptually distinct, additional sources of bias which may be termed small cell bias and incomplete data bias. If the numbers in a particular cell are too small (relative to the requirements of the technique being used) researchers are faced with a choice between a number of alternatives, all of which are to some extent unsatisfactory. They can: (1) proceed with the chosen analysis recognizing that the estimates may be unreliable; (2) amalgamate cells even when there are theoretical or statistical objections to doing so; (3) omit the cells with small numbers from the analysis. There are examples of each of these strategies in this book. Each introduces the possibility of bias. An example may assist.

Much of our analysis has been done on families where the respondent only or the respondent and spouse only are workers. We justified this decision (see Chapter 5) on the argument that the individual labour supply model is particularly inappropriate where there are additional workers. We have not analysed married workers' behaviour in households with additional workers because the numbers were too small. This means that at best our results apply to the sub-sample of our population without additional workers. To generalize from the sub-population studied to all married workers would be a form of small cell bias.

11

INCOMPLETE RESPONSE BIAS

As our techniques have become more sophisticated the data requirements have grown more complex and as a consequence our numbers have fallen. The combination of eliminating the smallest cells and incomplete inform-ation in other cells has meant that the numbers are so small, in absolute terms, as to call into question the reliability of the answers. Even if the numbers are not too small absolutely they are such a small proportion of the sample that they may be unrepresentative.

This problem of incomplete response bias, in principle, is the same as the problem of non-response bias. Providing absolute numbers are high enough a low response rate does not matter if respondents do not differ in any significant way from non-respondents. It is usually impossible to know the answer to this question which is why high response rates are im-portant. While we do not *know* if those we have studied differ from those we did not (except in a few cases where we have been able to repeat the same analysis on different samples) one would not expect behaviour to be the same. It seems reasonable to hypothesize that people who know a great deal of information about their budget constraints would be more likely to respond to changes in their budget constraint than people who know very little. Table 3.1 illustrates the way our numbers have shrunk (an analysis of the reasons for the loss is given in Chapter 7; see Tables 7.1, 7.5 and 7.9). In our analysis of households in Chapter 9 we end up analysing only 88 married men, or 10 per cent of all married men. If our 70 per cent response rate (see below) applies equally to married men this means we have analysed only 7 per cent of the sample of eligible married men. In retrospect it

Table 3.1

	Number Married Men	*Chapter*
Total	924	—
Interview approach	909[a]	4
Linearized budget constraint	505	—
Linearized budget constraint (2 workers only)	434	5
Endogeneity I	335	6
Endogeneity II	213	8

[a] The number is probably higher than this. In total the interview approach was able to make use of 2139 of a weighted total of 2153 cases. The number in the table assumes that all of the missing cases are married men.

seems clear that we should have made a greater effort to keep numbers up by calculating[1] answers to certain questions when the respondent did not give an answer.

RESPONSE RATES

The main fieldwork took place between 4 October and 6 November 1971. A total of 1913 interviews were completed and 66.3 per cent of those eligible were interviewed. We were disappointed by this response rate and after considerable discussion it was agreed that a second wave of fieldwork should take place. In this second wave, which lasted from 6 to 24 December 1971, fieldwork addresses were reissued for 103 constituencies. A different interviewer did the second wave interviews. The 103 constituencies contacted in the second round are starred in the list of constituencies in the Appendix. Unlike wave 1, the probability of selection in wave 2 was not equal. The resulting sampling fractions for the 155 interviews achieved in wave 2 are given in Table 3.2 (and further details is given in the Appendix).

Table 3.2   *Actual and Weighted Numbers on Wave 2 Interviews*

	1 in 4	1 in 2	1 in 9	1 in 1	Total
Actual	6	52	51	46	155
Weighted	24	104	66	46	240

The analysis in Chapter 4 uses weighted numbers while the analysis in all the other chapters employs unweighted data. The total number of interviews from waves 1 and 2 is 2008 actual interviews with the weighted total being 2153.

The combined response for waves 1 and 2 is given in Table 3.3. (A similar analysis of wave 1 and a reconciliation of wave 1 and wave 2 results are given in the Appendix.) It can be seen that 266 of the 9593 addresses issued were demolished, empty or not traced. Nearly 300 addresses were discounted because of non-contact, refusals, etc. This left over 9000 addresses co-operating at the sift or contact stage, of which over two-thirds had no eligible person (as defined in Chapter 2). Somewhat under 3000 people were eligible for interview, of whom slightly over 2000 were interviewed giving a response rate of 69.7 per cent *of those eligible* for interview. Some of the non-respondents at the sift stage presumably would have been eligible for interview. If the proportion of eligibles was the same for respondents and non-respondents at the sift stage this would imply that a further 98 people would have been eligible and this gives an adjusted response rate of 67.5 per cent.

NON-RESPONSE BIAS

We had hoped to achieve a higher response rate than was in fact achieved and so are concerned about the possibility of non-response bias. We are unaware of any national statistics relating to weekly paid workers so we have attempted two other ways of testing for non-response

Table 3.3   *Comparison of Waves 1 and 2*

| | | Wave 2 | |
		Unweighted	*Weighted*
Demographic Characteristics			
1	Age	_[a]	. —
2	Sex	—	—
3	Number in house	—	—
4	Number of adults	—	*(more with only 1 or 2 adults)[b]
5	Children in house	—	—
6	Social class	—	—
Answers to selected questions			
1	Main job – hours worked	—	—
2	Second job – hours worked	—	—
3	Gross pay	—	—
4	Household income	—	—
5	Subjective marginal rate of tax	—	—
6	Utility of work	—	—
7	Need for income without overtime	—	—
8	Family need for income	—	—
9	Soon get bored	—	—
10	Wish more leisure	*(more disagree)	*(more disagree)
11	Claimed effect of tax on overtime	—	—
12	High deductions mean I work less overtime	—	*(fewer agree)
13	High deductions mean I work more overtime	—	—
14	Overtime summary	—	*(see text)

[a] Dash indicates wave 2 not significantly different from wave 1 at 5 per cent level.
[b] Asterisk indicates wave 2 significantly different from wave 1 at 5 per cent level.

bias. The first method is based on an analysis of waves 1 and 2. It is assumed that those interviewed in wave 2, who were non-respondents in wave 1, may share some of the characteristics of those who were non-respondents in both waves. Thus if the characteristics of people in waves 1 and 2 are substantially different this implies that the true non-respondents may differ from respondents. We also have a limited amount of subjective information about some non-respondents.

Table 3.3 shows whether or not the results on wave 2 differ from the results on wave 1. This exercise has been done for both the weighted versions of wave 2. Where there is no significant difference a dash is shown. An asterisk indicates a significant difference at the 5 per cent level (with the material in parentheses indicating the way in which wave 2 differed from wave 1).

As far as the demographic data is concerned the only significant difference was in the number of adults in the household. The most noticeable difference is that in wave 1, 4 per cent of households had 1 adult (while in the weighted version of wave 2, 9 per cent had 1 adult). The corresponding figures for 2, 3 and 4+ adult households are: 2 adult, 48 per cent W1, 44 per cent W2; 3 adult, 26 per cent W1, 26 per cent W2; 4+ adult, 22 per cent W1, 20 per cent W2. This suggests there may be some under-representation of 1 adult households. At the end of wave 1 there were 208 addresses at which no reply had been received and the corresponding number after wave 2 was 115. These 115 addresses may well have contained a disproportionate number of 1 adult households who, for that reason, were difficult to contact.

There is no significant difference between waves 1 and 2 for most of the variables tested. For the factual questions – hours, second jobs and income – there is no significant difference. There is however a significant difference in the replies to some of the attitudinal questions. In the second wave a higher proportion (35 per cent compared to 29 per cent) *disagreed* with the statement that they wanted more leisure. A lower proportion in wave 2 (23 per cent versus 34 per cent) agreed with the statement that higher deductions made them work less overtime. Finally, the proportion of people in wave 2 (weighted) who said they sometimes worked overtime fell while the proportion claiming that they always worked overtime and the proportion claiming they never worked overtime both *fell*. It is difficult to discern any very consistent pattern of bias from these few cases, but it is possible on this evidence that non-respondents would have thought they had a strong income effect.

UNEMPLOYMENT AND NON-RESPONSE

It was suggested to us that non-response might be associated with unemployment; the hypothesis was that people in areas of high unemployment would be less willing to be interviewed about (their) work than people in areas where unemployment was low. To test this hypothesis we plotted non-response (excluding those ineligible for interview) against unemployment. The graph (not reproduced) appears to suggest a negative relationship contrary to the hypothesis.[2]

COMPARISON WITH 1971 CENSUS DATA

Given that our population consists of weekly-paid employees it clearly cannot be expected that it will be representative of the general population. Nevertheless it is of interest to see how our sample compares with the general population. Tables 3.4 – 3.6 provide comparisons of social class, industry and occupation between our data and the 10 per cent 1971 Census data. (In every case our data is significantly different statistically from the 1971 Census data). As expected our data contains fewer professional and managerial workers and a higher percentage of skilled and partly skilled workers. While the differences revealed in the tables

Table 3.4   *Social Class*

	Stirling 1971	*(10%) Census 1971*
Men		
Professional, etc., occupations	1	5
Intermediate occupations	3	17
Skilled occupations – nonmanual	6	11
Skilled occupations – manual	62	37
Partly skilled occupations	22	17
Unskilled occupations	5	8
Others (incl. Armed Forces)	1	5
Women		
Professional, etc., occupations	0	1
Intermediate occupations	5	14
Skilled occupations – nonmanual	37	30
Skilled occupations – manual	20	8
Partly skilled occupations	27	20
Unskilled occupations	11	6
Others (incl. Armed Forces)	0	22

Table 3.5 *Industry*

		Men Stirling	10% Census	Women Stirling	10% Census
1	Farmers, foresters, fishermen	4	4	1	1
2	Miners and quarrymen	2	2	0	0
3	Gas, Coke and chemical makers	1	1	0	0
4	Glass and ceramics makers	1	0	1	0
5	Furnace, forge, etc.	3	1	0	0
6	Electrical and electronics	5	3	3	1
7	Engineering and allied	23	16	6	3
8	Woodworkers	3	3	0	0
9	Leatherworkers	1	0	1	1
10	Textile workers	2	1	3	2
11	Clothing workers	1	0	5	4
12	Food, drink and tobacco	2	2	4	1
13	Paper and printing	3	1	3	1
14	Makers of other things	2	1	2	1
15	Construction workers	4	3	0	0
16	Painters and decorators	2	2	0	0
17	Drivers	3	2	0	0
18	Labourers	5	7	1	2
19	Transport and communications	13	8	2	2
20	Warehousemen, etc.	3	3	4	3
21	Clerical workers	3	7	20	27
22	Sales workers	4	7	14	12
23	Services, sport, etc.	4	6	27	22
24	Administrators, managers	1	5	0	1
25	Professional, technical, artists	2	11	4	12
26	Armed Forces	0	2	0	0
27	Inadequately described	1	2	0	4

are not unexpected they do drive home the point that our data does not represent the general population.

TRUNCATION BIAS

Whenever variables are restricted there is the possibility of truncation bias. The problem arises because of the random error in the model. The actual model tested is unlikely ever to explain all of the variation in the dependent variable, and typically in cross-section work explains considerably under half. The remaining variation in hours is attributed to random error: If this error is truly random it reduces the efficiency of the resulting estimates but does not bias them. However, if the error is

Table 3.6   *Occupation*

		Men *Stirling*	*10%* *Census*	Women *Stirling*	*10%* *Census*
1	Agriculture, forestry, fishing	3	3	1	1
2	Mining and quarrying	3	2	0	0
3	Food, drink and tobacco	3	3	8	3
4	Coal and petroleum	1	0	0	1
5	Chemicals and allied	2	2	1	2
6	Metal	6	3	1	1
7	Mechanical engineering	8	6	3	2
8	Instrument engineering	1	1	1	1
9	Electrical engineering	6	3	5	4
10	Shipbuilding, etc.	2	1	0	0
11	Vehicles	5	5	2	1
12	Metals (not 6)	2	3	2	2
13	Textiles	2	1	4	3
14	Leather, etc.	0	0	1	0
15	Clothing and footwear	2	1	5	4
16	Bricks, glass, etc.	2	2	1	1
17	Timber, furniture, etc.	3	2	2	1
18	Paper, printing, etc.	4	3	3	2
19	Other manufacturing	2	1	2	1
20	Construction	7	10	1	1
21	Gas, electricity and water	2	2	0	1
22	Transport and communication	12	9	3	3
23	Distributive trades	7	10	17	18
24	Insurance, banking, etc.	1	3	2	5
25	Professional and scientific	3	7	13	21
26	Miscellaneous services	5	7	15	15
27	Public administration and defence	6	7	5	5
28	Inadequately described	1	1	1	1

not random bias will occur. Figure 3.1 illustrates two examples of truncation bias. A particularly severe type occurs when income is used as a criterion for inclusion in the study. In the figure each dot represents an assumed observation. There are several observations at each wage because of random error. The true supply curve that would be plotted from this data is drawn in S_t. Suppose now that income was used as a criterion for sample selection and that all those with income in excess of Y_1 were omitted from the sample. The observations in the study would then lie below Y_1 in the diagram and the observed supply surve (S_o) would have a very different elasticity.

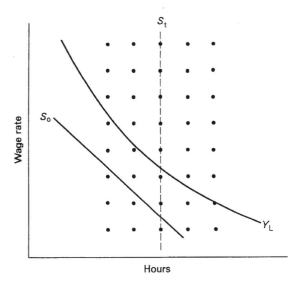

Fig. 3.1

We have a problem that is similar in principle but, we believe, less serious in practice. We have omitted people who worked less than eight hours. It may be noted that if the true supply were totally inelastic, as is assumed in Figure 3.1, omitting observations with low hours would affect the position of the observed supply curve but not its elasticity. This is relevant to the question of how important truncation bias is in practice because most evidence suggests that married men's supply curves appear to be nearly inelastic while those of married women have positive elasticity. This suggests that truncation bias might be more important for women than for men.

Table 3.7   *National Percentages of workers with low hours*

Hours worked	Women aged 18 and over including those whose pay was affected by absence	Men aged 21 and over including those whose pay was affected by absence
	(%)	(%)
Between 0 and 8	3.1	0.4
Between 8 and 16	5.8	1.4

Source: Department of Employment.

Another indication of the possible extent of truncation bias is given by the figures in Table 3.7. It can be seen that less than half of 1 per cent of men over 20 worked less than eight hours even allowing for absences. The corresponding figure for women is 3 per cent which suggests the problem may be more serious for women.

A related difficulty arises even when people who have worked zero hours are included in the sample. Random error cannot cause people to work fewer than zero hours which means that random errors may cause a cluster of observations at zero hours. Given lower participation rates for women the problem for women may be more severe than for men.

SUMMARY

There is little evidence of non-response bias; however, small cell bias and incomplete response bias may well be important. Truncation bias will exist in principle. The limited evidence we have looked at on truncation bias suggest it is more likely to be important for women than for men.

The extent to which the variables succeed or fail in measuring the concepts we were seeking is discussed in many of the chapters in Part Two and especially in Chapter 5.

NOTES: CHAPTER 3

1   For example, if any two of gross income, net income and deductions are given the third may be calculated. With more complex examples it is possible to calculate various parts of the budget constraint.
2   It was also suggested to us *after the graph was drawn* that London, Wales, the North and Scotland were all special cases, and if they were eliminated the hypothesis tends to be confirmed.

PART TWO   THE RESULTS

Chapter 4

The Interview Approach

This study of taxation and the incentive to work covers two distinct approaches. In one of these, which may be exemplified by the work of Break (1957), the object is to discover whether the individual claims that he is suffering an incentive or disincentive effect and to see whether this claim is plausible. In the other approach, the object is to explain work effort directly by inferring their reactions to tax from a cross-section analysis of a group of workers. Chapters 5 – 9 are devoted to this latter approach.

We designed our study so that we could use both of these approaches on a single body of data in the belief that if both approaches, which are almost wholly independent, gave similar results, then the results themselves would carry greater conviction. In the present chapter we concentrate exclusively on the first of these approaches, using overtime hours as the dependent variable. In the remaining chapters of the book the dependent variable is all paid hours. Overtime hours *exclude* both second job hours and hours worked at the basic rate. All paid hours is a preferable measure, but we used overtime hours because we had a question which directly asked respondents how tax had affected their overtime working. As explained below this choice had little effect on the results. However since the original version of this chapter appeared it has become clear that the term 'overtime' was interpreted in a variety of ways by women who frequently work part-time. For some women 'overtime' hours are hours worked at a premium hourly rate, for other women 'overtime' hours means any hours in excess of what they regard as normal. For example, a woman who worked two hours a day five days a week serving school dinners said she worked 'overtime' when she worked an extra two hours to cover for a colleague's illness. For other women the term 'overtime' was not relevant. For this reason the present version refers to men only.

We begin by describing the questionnaire in Section I, and in Section

II we examine the proportion of workers who say that taxation (1) has made them work more overtime, (2) made them work less overtime and (3) has not affected their behaviour. We study the position for all workers taken together and also for various demographic groups, since (for example) the effects are very different for single men and for married men with a family. We then go on to see whether the claimed effects are plausible in Section III, and in Section IV we examine the effects of constraints. We also indicate whether those who claim to work more or less overtime do in fact work a larger or smaller number of overtime hours than those who claim no effect, and in Section V we discuss the net effect. Since the study reveals that a very large proportion of workers claim no effect from taxation, we study in Section VI some of the reasons for this, such as their not being regular tax payers, or their inability to vary the number of hours which they work.

I   THE QUESTIONNAIRE

In our survey some 2,000 weekly-paid workers were asked detailed questions about their work behaviour. The introductory statement made it clear that the survey was about work but it did not mention taxation. The interviews lasted on average about an hour and a quarter. In the first part the subject of taxation was never mentioned by the interviewer. Topics included what the respondent liked and disliked about his job; whether or not his wife worked; how much overtime he worked; what he did in the way of do-it-yourself activities, etc. There were quite a number of open-ended questions where the respondent was asked to explain why he did or did not do a particular thing. The respondent could of course mention taxation, but most did not.

After obtaining this background information and before bringing up the subject of taxation the respondent was handed a self-completion section in which he had to agree or disagree with twenty-eight statements on a five-point scale. The fourth of these statements was 'High deductions from my pay mean I don't work much overtime because it is not worth while.' The nineteenth stated 'High deductions from my pay mean that I have to work overtime to make ends meet.' When the respondent had filled in this self-completion questionnaire the interviewer said ' . . . would you look at your answers to statements four and nineteen and explain why you answered as you did to these two statements'. The respondent was thus forced to recognise that the effect of taxation and other forms of deduction could work in either direction. A large number of questions about the effects of taxation on hours, effort, second jobs, etc., followed, and there were questions about knowledge of the tax system. Right at the end of the questionnaire the respondent was given a final self-completion questionnaire. This referred to possible types of effect from taxation and the respondent was asked to agree with one of three statements about each. In one case the choices were

(1)   Tax has made me work more overtime   (abbreviated 'more'),
(2)   Doesn't apply/Neither   (abbreviated 'neither').
(3)   Tax has made me work less overtime   (abbreviated 'less').

The replies form the starting point for the present analysis.

II   CLAIMS ABOUT TAXATION

The main results are shown in Table 4.1. In this section we concentrate on the claimed effects which are shown in part I of the table. The layout of the table is as follows. In the left-hand column we show various demographic groups: all men, single men, married men without children, and married men with children. Next we show the claim: 'less', 'neither' and 'more' overtime. In the remainder of the table we show for each section the number and percentage of people making each claim, and the average number of overtime hours worked 'last' week by this group of people. The table also indicates when the number of hours worked by those claiming an effect differs from the number of hours worked by those claiming no effect by an amount which is statistically significant at the 5 per cent level.

Perhaps the most interesting result of all is that 74 per cent of the men claimed no effect from taxation. It can be seen that 11 per cent claimed tax made them work less overtime and 15 per cent that it made them work more overtime. Judging by the large percentage of 'neithers' and the fact that those claiming opposite effects would tend to cancel each other out, it would appear that the aggregate net effect is small. We estimate that the aggregate net effect lies between + 0.3 and + 0.8 overtime hours per week for men, that is, an increase, somewhere between 8 per cent and 20 per cent in overtime, equivalent in very round terms to an increase of about 1 per cent in hours worked. When we look at men by marital status and the presence or absence of children the claims change, though the proportion claiming 'neither' is always by far the biggest. The proportion of single men claiming 'less' (13 per cent) is greater than the percentage claiming 'more' (10 per cent). For married men without children the

Table 4.1 Claimed effects of tax on overtime hours and actual mean overtime hours worked

Demographic group	Claim	I. All claims			II. High plausible[c]			III. High plausible and unconstrained[c]		
		(N)	(%)[a]	Mean over-time (hrs)	(N)	(%)[a]	Mean over-time (hrs)	(N)	(%)[a]	Mean over-time (hrs)
All men	Less	149	11	3.5	88	7	3.4	61	9	2.8[b]
	Neither	987	74	4.2	987	79	4.2	470	69	6.2
	More	205	15	9.0	173	14	10.6	151	22	10.6[b]
Single men	Less	44	13	2.5	25	8	2.8	19	12	2.3
	Neither	259	77	2.2	259	84	2.2	123	75	3.5
	More	32	10	3.1	24	8	3.8[a]	23	14	4.0
Married men without children	Less	54	12	3.8	33	8	4.1	22	10	3.1
	Neither	339	73	4.3	339	78	4.3	153	68	5.9
	More	69	15	9.9[b]	60	14	11.3[b]	51	23	11.2[b]
Married men with children	Less	45	9	3.8	26	6	2.3[a]	17	6	1.8[b]
	Neither	353	72	5.6	353	77	5.6	182	68	8.6
	More	94	19	9.5[b]	80	17	11.2[b]	69	26	11.1[a]

[a] Significant at 5 per cent.
[b] Significant at 1 per cent.
The significance test on the difference between means compares the 'less' ('more') mean of overtime hours worked with the 'neither' mean of overtime hours worked. See Kendall and Stuart (1967) and Aspin (1949). As we have no knowledge that overtime hours are normally distributed, we have drawn no conclusions when the test statistic is close to the critical value.
[c] For definition of 'high plausible' and 'constrained' see Sections III and IV, respectively.
[d] Percentages are of the demographic group in the relevant column. Thus in the high plausible column the 173 men claiming 'more' are 14 per cent of all high plausible men, but on 13 per cent of all men.

percentage of 'more' claims (15 per cent) is greater than the percentage of 'less' claims (12 per cent). For married men with children the predominance of the 'more' claims (19 per cent) as opposed to 'less' claims (9 per cent) is greater still. This is perhaps what one would expect in the light of the increasing financial commitment of married men, particularly those with children. Even in this case, however, the proportion of 'more' is still quite small.

Before drawing conclusions from the number of people who claimed effects from tax we wished to see if their work effort varied in a way that was consistent with their claims. There are a very large number of measures of work effort which might be chosen. Even if one leaves aside attempts to measure effort per hour and concentrates entirely on measures of the length of time spent working, there are a variety of possible measures. These include participation rates,[1] hours of overtime worked, total hours worked at the main job, second job hours, all paid hours. These measures could be applied to each adult member of the household and one could look for interrelationships between the labour supply of one member of the household and the labour supply of other members. In the present chapter we concentrate entirely on hours of overtime worked 'last' week[2] and we should offer some justification for choosing this particular measure of labour supply.

We choose overtime hours primarily because we have a reliable question asking about the effects of tax on overtime hours, and also because this is an area in which much of the controversy lies. However, it could be argued that the differences in mean overtime hours actually worked between 'more' ('less') claims and 'neither' claims provide no basis for estimating the magnitude of the effect of tax on total hours worked even if everyone was telling the truth and the sampling error was zero. In the first place the differences in mean overtime hours worked between groups with different claims might be simply due to differences in the standard working week. To see if our conclusions are affected by the length of the standard working week we repeated the analysis comparing mean total hours worked in the main job instead of overtime hours. Our main conclusions were not affected.[3]

Secondly, the differences in mean overtime hours worked between groups with different claims does not take into account the possibility of substitution between the main job and a second job, thereby perhaps invalidating any inference about the effect of tax on total hours in all paid jobs based on findings about the effect of tax on overtime hours. Those with a second job did in fact work fewer hours of overtime on average than those with no second job. A replication of the analysis comparing the overtime claims on mean total hours worked in all paid jobs did not alter the broad conclusions. Thus while we believe that this study should be interpreted in terms of the tax effect on overtime hours only and not on total hours in all paid work, there is some suggestive evidence to permit a tentative inference concerning the effect of tax on total hours worked for men.

If we accept overtime hours as a measure of work effort we still need a standard against which to measure the strength of the claimed effects. Ideally, we should like to know for each employee how many hours they would have worked had tax not affected the amount of overtime worked. Quite obviously it would be impossible to collect this sort of information in a reliable way, so we have had to approach the problem somewhat differently. Our comparison assumes that the number of hours overtime worked by the 'neither' group is a measure of the number of overtime hours people would have worked had there been no tax effect.[4] As can be seen 'neither' hours rises both by family size and by the presence or absence of constraints, and this affects our conclusions.

Table 4.1 indicates how average overtime hours differ among people making different claims, but it should be noted that differences in overtime hours cannot be taken as proof of a tax effect. It is conceivable, for example, that people claimed 'more' because they worked a lot of overtime, which would imply that the direction of causation is from hours to claims rather than from claims to hours. All we can say is whether the behaviour is, or is not, consistent with the claims.

Table 4.1 in fact does reveal broad consistency between behaviour and claims. In Part I the variation in overtime hours is consistent with the claims except in the case of single men claiming 'less'. Apart from single men, those claiming 'more' work significantly longer overtime hours than those claiming 'neither'. It is also interesting to note that among those who claim 'neither', the number of overtime hours worked by married men with children is greater than the number worked by married men without children, which in turn is greater than that worked by single men.

There are a variety of reasons why these claimed effects should not automatically be taken at their face value. Some of these are discussed in the sections which follow.

III   PLAUSIBILITY OF CLAIMS

Having looked at employees' claims about the effects of taxation we of course are faced with the crucial question: can we believe the answers? It is our impression, although of course we cannot prove it, that asking our question about claimed effects at the end of the interview is likely to get as near to an individual's perception of the truth about the effect of taxation on overtime as it is possible to get in an interview situation. The respondent by this time has had ample opportunity to blow off steam, to try out unthought-out preconceptions of the effect of taxation, and he has been confronted with his answers to earlier questions, which should reveal to him any inconsistency in his position. In other words we believe the answers to this question are likely to be very much more reliable than they would have been had the question been asked cold at the beginning of the interview. It is of course still possible that some respondents were deliberately trying to mislead us, or (more likely in our view) were still not certain how, if at all, taxation affected their work.

We believe that the answers to these questions are sufficiently reliable to provide a useful starting point for our analysis of the claimed effects of taxation on overtime. Our task is to decide whether these claims, made at the end of the interview, are plausible. In deciding whether a claimed effect was plausible or not, our criterion in the broadest terms was consistency with earlier statements. We adopted the general rule that an employee's claim was plausible unless demonstrably inconsistent with earlier statements. Thus people were assumed to be plausible if, as in the case of the 'neither' group, there was no evidence to contradict their claim.

Clearly the more 'hoops' we put someone through before labelling his behaviour consistent and hence plausible the smaller proportion of plausible replies we will have. Equally clearly, changes in the criteria will change the proportions judged to be plausibly suffering from an incentive or disincentive effect. It would have been worrying to us if slight changes in our criteria of plausibility had resulted in dramatic changes in the number judged to be plausible. Fortunately this did not happen.

The criteria used in the present chapter are set out in detail in the 'tax tree' on p. 32-3, which shows not only the criteria for deciding plausible claims but also the criteria for constrained effects.[5] The interested reader can work his way through the table and see in detail how each of the judgements has been made. For example, people who claimed they worked less were judged to be implausible if they would not work more overtime at a higher overtime rate than they were currently being paid. Also, in general, someone claiming he worked more was judged as implausible if he had not worked some overtime during the past four weeks.

Those judged to be plausible by the criteria outlined above are shown in part II of Table 4.1. It can be seen that on the whole a larger proportion of men claiming 'more' were judged to be plausible (173 out of 205) than of men claiming 'less' (88 out of 149). It is interesting to note that the ratio of plausible 'more' claims to plausible 'less' claims is highest for those married men who have children and lowest for single men, who now have the same proportion of plausible 'less' claims as of 'more' claims. It can also be inferred from the table that those with plausible claims, whether 'more' or 'less', worked more overtime than those with implausible claims except in the case of married men with children. Single men claiming 'less' in fact worked slightly more overtime than those claiming 'neither' but in most cases those claiming 'more' do in fact work a significantly larger number of hours than those claiming 'neither'.

IV   CONSTRAINTS

In practice employees may not be free to choose the amount of overtime that they would like to work, for a variety of reasons. Perhaps the clearest and most common form of constraint is that an employee may be required by his employer to work longer or shorter hours than he wishes to work, as a condition of employment.[6] Thirty per cent were constrained by this definition. In addition to the situation, which we have called a 'work' constraint, there are two other classes which may be considered constrained as well. One of these is what we have called the 'pay' constraint. If a person's pay does not change because of the number of hours he works then the tax system cannot really be making him work more or less overtime.[7] We have, with one exception, treated all workers not paid extra for overtime as being constrained. The exception is where people who are not paid extra for overtime said they chose the job because it did not have any overtime. Nine per cent of men had a pay constraint. The final type of constraint we used is a constraint which we have termed 'personal'. An employee may wish to work overtime but because of reasons of health or family commitments (*e.g.* a married woman with a young child) may not be able to work overtime. They are constrained by personal factors. Six per cent of men and 15 per cent of women had a personal constraint.

In part III of Table 4.1 we have excluded those who are constrained by any of the three definitions above. We have done this for both those who have claimed an effect from taxation and those who have claimed that taxation did not affect their behaviour. The table implies that the high proportion of 'neither' claims is partly caused by constraints, but the figure for 'all men', for example, is only reduced from 79 per cent in part II to 69 per cent by eliminating those who are constrained. For those who claimed 'less' the effect of constraints appears to be to reduce the difference in hours between those claiming 'less' and those claiming neither'. For those who claimed that tax made them work more overtime the effect of constraints seemed minimal. Perhaps the most dramatic result of separating out the unconstrained is in the overtime hours worked by those claiming 'neither'. It can be inferred that in every demographic group those claiming 'neither' worked more overtime if they were unconstrained than if they were constrained. The largest change is among the married men with children, where the average overtime hours of those claiming no effect rises from 5.6 for both constrained and unconstrained to 8.6 for the unconstrained alone. It is this increase in the overtime hours worked for the 'neither' unconstrained married men with children which results in the difference between 'neither' and 'less' mean overtime hours outweighing the difference between 'neither' and 'more' overtime hours.[8]

V NET EFFECT

We now turn to estimating the net effect of the income taxation on overtime. For the purpose of this argument let us assume that the figures in Table 4.1 are entirely accurate in every respect. Even given these rather sweeping assumptions our task is by no means straightforward for there are a large number of bases on which calculations of the net effect might be made. We propose to discuss two of these possibilities. First let us assume that the only men affected by taxation are the 61 plausible unconstrained now claiming 'less' and the 151 plausible unconstrained now claiming 'more'. Taking the differences in overtime worked by these 212 people from the mean overtime hours worked by the 'neither' group and dividing by the total number of men (including those whose answers were considered implausible) gives a net effect +0.3 overtime hours. This amounts to 8 per cent of overtime hours or about 0.75 per cent of total hours

This first method assumes that all constrained employees are unaffected by tax, which is almost certainly false. A simple example may make the point clear. Suppose a man has a job in which he can choose how long to work provided he works at least 40 and not more than 45 hours. Let us imagine that in the absence of taxation he chooses to work 42 hours and is thus unconstrained. If the introduction of tax made him wish to work 39 or 46 hours he would actually work 40 or 45 hours and would now be constrained *because* of the tax system.

Our first estimate of the net effect assumed *no* constrained people are affected by tax. On our second estimate we make the opposite assumption, that *all* constraints arise as a result of the tax system. We therefore included all high plausible respondents in the calculation; one very important consequence of this is that the average number of overtime hours worked by the 'neither' group, which is taken as the yard-stick, is reduced from 6.2 to 4.2. In this case the average net effect for all males is + 0.8 overtime hours, which is equivalent to 20 per cent of total overtime or nearly 2 per cent of total hours.

The best estimate probably lies somewhere between these two figures: a very rough guess as to the net effect of tax on the amount of overtime worked by weekly-paid males thus might be about half an hour a week. Half an hour expressed as a percentage of mean hours worked in all paid jobs (45.2 hours) for the whole male sample is a little over 1 per cent.

This estimated net effect of tax on overtime is clearly small and it *may* be the case that because it is small there are no important policy conclusions to be drawn from the study – except that the net effect of tax on overtime is small (which is clearly important in itself). We are not however, prepared to draw this inference at this stage. One reason for this is that we wish to look at the quantitative figures from our second approach in order to see if they agree with our present figures. A second reason is that we should be able, using our other approach, to estimate by how much particular tax changes will affect hours worked. Finally, even if the net average effect is small it may not be unimportant. Income tax does not, as we have seen, have a uniform effect on all groups and so *if* the authorities wish to influence the amount of overtime worked they can make tax changes that affect different groups in different ways. This is another matter we are exploring in our second approach, where we are trying to estimate not only how tax changes might affect different demographic groups but also changes in the degree of progression in the tax system might affect work effort among the 'rich' and the 'poor', both separately and in terms of its likely net effect.

VI   LIMITATIONS

There are clearly limitations to these findings. First, there are certain general matters which apply to both approaches used in this study such as the fact that the sample is not representative of the population generally and that the results are from a cross-section study. Like most, but not all, of our work there is no household model employed.

Second, there are obvious limitations to the interview approach. People may try to mislead the interviewers. We think this is not likely to be a serious problem given both the complexity of the questionnaire to be a serious problem given both the complexity of the questionnaire and that taxation was not mentioned at the outset. Potentially much more serious is the possibility that even after careful thought people may not understand how they have been affected by tax. Budget constraints – can become extremely complex. The interview approach relies on the individual to sort out in his own mind all of the complex ways in which he is affected by tax and give an answer to simple questions such as the one forming the starting point for the present analysis. The respondent may not understand his own decision-making process (but he conceivably could understand it better than the econometric modeller).

The other obvious limitation to the interview approach is that it cannot provide numerical estimates of price income and substitution[9] elasticities. This in turn makes it difficult to use the results for policy purposes.

Our basic justification – about a decade ago – for using two approaches was that no single approach could be expected to be free from objection but we believed that if two approaches led to similar conclusions this would reinforce the acceptability of both. This issue is discussed briefly in Chapter 10.

There is one related issue that should be mentioned here. Some readers of the original version of this chapter drew an incorrect inference from our conclusion that the net effect of tax was to increase labour supply. The inference that was drawn was that because the net effect of tax was to increase labour supply there could be no objection to raising income tax rates. This inference is mistaken. For purposes of argument let us assume that our conclusions were firmly established, and thus would be based on the net effect of the 1971 tax system on a group of workers. For reasons which are explained in detail in Chapter 12 different methods of raising taxes would have very different effects. For example, an increase in the basic rate of tax would be expected to have a different effect from a reduction in the allowances. Because the interview approach does not lead to numerical estimates of elasticities these effects cannot be calculated. While it is a defect of the interview approach that these elasticities cannot be calculated, their existence should not be assumed away.

NOTES: CHAPTER 4

1 We cannot study participation rates among our respondents because our population has by definition a 100 per cent participation rate.
2 Hours of overtime worked 'last' week might be atypical in a way that biased the results. As a partial check against this possibility we repeated the analysis

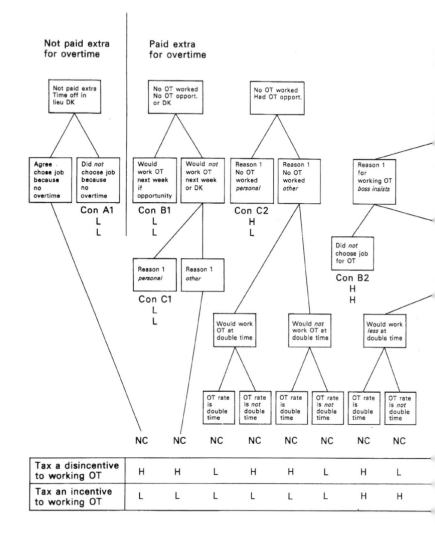

TAX TREE

Con A pay constraint
Con B work constraint
Con C personal constraint
NC   non constrained
H   high plausible
L   low plausible

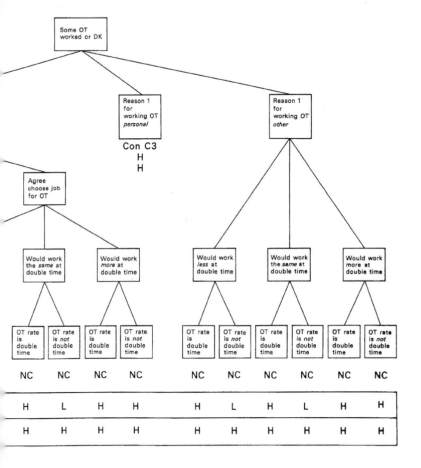

for overtime hours in the preceding week. Our conclusions are not materially affected.

3   The largest change in results found was for married men with children who were both plausible and unconstrained. In this case mean total hours were 43.9 for those claiming 'less', 48.4 for those claiming 'neither' and 52.9 for those claiming 'more' (see Table 4.1). It was this group that appeared to be out of line with the general pattern on overtime hours, but this aberration disappears when using total main job hours.

4   Our 'neither' group includes non-taxpayers as well as taxpayers. Especially in view of the evidence below that non-taxpayers claim fewer effects from tax, it might be thought that this would bias our results because, for example, non-taxpayers with low wages and large families may work long hours and hence bias the average number of 'neither' hours upwards. To remove possible bias we replicated the analysis excluding non-taxpayers from the 'neithers'. The results, indicate that the conclusions are unaffected. (We did not remove non-taxpayers from the claimed effects, for example, people near the tax threshold might work less in order to avoid paying tax.)

5   See Section IV.

6   This constraint is likely to be strongest in the short run because if a person is unable to work the number of hours he wishes in his current job he may be able to switch to another job which offers him the number of hours he wishes to work. Thirty per cent of the sample indicated that the amount of overtime offered had influenced their choice of jobs. It should be noted that there is no reason to assume that a person's claim is implausible because he is constrained. Indeed someone may be constrained because the tax system causes him to wish to work either shorter or longer hours than his employer is willing to offer.

7   This may well be a short-term constraint because if a person was constrained by the 'pay' system to work less than he wanted to he could change his job and work for an employer where he was paid more when he worked longer hours. It is also conceivable that even when working for his original employer he would think it worthwhile in the long run to work longer hours even if there was no immediate benefit to his income, for he could increase his chances of promotion and hence his long-run income.

8   See, however, n. 4 above.

9   Holland (1977) has however attempted to estimate the substitution effect directly.

Chapter 5

The Basic Model

Since 1976 several different strands of our project have developed semi-independently, each tackling a separate problem and/or a separate group of workers. Each of these strands can be seen as a development leading on from Brown, Levin and Ulph (1976). These recent developments are the subject matter of Chapters 6 - 9. The purpose of the present chapter is twofold. First, it explains the state of our thinking in 1976 which serves as the basis for subsequent comparison. Secondly, it deals with a number of matters of definition so as to avoid unnecessary repetition in subsequent chapters. This does *not* mean that all variables are defined in precisely the same way in every chapter. As will become clear various definitions have been changed for several reasons. It appears likely that these definitional questions are amongst the most important cause of the variations in elasticities that we have found. For this reason we pay considerable attention to them.

Because of its 'historic' role in the development of the project parts of the earlier article are reproduced in full - including known errors and omissions. These parts of the article are indicated in the relevant section headings, where the article is cited as BLU 1976.

THE ELEMENTARY THEORY OF LABOUR SUPPLY (BLU 1976)

In the standard textbook model of labour supply it is assumed that there is a single independent individual and two homogenous commodities. One of the commodities is called leisure and is measured in time. The other commodity is a consumption good called income. The individual is endowed with one unit of time which we take to be 168 hours since we will be discussing the number of hours worked a week. That part of an individual's time which is not spent in leisure we call work. The individual also has an endowment of N units of non-employment income which may be positive, zero or negative (if, for example, he has net debts or faces a

Parts of this chapter (indicated by BLU 1976 on the section headings) which are extracts from an earlier paper were written jointly by C. V. Brown, E. Levin and D. T. Ulph. The remainder of the chapter is by C. V. Brown.

poll tax). The physical consumption possibilities open to the individual comprise all combinations of non-negative income and leisure provided that the consumption of leisure does not exceed one unit. We assume the

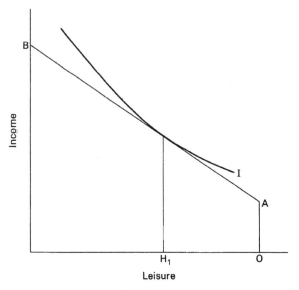

Figure 5.1

individual has a preference ordering over these possibilities which satisfies all the usual conditions. The price of income is assumed to be 1. Finally, it is assumed that there is a budget constraint determined by non-employment income and an exogenously given wage rate. The individual's consumption of income cannot exceed the value of his non-employment income plus the value of his hours spent in work.

The individual then maximises his utility subject to his budget constraint and so generates a supply of labour function which we call the simple supply function. This is the supply function that we wish to estimate and although it is not always clearly specified we think it is this supply function that most people think of when they speak loosely of 'the supply of labour' and which is most often estimated in individual labour supply models.

In this model a change in the wage rate gives the price effect (P), a unit change in non-employment incomes gives the income effect (Y) and the substitution effect (S) is found in the usual way $(S = P - YH$, where H is hours worked).

The model is illustrated in Figure 5.1 which has income on the vertical axis and leisure on the horizontal axis. The individual starts off at O where he has 168 hours of leisure and some initial non-employment income OA. Given a wage rate he can trade leisure for income along the line AB (his budget constraint). How much he trades is determined by his preferences represented by a series of indifference curves. For the case illustrated the individual would work OH_1 hours.

LINEARIZATION OF THE BUDGET CONSTRAINT (BLU 1976)

This first major problem of applying the simple model is that with a progressive tax system and with the possibility of an overtime premium for hours worked in excess of the standard working week the individual will face a complex trade-off between income and hours worked. Figure 5.2 illustrates the budget constraint that would confront the individual if he hit a tax threshold at OC (and paid some basic rate of tax thereafter) and if after working a standard week of OH_0 he could earn an overtime premium. In these circumstances the budget constraint would be ABDE and the individual would work OH_1 hours.

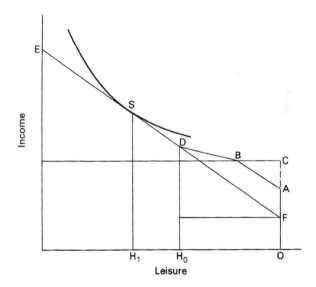

Figure 5.2

It is crucial to our procedure[1] to note that point S which is the point the individual chooses when faced with the budget line ABDE is also the point he would have chosen had he faced the budget line FE. Thus point S is the point he would have chosen had he been in the standard textbook world with non-employment income of OF and facing a net wage given by the slope of FE. It would seem therefore that if we make an adjustment to non-employment income to allow for the non-linearity of the budget constraint, and measure the increase in the *net* income an individual would receive for working an extra hour, we could estimate the simple supply function by regressing hours of work on the marginal wage rate and adjusted non-employment income. However, econometric objections have been raised against such a procedure and we discuss these in the next section.

ECONOMETRIC OBJECTIONS (BLU 1976)

There have been two objections raised to the procedure discussed in the previous section,[2] and they can be illustrated by means of Figure 5.3. Here the individual faces the non-linear budget constraint OA and is in equilibrium at the point S. As in the previous section we can think of the individual's equilibrium as being that which would obtain had he faced a wage rate given by the slope of FE (the net marginal wage rate) and non-employment income OF (his adjusted non-employment income).

The first objection notes that the marginal wage rate and adjusted non-

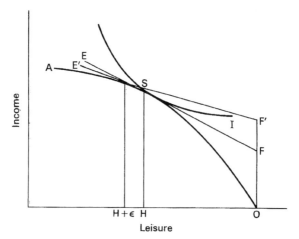

Figure 5.3

employment income are correlated with the error term of the regression, that is, that the simple labour supply equation is subject to endogeneity bias. To see this, suppose we took a second individual, identical to the first, who just because of the random error of the model worked OH + ϵ hours and not OH hours. For this individual we would compute a non-employment income term OF$'$ > OF and a wage term given by the slope of F$'$E$'$ < slope of FE. Hence there are spurious correlations between the error term and the independent variables.

The second objection is that if there are any errors in the measurement of hours then when we calculate OF = HS – OH × slope FE we will induce a negative correlation between the errors in the measurement of hours and the measurement of non-employment income.

However, both of these objections rely heavily on the strict concavity of the budget constraint OA in Figure 5.3. When, as in Figure 5.2, the budget constraint is piecewise linear, then as long as the random error is not large enough to carry the individual onto a different linear segment of the budget constraint there will be no relation between the random error and the independent variables. Moreover, even if the error does carry the individual onto a different linear segment, when there is an overtime premium as well as a progressive tax system, a small increase in hours will sometimes be associated with a rise in the marginal wage rate and sometimes with a fall. For both these reasons the correlation between the error term and the independent variables is likely to be much smaller in a situation as depicted in Figure 5.2 than that shown in Figure 5.3. Moreover for Great Britain where most weekly-paid workers pay tax at the standard rate (if at all) and there is a great deal of overtime, it is Figure 5.2 which is likely to be more relevant than Figure 5.3. This is in contrast with the situation in the United States, where tax bands are narrower and less overtime is worked, so that Figure 5.3 is more likely to be relevant than Figure 5.2 and endogeneity bias to be a more serious objection to adopting the procedure outlined in the previous section.

Piecewise linearity also enables us to avoid errors in the measurement of adjusted non-employment income arising out of errors in the measurement of hours of work. For notice that in Figure 5.2, we could calculate adjusted non-employment income as OF = $H_0 D$ – OH_0 × slope of FE where OH_0 is the standard working week and $H_0 D$ is the individual's net income earned by working the standard working week. OF can thus be calculated without employing hours of work directly and so will be unaffected by any errors arising in the measurement of hours.

As an illustration of how the computation could be carried out in practice, consider an individual who has non-employment income of N and is paid a basic wage rate w. If he works more than the standard working week S he is paid for these extra hours at the gross wage rate ow where o is the overtime premium. The gross income, GY, of someone working overtime is therefore

$$GY = wS + ow\,(H - S) + N = owH + w(1 - o)S + N. \qquad (1)$$

If, moreover, he pays tax at the rate t on that part of his gross income which exceeds his tax threshold T then the net income, NY, of somebody paying tax is

$$NY = T + (1 - t)(GY - T) = tT + (1 - t)GY. \qquad (2)$$

Substituting (1) into (2) we have, for someone paying tax and working overtime,

$$NY = (1 - t)\,owH + tT + (1 - t)w(1 - o)S + (1 - t)N. \qquad (3)$$

So the marginal wage rate and adjusted non-employment income terms are given by

$$\text{marginal wage rate} = (1 - t)ow \qquad (4)$$

$$\text{adjusted non-employment income} = tT + (1 - t)\,w(1 - o)S + (1 - t)N \qquad (5)$$

neither of which contains H explicitly. Indeed to calculate these we need only know if he paid tax and worked overtime without even using his hours of work directly.

In conclusion, therefore, we would argue that for weekly-paid workers in the UK we can avoid the negative correlation problem arising from errors in the measurement of hours of work, and that while there could be a problem of endogeneity bias this is likely to be a far less serious problem than with US data. However, there remain a number of conceptual and practical problems in the measurement of the variables and we now turn our attention to these.

DEFINITIONS OF VARIABLES

In this section we discuss the conceptual and practical problems we encountered in measuring these variables. It should be noted that in some cases the terminology used here is *not* the same as that in BLU 1976.

Hours

We needed to record the number of hours people would like to work given their budget constraints, and we used all paid hours worked 'last' week as our measure. We included both main job hours and any second job hours in all paid hours, believing that the inclusion of second job hours is an improvement on the normal practice of including main job hours only. Nevertheless it does present a problem because it does not make sense for all three of the following assumptions to be satisfied simultaneously: (1) people have two jobs with differing wage rates; (2) they are free to choose their hours in both jobs; and (3) they are indifferent between the two jobs. If (2) and (3) hold, the utility maximizing individual would choose the job with the higher net wage rate and would work zero hours in the other job. Thus if people have two jobs it is likely to be the case that either (2) or (3) does not hold. An individual might have a second job with a higher net wage rate (perhaps because of tax evasion) but with only limited hours of work possible. Alternatively someone might have a second job with a lower net wage rate because they were unable to work as many hours as they wished in their main job. The method of handling this problem in BLU 1976 is discussed below.

It has been argued, for example, by Hanoch (1976), that hours worked last week is inadequate because it does not allow for the possibility that individuals achieve their desired annual equilibrium number of hours and their desired pattern of leisure by working some weeks and not others. This argument has some force but our procedure has a number of advantages. In practice it would be impossible to expect people to remember the exact number of hours they had worked in each of the last 52 weeks. Therefore a typical procedure is to define annual hours as the product of 'usual' hours last week and weeks worked. This produces the difficulty that both usual hours and weeks worked are potentially ambiguous concepts. Would someone asked for their 'usual' hours understand this to mean usual *paid* hours (see below)? modal hours? mean hours? Does weeks worked include paid weeks of holidays? paid public holidays? casual days off? Even if these difficulties are overcome constructing an annual budget constraint properly would be impossible.[3] There is also the comforting possibility that varying annual hours by taking some weeks off may not be particularly serious in the UK because seasonal employment possibilities are less common than in the USA.

In our view a more serious problem is that actual hours worked last week may not be the equilibrium hours for that week. Various definitions of constraint were discussed in Chapter 4 and the problem is discussed further below.

The actual measure of hours we have used in all of our regressions is 'Actual hours worked last week in all paid jobs' from the Household Composition section of the questionnaire. There are a number of other measures we might have used from our questionnaire with perhaps the second most promising being the sum of second job hours and main job hours recorded on the last pay slip. The two measures do *not* give the same answer. We preferred the measure we chose for two reasons. Hours on the last pay slip may not refer to 'last' week. Hours on the pay slip may be hours for which a person is paid rather than number worked (e.g. 5 hours of overtime at double time may be recorded as 10 hours at single time).

The wage rate (w)

The appropriate wage rate for this model is the slope of the segment of the budget constraint on which equilibrium occurs. Several examples follow. For a person not paying tax and not working overtime it is the gross basic wage rate (Q49b). For someone paying tax every week (Q99) but not working overtime it is the gross wage times (one minus the tax rate). For a taxpayer working overtime it is the basic wage rate times the overtime premium (Q20) times (one minus the tax rate). In some cases it was possible to calculate the required wage rate in several ways. To minimize loss of numbers due to missing data we calculated the wage in other ways when our first choice of data was missing. For example, the wage rate of a taxpayer working overtime was calculated as the gross wage for working overtime (Q61a) times (one minus the tax rate) if Q20 or 49 was missing.

For people with second jobs our definition of the wage rate depended on whether or not they were constrained in their main job. If they were unable to work as long as they wished in their main job we used the second job wage rate. If people could work as long as they wished in their main job we used the lower of the two wage rates as the marginal wage. The second job wage rate was defined as second job income (Q45) less expenses (Q44b) all divided by second job hours.

This definition of the wage rate generally avoids the problems (the exception is the second job wage rate) of wage rates being defined as income divided by hours. Wage rates defined as income divided by hours have several problems. The underlying models are theoretically indeterminate because the average wage rate so defined is not uniquely related to positions of equilibrium (Brown, Levin and Ulph, 1974; Brown, 1980). This wage rate is artificially depressed as a result of measurement error in hours. The average wage also suffers from endogeneity bias even for someone who remains on the same segment of their budget constraint.

While our definition of the wage rate avoids many problems from earlier studies it does have several deficiencies. A person's objective budget constraint includes their entitlement to state transfer earnings including the implied tax rate on means-tested transfers. This means that the net marginal wage should reflect the loss of transfers where appropriate. We have ignored the state transfer system altogether (i.e. in our intercept as well as in our wage rate) partly because our information was incomplete and partly because we had direct information which suggested that most of our respondents did not recognize that they would lose their entitlement to means-tested benefits if their earnings rose.

The second problem with the wage rate concerns the treatment of people at kinks. Consider the typical budget constraint shown in Figure 5.2. In principle people free to choose their hours should not be at convex kinks such as D (though they could be if they are constrained) but could well be at concave kinks such as B. The wage rate for people at kinks was defined as the slope of the segment of the budget constraint before the kink (i.e. the slope of BA for people at B and the slope of BD for people at D). The problem of wage rates at kinks is considered further in Chapter 8.

The intercept

The basic labour supply model outlined above implies that the intercept should include true non-employment income plus an adjustment term to take account of non-linearities in the budget constraint. As is explained in detail below we have measured something we call 'other income' which is a seriously inadequate proxy for true non-employment income. We have adopted two approaches to the treatment of this other income, in both of which we have encountered difficulties. In BLU (1976) we entered the adjustment term and other income into the equation as separate variables. In most of our subsequent work we have used a single variable, we call the intercept, which is the sum of the adjustment term and other income.

The adjustment factor (A)

One component of the intercept is an adjustment factor to take account of non-linearities in the budget constraints. The calculation of this adjustment factor for a typical budget constraint is illustrated in Figure 5.4, where it is assumed that true non-employment income is BC. The adjustment factor $CJ(= A)$ could be calculated as $A = C''E - w(BH)$ but this is open to the objection that error in the measurement hours will cause a negative correlation between hours and the adjustment term. We have therefore measured the adjustment term using hours at the previous kink, that is, $A = C'F - w(BS)$.

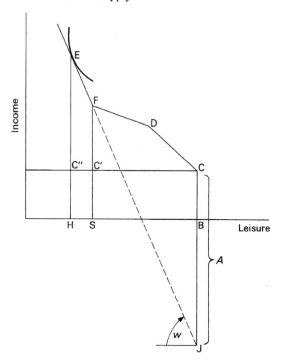

Figure 5.4

'Other income'

'Other income' includes the employment income of other members of the family, state (and private) transfer income, interest, dividends and rent received (e.g. for subletting) plus the direct services of physical assets such as housing and other consumer durables.

If, as seems probable, labour supply decisions are made on a family or household basis then the labour income of other household members is not true non-employment income. Such income ought to be handled in a household model. With an individual model it should be recognized that this income is endogenous, that is, it depends in part on how much the individual works. The position with means-tested state transfer income is similar. The longer a person works the higher his income will be and this will reduce his entitlement to state transfer income. This income ought to be handled by modelling the state transfer system in budget constraints, but, as stated above, we have not done this.

While dividend and interest income and outgoings may appear to be free from endogeneity bias this could well not be true either. Fleisher, Parsons and Porter (1973) have argued that if the stock of financial assets is not at its equilibrium level people will change their labour supply to reach this level. Brown, Levin and Ulph (1974) made a similar point when they argued that borrowing and working decisions may be simultaneous. Solving these problems probably means going beyond the confines of a static model.

In addition to these theoretical problems there are likely to be several measurement problems. There are problems of imputing income to holdings of real assets, of distinguishing between real and money income and outgoings.

Our own measure of other income suffers from particularly severe measurement problems. The difficulties stem from our decision at the outset to use both the interview approach and the cross-section econometric approach on a single set of data. With the interview approach it is essential to provide some checks for the plausibility of the claims about the effects of taxation. This means collecting the information for the checks before the respondent knows the interview is about taxation. If we interviewed more than one person in each house, all but the first would be likely to know that taxation was our major interest. This meant only one interview per family, which in turn meant that information about other family members had to come second hand. This had several undesirable consequences, some of which were not foreseen. Ideally we would have liked detailed information about the employment and 'other' income of all household members. But we recognized that asking detailed information of wives about husbands or of working children about parents could lead to non-response, both because the relevant information was not known and because the respondent would be reluctant to reveal details about other members of the family. In an attempt to minimize this problem we asked one question about the total net income of all household members.

This question (Q83)[4] asked for total household income in bands in the least threatening form of wording possible. 'Other income' in BLU was constructed as follows. For each band an assumed figure[5] for total household income was assigned. To find the total income of the household, excluding the employment income of the respondent, we subtracted net main and second job income. The remainder should have been the sum of household state and private transfer receipts, the employment income of other household members, rental interest and dividend income. On the most optimistic assumptions (which were not justified – see below) it was clear that there would be a great deal of measurement error in the other income variable because total net household income was given in bands.

Given these conceptual and practical difficulties we argued (BLU)

> For the reasons given above we do not think this variable is conceptually equivalent to non-employment income and would not expect a unit increase in other income to affect hours of work in the same way as a unit increase in true non-employment income. However, whether or not we have measured non-employment income correctly, we would expect a unit increase in the intercept to act in the same way as a unit increase in true non-employment income. We have therefore entered other income and the intercept into the regression as two separate variables and have calculated the income effect using the derivative of hours with respect to the intercept.

This view has not been taken in much of our work where 'other income' has been combined with the adjustment term in the intercept. Both methods suffer from the endogeneity of the 'other income' term. While we have made very considerable efforts to deal with other aspects of the endogeneity problem this aspect has been entirely neglected.

It has become clear in subsequent work that the family income question was misunderstood by a significant proportion of respondents. Because of the banding of family income it is possible for measured family income to be negative, However some people reported that net family income in total was less than their own net income. This suggests that the question was interpreted as net family income excluding the respondents own income. In Chapter 8 the predicted value for other income has been used when the measured value is negative.

TERMINOLOGY AND NOTATION – SUMMARY

Hours (H) is hours worked last week.
The Wage (w) is the net marginal wage rate.
The Adjustment term (A) is the adjustment for non-linearities arising from income taxation, overtime premia and second jobs.
Other income (Y) is net family income less respondents income.
The intercept (I) is the adjustment term (A) plus other income (Y).
The Sample. Our regressions are based on the 434 married men in the sample who come from households where the husband alone or the husband and wife only are workers, where the man is under 65, worked at least 8 hours 'last' week, where there is enough information to calculate our variables and where there is a positive hourly marginal wage rate.
Functional form. The functional form employed in BLU was

Table 5.1 The Basic Model – Results

Column groups: columns 1–4 fall under **Husband Only or Husband and Wife Both Work**; columns 5–7 fall under **Husband Only Works**.

Column headings:
1 = All; 2 = Not Constrained; 3 = Not on Bonus; 4 = All; 5 = Not Constrained, Not on Bonus; 6 = Not Constrained, Not on Bonus, Children under 11; 7 = Not Constrained, Not on Bonus, No Child under 11.

	1 All (A)	1 All (B)	2 Not Constr. (A)	2 Not Constr. (B)	3 Not on Bonus (A)	3 Not on Bonus (B)	4 All (A)	4 All (B)	5 (A)	5 (B)	6 (A)	6 (B)	7 (A)	7 (B)
Marginal wage rate	-14.3[a] (4.80)	-18.3[a] (4.60)	-19.6[a] (5.43)	-24.1[a] (5.18)	-29.2[a] (6.33)	-31.2[a] (5.94)	-8.34 (7.54)	-15.5[a] (7.25)	0.893 (21.3)	-23.5 (20.2)	113[a] (56.3)	95.5 (30.0)	-34.6 (25.9)	-36.6 (26.3)
Marginal wage rate squared	3.63 (2.05)	4.62[a] (1.96)	5.49[a] (2.20)	6.78[a] (2.09)	8.54[a] (2.65)	8.07[a] (2.48)	0.118 (4.14)	3.00 (3.94)	-11.0 (14.5)	3.59 (13.7)	-106[a] (46.1)	-95.2[a] (40.8)	8.15 (17.2)	9.39 (17.4)
Intercept	-0.959[a] (0.143)	-0.907[a] (0.137)	-1.04[a] (0.159)	-1.02[a] (0.150)	-1.26[a] (0.274)	-1.31[a] (0.265)	-0.966[a] (0.2)	-0.976[a] (0.190)	-1.04 (0.651)	-1.14 (0.599)	2.47 (1.4)	2.0 (1.27)	-2.53[a] (0.89)	-2.47[a] (0.943)
Intercept squared	0.0105[a] (0.00212)	0.00888[a] (0.00203)	0.00973[a] (0.00221)	0.00843[a] (0.00211)	0.00269 (0.00960)	0.00427 (0.00897)	0.00941[a] (0.00247)	0.00789 (0.00235)	-0.00619 (0.0153)	-0.00527 (0.014)	-0.0648 (0.0267)	-0.0543 (0.0242)	-0.00156 (0.0938)	-0.00093 (0.0956)
Marginal wage rate x intercept	0.644[a] (0.118)	0.582[a] (0.113)	0.662[a] (0.124)	0.624[a] (0.118)	0.790[a] (0.393)	0.956[a] (0.374)	0.556[a] (0.188)	0.554[a] (0.178)	0.312 (1.00)	0.467 (0.924)	-5.67[a] (2.35)	-4.91[a] (2.16)	2.2 (1.53)	2.12 (1.58)
Other income	-0.114[a] (0.048)	-0.146[a] (0.045)	-0.148[a] (0.054)	-0.189[a] (0.051)	-0.125 (0.065)	-0.159[a] (0.062)	-0.119[a] (0.057)	-0.145[a] (0.053)	-0.063 (0.087)	-0.101 (0.082)	0.143 (0.154)	0.00388 (0.14)	-0.223[a] (0.09)	-0.235[a] (0.093)
Job satisfaction		0.149[a] (0.041)		0.187[a] (0.045)		0.108 (0.06)		0.110[a] (0.049)		0.113 (0.085)		-0.00169 (0.114)		0.117 (0.123)
Need		0.323[a] (0.062)		0.350[a] (0.07)		0.487[a] (0.094)		0.397[a] (0.079)		0.607[a] (0.139)		0.874[a] (0.198)		0.094 (0.240)
Constraint		-2.97[a] (0.967)				-1.82 (1.38)		-3.87[a] (1.19)						
Constant	55.3	47.9	58.4	48.9	62.0	52.9	53.3	47.3	52.6	48.3	21.4	12.1	64.9	60.7
N = No. of cases	434	434	337	337	210	210	284	284	102	102	57	57	45	45
R^2	0.116	0.214	0.144	0.240	0.194	0.309	0.152	0.269	0.196	0.342	0.251	0.467	0.453	0.469
$\bar{R}^2$	0.104	0.197	0.128	0.222	0.170	0.278	0.134	0.223	0.145	0.285	0.162	0.367	0.367	0.351
F	9.35[a]	12.9[a]	9.23[a]	12.9[a]	8.13[a]	9.93[a]	8.25[a]	11.25[a]	3.86[a]	6.04[a]	2.80[a]	5.26[a]	5.25[a]	3.98[a]
Hours	47.4	47.4	48.2	48.2	48.1	48.1	47.9	47.8	50.7	50.2	52.7	52.4	49.6	49.6
Price effect	-9.72[a]	-12.7[a]	-13.2[a]	-16.4[a]	-20.0[a]	-22.6[a]	-7.68	-11.8	-12.0	-20.2	-2.07	-7.84	-23.7	-28.9
Income effect	-0.596[a]	-0.580[a]	-0.668[a]	-0.680[a]	-0.817	-0.779	-0.653[a]	-0.667[a]	-0.844	-0.864	-0.643	-0.700	-1.37	-1.35
Substitution effect	18.5	14.7	19.0	16.4	19.2	14.9	23.6	20.1	30.9	23.2	31.8	28.8	44.3	38.0
Price elasticity	-0.107	-0.140	-0.144	-0.179	-0.232	-0.261	-0.085	-0.131	-0.013	-0.227	-0.023	-0.089	-0.253	-0.308
Income elasticity	-0.016	-0.016	-0.011	-0.011	-0.008	-0.007	-0.013	-0.013	-0.025	-0.026	-0.023	-0.025	-0.029	-0.028
Substitution elasticity	0.204	0.162	0.209	0.180	0.224	0.173	0.261	0.223	0.343	0.261	0.357	0.325	0.472	0.405
Elasticity of substitution	0.274	0.218	0.287	0.247	0.317	0.245	0.356	0.303	0.510	0.387	0.543	0.494	0.689	0.591

[a] Significant at 5 per cent level. (We know of no test of the significance of the substitution effect or of elasticities.)

$$H = a_1 + a_2 w + a_3 w^2 + a_4 A + a_5 A^2 + a_6 wA + a_7 Y + E$$

and the coefficients a_1 to a_7 were estimated. It may be noted that this function form allows for non-linear effects of both the wage and the adjustment term, and for interactions between the wage and intercept. It assumes that other income has a linear effect on labour supply. The results are given in column 1A of Table 5.1. In Table 5.1 the price (E_p), income (E_y), and substitution (E_s) are calculated as follows:

$$E_p = \frac{w}{H} \frac{\partial H}{\partial w}$$

$$E_y = \frac{A}{H} \frac{\partial H}{\partial A}$$

$$E_s = \frac{w}{H} \frac{\partial H}{\partial w} - \frac{\partial H}{\partial A}$$

Applicability of the Model. One of our main objectives in BLU 1976 was to explore the suitability of our simple model to groups of people, where the model is not strictly relevant.

NON-HOURLY PAYMENT SYSTEMS (BLU 1976)

A different set of difficulties arises with those people in our sample who are paid by piece-rate, bonus or commission. Under such schemes individuals will simultaneously determine both the number of hours they work and their effort level. The effort level will determine their effort payment which will enter into their observed hourly wage rate. While it is still appropriate to ask how an individual will change his hours of work holding his effort level constant it would only be possible to answer this question using our regression if we had some way of holding effort constant. We are currently working on this problem, and will report our results at greater length in a subsequent paper. As a first step towards improving our present results, we can eliminate from our sample, those people who are paid on some form of bonus scheme, thus making the implicit assumption that all who remain work at some common effort level. The results of this exercise are reported in regression 3A. It can be seen that there has been some improvement in the adjusted R^2. The price and income effects (and elasticities) have changed rather more than when we removed constrained people but we do not know if this is a significant difference.

WORKING WIVES (BLU 1976)

Finally, we have applied an individual model to a household situation. It seems likely that in this situation there will be complex interactions between the wage rate of the husband, the husband's hours, the (actual or potential) wage rate of the wife and the wife's hours. In using an individual model on households there is an implicit assumption that the husband's behaviour does not affect the wife and that the only effect of the wife's behaviour on the husband is through an income effect. The individual model is less obviously inappropriate when the wife is not working for in this case our other income will more closely approximate true non-employment income to the household, *if* (as must be assumed) the wife's potential wage rate is well below the threshold wage that would cause her to undertake market work. The regression when only the husband works is given in 4A. Adjusted R^2 rises and the elasticity of substitution increased but we do not know if the increase is significant.

CONSTRAINTS (BLU 1976)

The first such subset we wish to consider consists of people who are constrained in their choice of hours of work. The model as outlined in the second section of this chapter assumed that people could choose to work in a week any number of hours between 0 and 168. There are many reasons why this assumption may be inappropriate (some of these are discussed in Chapter 4). We have concentrated on the difficulty that arises when individuals find that in a particular job there is either some minimum hours of work requirement or an upper limit to the number of hours for which the employer will hire them. In particular, it might be that many individuals are confronted with a single fixed number of hours set by the employer. When such situations arise it may well be that an individual's actual hours of work will differ from those he would choose to work given the free choice open to him in our model.

There are two problems when individuals are constrained in this sense. The estimates will be biased through error in the dependent variable. Then there is the identification problem; if hours are determined by the employer rather than the employee the regressions may measure the demand for labour rather than the supply of labour.

There are a number of ways in which one might try to circumvent these problems, but we chose to try to eliminate from our sample those people whom we could identify as being constrained, in the sense that they were not working the number of hours they wished to work. Our criterion for identifying such people is given at the end of the chapter.[6]

The first point to note in our results is that even using a broad definition of constraint only 22 per cent of our sample were constrained through employment requirements.

The second point is that when we compare our results as given in regression 2A with those for the sample as a whole, there has been no dramatic improvement in the adjusted R^2. Furthermore, the price, income and substitution elasticities do not appear very different.[7] The impression, then, is that constraints make very little difference to our results. There could be two reasons for this. On the one hand, individuals who are prevented from working as much as they would like in their main job may choose a second job (our dependent variable is hours worked in all paid jobs). Indeed, there may be a number of other dimensions (for example, choice of occupation, or choice of employer) on which the individual can move to avoid constraints. On the other hand, if many of our constraints are not of the rigidly fixed number of hours kind but of the upper or lower bound on hours kind, and if these bounds are fairly uniform, widely spread and set by 'custom' then workers under those constraints may nevertheless be employed for close to their desired number of hours. Further research will be required to settle these questions.

The similarity between the results for the whole sample and for the unconstrained sub-sample suggest that the identification problem *may* not prove to be important. This argument, however, is not conclusive. It is conceivable, for example, that people in different regions have different tastes and hence different supply curves. What appears to be a movement along a supply curve thus might in fact be a shift between one supply curve and another. A rigorous test of this possibility would require running separate regressions for areas where one hypothesises tastes might differ. This is not possible without a much larger data set.

PREFERENCES (BLU 1976)

We have attempted to control for tastes directly by inserting variables designed to measure need and job satisfaction. We have therefore constructed a composite need variable measured in £'s per week which depends on supplementary benefit levels, housing costs, the imputed rent of owner-occupied housing, HP payments and money required for specific savings targets. Supplementary benefit levels were included as an official measure of minimum needs depending on household size and composition. Weekly rent or mortgage payments were included because housing costs vary in different parts of the country and because in the short run it is a fixed outgoing. A crude estimate[8] of the imputed rent of owner-occupied housing was included on the assumption that such income reduced needs. HP payments and specific savings targets were included as people with such contractual (HP) or specific savings plans seemed likely to have different tastes. It seems likely that some items in this index (e.g. target savings and HP payments) can be changed more frequently than others (e.g. family size) and thus the index in its present form is only relevant to short-run labour supply analysis.[9]

Our other taste variable is job satisfaction. The individual labour supply model ignores job satisfaction but it seems likely that people who like their work will wish to work longer than people who dislike their work. We measured job satisfaction on five well-designed scales called the *Job Description Index*[10] and we used the scale relating to the job itself in our regressions. The scale attempts to measure the extent to which people enjoy their work, by asking them to agree or disagree with a variety of statements about their work. The first four (of eighteen) items respondents are asked to consider are 'fascinating', 'routine', 'satisfying', 'boring'.

We have argued that the problem of constraints does not appear to be a serious one. However, we wished to see if constrained people worked longer or shorter hours than those who were not constrained. For this purpose we entered a dummy variable for constrained (using the same definition reported above).

We have stepped in the variables representing need, job satisfaction and constraints into our regressions and the results are presented in the B regressions in the table. The addition of the tastes variables increases the proportion of the variance explained and increases the significance of the equation in most cases. While there is no evidence of any dramatic change in elasticities, the absolute value of the price elasticity rises in every case when the taste variables are entered, but the elasticity of substitution falls. The coefficient on need is positive and almost always significant. The coefficient on job satisfaction is (nearly always) positive.

SUMMARY

In this chapter a number of definitional matters have been discussed and our early results have been repeated. These results are in principle endogenous and while this was recognized at the time it was thought that in practice 'this is likely to be a far less serious problem than with US data'. In two independent examinations of the endogeneity problem this optimistic view is upheld by Ruffell (in Chapter 8) but contradicted by Ashworth and Ulph (in Chapter 6).

NOTES: CHAPTER 5

1 In Brown, Levin and Ulph (1974) we first presented our procedure and demonstrated its logical and empirical superiority to that of Kosters (1969). A logically equivalent, but not identical, procedure was proposed by Hall in Cain and Watts (1973), which contains other examples of the Kosters procedure. Some of our subsequent comments on empirical difficulties have been anticipated by Greenberg (1972), De Vanzo and Greenberg (1973) and Killingsworth (1973).

2 See, for example, Kurz *et al.*, (1974).

3 It would have to make allowance for job changes, changes in the nominal rates of pay over the year, changes in real wage rates due to inflation, the presence of overtime opportunities in some weeks but not in others, changes in tax allowances, tax rates, social security changes, etc.

4 "The amount that any one person works sometimes depends on how much money is coming into the house from *all* sources. Could you show me the group on the card that gives the total amount of money normally coming into the house each week, counting all wages and salaries after deductions and other things like family allowances, pensions and so on. If anyone is paid monthly can you divide by four when adding it in?"

5 This assumed figure was above the middle of the band for households in the lower bands and below the middle of the band for high band households because the distribution of individual income suggested this was appropriate.

6 Our definition of 'constrained' depends on whether or not the person worked overtime in the 'last' four weeks. For those who did work overtime, a person is regarded as constrained if he would have liked to work either more or less overtime and if the amount of overtime he worked was determined by the employer. For those who did not work overtime, a person is classed as constrained if he did not have the opportunity to work overtime *and* said he would have worked overtime if presented with the opportunity.

7 Had we been trying to test the homogeneity of our sample we could have adopted standard tests to see if our regressions really were different. However, we are trying to judge the appropriateness of a model to different samples, and we know of no test of the difference in equations for such a case. We have run a regression on the constrained only, and found that the regression is not significant.

8 The estimate was made as follows. We first computed for all rented accommodation the average rent for houses with various numbers of rooms. We then assumed that the imputed income of an owner occupier was equal to the average rent paid by people renting that number of rooms.

9 For some purposes (e.g. longer-run estimates) it might be better to include only supplementary benefit levels plus possibly the housing items. We have run various definitions of the needs variable. The more inclusive definition in the text gives a higher R^2 and F than narrower definitions of need but the differences are not dramatic.

10 The scales relate to work (i.e. the job itself), pay, promotion, people (at work) and supervisors. The scales are discussed in Smith *et al.* (1965) and are evaluated in Robinson, Athanasious and Head (1969) where it stated 'the instrument which appears to us to have the best credentials is the *Job Description Index.* Lengthy extensive and competent research went into the construction of this instrument ... ' (P. 101).

Chapter 6

Endogeneity I
Estimating Labour Supply with Piecewise Linear Budget
Constraints

INTRODUCTION

The classical theory of individual labour supply derives a supply of labour
function relating the number of hours an individual wishes to work to his
wage rate and the level of his unearned income. One of the major problems
that investigators have faced in trying to estimate this relationship is that
in practice individuals do not face the simple linear budget constraint on
which the theory is based, but rather a piecewise linear budget constraint
comprising a multiplicity of linear segments. There are a number of factors
that give rise to such a form of budget constraint. First, there is the
existence of a progressive tax schedule which displays constant marginal
tax rates within various income bands. Secondly, there is the existence of
overtime which implies that an individual's gross hourly wage rate is higher
for hours beyond the standard work week. Finally there is the presence of
upper constraints on the number of hours an individual can work in a given
job. This implies that if the individual wants to work longer than these
given number of hours he either has to take another job paying a possibly
different gross wage, or can find no other job in which case his wage beyond
this point is effectively zero.

A widely adopted procedure for estimating the supply function in these
conditions is to take a linear approximation to the budget constraint at
the individual's actual hours of work; that is, to enter as independent
variables in his supply function the net marginal wage rate and the imputed
level of non-employed income derived by assuming that the linear segment
of the budget constraint on which the individual actually works extends
over his entire range of possible hours of work. Probably the first to use
such a method was Hall (1973) who applied it to a sample of US workers.
It was also used by Brown, Levin and Ulph (1976) for a sample of UK
married male workers (see Chapter 5).

The problem with this procedure is that it takes the segment of the budget constraint on which the individual operates as exogenous, whereas this really depends on the hours the individual chooses to work and should be explained simultaneously with hours of work. As is now widely recognised failure to do so can result in the estimates being biased.[1]

The main object of this chapter is to report a procedure for obtaining labour supply estimates which are free from endogeneity bias, and to use this procedure to determine the magnitude of the errors in the earlier labour supply estimates for the UK which had been obtained by Brown, Levin and Ulph (1976).

At an advanced state of the research, however, we discovered that Wales and Woodland (1979) and Burtless and Hausman (1978) had developed procedures for circumventing endogeneity bias which are very similar to our own.

Our procedure differs from that of Wales and Woodland in that we employ an indirect utility function to represent preferences rather than a direct utility function. This allows us to employ a more general functional form than the CES function employed by Wales and Woodland. Burtless and Hausman start from a constant elasticity supply function which they integrate to obtain an indirect utility function. While this is again a more limited function form than we employ it permits them to use random coefficients in order to allow for heterogeneity in individual preferences, which we ignore altogether in our work. On the other hand, the people in our sample faced non-linearities in their budget constraints arising from all three factors mentioned in the opening paragraph, and had as many as four segments to their budget constraints. While it is in principle possible to extend the Burtless/Hausman procedure to this case, in practice, calculating the probability that an individual's optimum occurs on any particular segment of the budget constraint or at a kink point becomes considerably more complicated.[2] In this case one loses a lot of the computational advantage of starting with the more restrictive functional form, and it remains an open question whether the Burtless/Hausman procedure or some modification of the procedure proposed here would best allow for both a multi-segment budget constraint and heterogeneous preferences. We hope to report on this at a future date.

In the next section of this chapter we will outline our model and its stochastic specification, and in the following section will discuss the construction of our samples and the data we employ. In the subsequent section we will present our estimates, and a comparison of the various estimating methods which they enable us to make.

We have undertaken three types of comparison. First, we have used a given functional form to compare the estimates one obtains using the 'linear approximation of the budget constraint' approach as against the 'full information approach'. Here we confirm the finding of Wales and Woodland that the endogeneity bias of the first approach leads to underestimation of the elasticity of substitution. Secondly, we compare our general functional form with the restricted CES form employed by Wales and Woodland, and show that the restriction can again lead to underestimating the elasticity of substitution. Finally, we compare the general functional form for the supply function adapted here to the quadratic approximation used by Brown, Levin and Ulph and others. We show that once again, the restricted functional form leads to lower estimates of the elasticity of substitution. We conclude that the Brown, Levin and Ulph estimates of the elasticity of substitution were too low for two reasons – endogeneity bias and restrictive functional form. Our finding is that when one uses a general functional form and removes endogeneity bias one obtains an estimate of the elasticity of substitution of about 0.55 for both men and women. This is a good deal higher than many previous estimates, and, if accepted, can have important implications for what one might take to be the optimal tax rate (see Stern, 1976).

THE MODEL AND ITS STOCHASTIC SPECIFICATION

The essence of the procedure adopted by Wales and Woodland, Burtless and Hausman, and ourselves is as follows. For each individual we construct his entire piecewise linear budget constraint. We then introduce an explicit representation of individual preferences whose parameters we wish to estimate. The representation is chosen so that for every set of parameter values and for every individual we can explicitly solve for the hours of work which maximize utility subject to the piecewise linear budget constraint. We then obtain maximum likelihood estimates of the parameters. As pointed out in the Introduction, the three methods differ in the way they represent individual preferences.

The basis of our procedure is an indirect utility function of the form

$$v(p,q) \equiv \text{Max } v\,(c,l) \qquad \text{s.t. } p\,c + q\,l \leqq 1 \atop \qquad\qquad\qquad c \geqq 0 \atop \qquad\qquad 0 \leqq l \leqq 1 \tag{1}$$

Here p and q are the normalized prices $p = 1/(W+N)$, $q = W/(W+N)$, where W is the wage rate and N is the level of non-employment income. Units are chosen so that the maximum amount of time available to the individual is 1 unit.

From (1) one derives the supply function

$$H(p,q) = 1 - \frac{\partial v/\partial q}{p\partial v/\partial p + q\partial v/\partial q} \tag{2}$$

The ith segment of individual j's budget constraint is characterised by its normalised prices p^j_i, q^j_i, and by the upper and lower bounds on the hours of work $\overline{H}^j_i$, $\underline{H}^j_i$. If n^j is the number of segments on the jth individual's budget constraint, and if p^j, q^j, $\overline{H}^j$, $\underline{H}^j$ are the associated n^j-dimensional vectors $X^j = (n^j, p^j, q^j, \overline{H}^j, \underline{H}^j)$ is the vector which completely characterises his budget constraint.

To find the hours of work associated with a given X vector one proceeds as follows.

For the ith segment, calculate

$$H_i = H(p_i, q_i) \tag{3}$$

If $\underline{H}_i \leq H_i \leq \overline{H}^i$ then H_i is a possible point of global utility maximization.[3] Having found the possible interior solutions, it only remains to check the possibility that the utility maximum occurs at a kink point.

As long as the utility function is monotonic in consumption and leisure, the utility maximum can never occur at a point where the marginal wage rate is increasing with hours of work, so we need only be concerned with the case where the marginal wage rate is decreasing. If such a point occurs at the boundary of the segments i, $i + 1$, then it is easy to see that this kink point will be a local maximum if and only if[4]

$$H_{i+1} = H(p_{i+1}, q_{i+1}) < \underline{H}_{i+1} = \overline{H}_i < H(p_i, q_i) = H_i \tag{4}$$

The calculations in (3) and (4) are straightforward to undertake.

Having determined possible points of global utility maximization it only remains to choose that point which yields maximum utility. The utility levels at *local interior* maxima are easily computed by inserting the p_i, q_i of the associated segment into the indirect utility function. The only problem, then, is that at kink points one first has to find the appropriate prices to substitute into the indirect utility function. These are found in the following way.

Suppose that at the point $\tilde{H} = \underline{H}_{i+1} = \overline{H}_i$,(4) is satisfied. Then the level of consumption, $\tilde{c}$, which prevails at H is given by

$$p_i \tilde{c} + q_i (1 - \tilde{H}) = 1 \tag{5}$$

or alternatively

$$p_{i+1}\, \bar{c} + q_{i+1}\, (1 - \bar{H}) = 1$$

The prices p, q which support $\bar{H}$ are then given by the two equations

$$\bar{H} = H(\bar{p}, \bar{q}) \tag{6}$$

$$\bar{p}\, \bar{c} + \bar{q}\, (1 - \bar{H}) = 1 \tag{7}$$

It is possible to solve (6) and (7) by a simple and efficient iterative procedure.[5,6]

One can therefore compute utility at all the local optima and hence find the global point of utility maximization. By this procedure we generate the supply function

$$H = \phi\,(X) \tag{8}$$

It is crucial to recognise that although the value of H given by (8) will satisfy the condition

$$H = H\,(\hat{p}, \hat{q}) \tag{9}$$

where $(\hat{p}, \hat{q})$ is *either* one of the p_i, q_i in X *or* a value of $(\bar{p}, \bar{q})$ computed from some of the p_i, q_i in X, a change in the values of the parameters of the utility function could alter H as given by (8) in a very different way from that given by (9), since such a change could alter the prices at which the utility maximum is achieved as well as the utility maximising number of hours for any given set of prices.[7]

To complete the specification of the model of estimation purposes, it remains to select a particular functional form for $V(p,q)$ and to specify the error structure of the model.

The functional form we chose was a Generalized Constant Elasticity of Substitution (GCES) function of the form

$$V(p,q) = \begin{cases} \dfrac{1}{1-\theta_6}\left[\theta_1\, p^{1-\theta_6} + \cdots + \theta_5\,(p+q)^{1-\theta_6}\right] & \theta_6 > 0, \theta_6 \neq 1 \\[2mm] \theta_1 \log p + \cdots + \theta_5 \log\,(p+q) & \theta_6 = 1 \end{cases}$$

This has the property that for any $\theta_6 > 0$ and for any indirect utility function it is possible to find values of the remaining five θ coefficients which will make the GCES function a local second-order approximation to the true utility function. Furthermore if $\theta_i < 0$, $i = 1, \ldots, 5$ the function is everywhere decreasing in both its arguments and is quasi-convex, which are properties that indirect utility functions must satisfy. As usual with these second-order approximations, however, if $\theta_i > 0$, for some $i = 1, \ldots, 5$ then the function may only be locally well-behaved. We will return to this point later.

The main reason why we selected this generalized functional form rather than others which have been proposed is that unlike the translog, the generalised Cobb–Douglas and the generalised Leontief, this function does not reduce to a specific CES function on imposing the additivity ($\theta_5 = 0$) and homotheticity ($\theta_3 = \theta_4 = 0$) conditions (e.g. both the translog and the generalised Cobb–Douglas reduce to Cobb–Douglas functions). Thus if the underlying function just happens to be CES but with elasticity of substitution different from 1, then this functional form should identify it while others will not.

If we bring the parameters of the indirect utility function explicitly into the model, we can now write (8) as

$$\hat{H}_j = \phi\,(X_j, \theta) \qquad\qquad (10)$$

where $\hat{H}_j$ are the predicted hours of individual j and X_j are the observed parameters of his budget constraint.

The stochastic specification of the model is then

$$H_j = H_j + \epsilon_j = \phi\,(X_j, \theta) + \epsilon_j \qquad\qquad (11)$$

where the ϵ_j are assumed to be independently and normally distributed with zero mean and constant variance.[8]

We seek maximum likelihood estimates of θ. Given our normality assumptions maximum likelihood estimates are equivalent to least squares estimates. Unfortunately, in order to establish claims for the consistency of the maximum likelihood estimates and to justify the use of tests such as the likelihood ratio test we must be convinced that the maximum likelihood estimator has certain properties. These properties include that 'the derivatives with respect to θ of log $f(\quad)$ exist up to third order. This should hold for all values of x (apart possibly from a finite number of x-values) and for every θ belonging to an interval A that contains θ_0 as an interior point',[9] and that the third-order derivative of log f is bounded.

Unfortunately in our case we cannot be sure that our likelihood function is continuous at the kink point where the marginal wage rate is rising.[10] It can, however, be shown using a proof derived from work by Holly (1978) that although there is a discontinuity at this point the true maximum will never occur at discontinuity. We can therefore assume that we can approximate the true likelihood function by one that is continuous and differentiable and that follows the true likelihood function as closely as possible and is identical close to the maximum,[11] – while accepting that there is still no guarantee that the likelihood ratio test is necessarily valid (if we can make this assumption then the estimates we derive will be consistent). Having established consistency we proceed to consider the data and the results which the model generates.

THE DATA

Our estimation procedure requires that we construct the entire budget constraint for each individual. Now while in the empirical work of Wales and Woodland the piecewise linear nature of the budget constraint comes only from the presence of progressive taxation[12] we have allowed for the other factors mentioned in the Introduction, namely, overtime, more than one job, and constraints on the hours an individual can work in any job. This means that an individual can have up to four segments to his budget constraint, with four possible boundary points occurring at zero hours of work, the point where he begins to work overtime, the point where he switches on to a second job and his tax threshold. However, unlike the case in which there is only progressive taxation and so, given his gross wage, a predetermined number of hours an individual has to be working to be in any one tax bracket, it is less obvious in which sequence our segments should occur except that an individual has to work his basic hours before he is entitled to work overtime. There are in fact a very large number of sequences in which one can place them depending on the varying relationships of the second job wage rate to the basic and overtime rates in the main job, and the various possible ways in which the individual could be constrained in his decisions in both the main job and the second job. Even if we had all the information we wanted on this (which we did not have, since we had no information on possible constraints on the choice of second job hours) we would still face the possibility that some people's decision to work a second job could only be explained by the assumption that they enjoy working there in preference to additional hours in the main job – a possibility not allowed by our simple model with homogeneous labour.

Consequently in order to design the budget constraint for each individual we imposed the following two requirements on those who worked a second job in order to be included in our sample. Individuals had to have a gross wage in their second job which was lower than the overtime hourly rate, and they had to have indicated that they would have liked to work more hours of overtime in their main job than they had been able to do. With this restriction we then ordered the segments so that the individual worked his standard working week first of all, then his overtime hours and then his second job.

It is worth mentioning that constraints on the overtime hours of those working a second job are not the only form of constraints allowed for in our work. We have also allowed for individuals who may wish to work more hours of overtime but have no second job to go to. To these individuals we have given a final segment which has a zero marginal wage rate beyond their total hours of work in their main job. We have similarly treated these individuals who said they wished to work overtime but had no opportunity to do so. We have not however tried to allow for the possibility that individuals may be constrained to work longer hours than they would otherwise wish.

Apart from the restrictions on second job workers mentioned above, our sample of married male workers is identical to that of the Brown, Levin and Ulph study. The effect of the restrictions has been to reduce the sample size from 434 to 335. Our second sample was of married women workers who were selected on exactly the same basis, giving us a sample of 74.

Our procedure requires that for each individual we identify the number of segments to his budget constraint and for each segment the boundary points (hours of work and income) the marginal wage, and the associated level of non-employment income.

The calculation of the marginal wage rates and levels of non-employment income are exactly as described by Brown, Levin and Ulph with one major exception. Brown, Levin and Ulph exclude from their measure of non-employment income all income accruing to the individual from sources other than their work – what they called 'other income' – largely because while such income does not flow directly from the individual's work, it is none the less unlikely to be independent of the decision he makes as to how long to work. This leaves in their measure of non-employment income simply the adjustment term for the non-linearities in the budget constraint, and this variable was entered with the regression independently of 'other income'. Under our technique we cannot allow for such a distinction and so our measure of non-employment income includes other income.

RESULTS

Our results are presented in Table 6.1 for men and Table 6.2 for women. The first regression in each table is of exactly the basic form as the regressions that appear in Brown, Levin and Ulph. For men this regression was run in order to explore the effect that changing the sample size has made, and so that a comparison between the different approaches can be made for exactly the same sample. As mentioned in the previous section, we are unable to adapt the Brown, Levin and Ulph procedure of distinguishing between non-employment income and other income, so the second regression gives the result of using their functional form (a quadratic approximation to the supply function) when other income, as calculated by Brown, Levin and Ulph, is amalgamated into non-employment income. We call this the comparative quadratic form. Since neither of these approaches was used in a context in which one utilises the full budget constraint (what we have called the non-endogenous estimates in the tables) rather than a linear approximation to it (the endogenous method) the cells in the bottom half of the table below these two regressions types are empty.

The last three columns present results derived by using, respectively, an unrestricted GCES form, a GCES form with $\theta_1, \ldots, \theta_5 > 0$ and finally a CES form (i.e. with the additional restrictions $\theta_3 = \theta_4 = \theta_5 = 0$). All of these estimates are obtained using both an endogenous and non-endogenous treatment of the budget constraint.

For each set of estimates we give the minimized sum of squares and the adjusted R^2 when a linear regression has been employed. Using the mean values for the marginal wage rate and non-employment income each person faced on the segment on which he was actually working we computed the hours of work, price, income and substitution elasticities and the elasticity of substitution that would be predicted by the estimated coefficients. In the case of all functional forms the mean marginal wage rates were 82.051 for men and 46.536 for women. For the GCES, restricted GCES and CES forms the mean values of the non-employment income were 3.486 for men and 16.543 for women. In the case of the Brown-Levin-Ulph quadratic form the mean values for the intercept were 1.509 for men and 1.793 for women and for the comparative quadratic form the mean values for the intercept were 7.055 for men and 22.567 for women. Each table also shows the value for the mean hours of work[13] worked by the sample (the value of $\bar{H}$), so that by comparing this with the predicted hours of the various regressions we get some impression of the ability of the various forms to predict.

TABLE 6.1 *Labour Supply Estimates for Men Sample ($\overline{H} = 0.28$)*

Functional Form	Brown–Levin–Ulph Quadratic Form	Comparative Quadratic Form	Generalised CES	Restricted Generalised CES	CES
Endogenous Treatment of Budget Constraint					
Sum of squares	0.65	0.68	1.01	2.36	3.03
$\overline{R}^2$	0.18	0.13	—	—	—
Predicted hours Price elasticity	0.28	0.29	0.29	0.28	0.28
Income elasticity	-0.00	0.06	-0.13	-0.38	-0.38
Substitution elasticity	-0.02	-0.02	-0.05	-0.09	-0.09
Elasticity of substitution	0.31	0.15	0.23	0.19	0.19
	0.41	0.20	0.30	0.24	0.24
Non-Endogenous Treatment of Budget Constraint					
Sum of squares	—	—	1.62	3.07	3.04
Predicted hours Price elasticity	—	—	0.24	0.22	0.28
Income elasticity	—	—	-0.07	-0.16	-0.33
Substitution elasticity	—	—	-0.10	-0.12	-0.10
Elasticity of	—	—	0.50	0.48	0.29

TABLE 6.2 Labour Supply Estimates for Women Sample ($\bar{H} = 0.22$)

	Functional Form	Brown–Levin–Ulph Quadratic Form	Comparative Quadratic Form	Generalised CES	Restricted Generalised CES	CES
Endogenous Treatment of Budget Constraint	Sum of squares	0.09	0.09	0.08	0.33	0.38
	$\bar{R}^2$	0.09	0.11	—	—	—
	Predicted hours	0.20	0.20	0.25	0.25	0.52
	Price elasticity	−0.21	−0.09	0.19	0.21	0.12
	Income elasticity	0.00	−0.10	−0.14	−0.12	−0.10
	Substitution elasticity	−0.23	−0.04	0.29	0.30	0.26
	Elasticity of substitution	—	—	0.22	0.22	0.44
Non-Endogenous Treatment of Budget Constraint	Sum of squares	—	—	0.41	0.49	0.48
	Predicted hours	—	—	0.22	0.20	0.30
	Price elasticity	—	—	0.63	0.57	0.32
	Income elasticity	—	—	−0.35	−0.41	−0.27
	Substitution elasticity	—	—	0.84	0.81	0.55
	Elasticity of substitution	—	—	0.55	0.50	0.49

The estimation procedure we employed for the non-linear forms was to randomly generate about 400 vectors of parameter values and evaluate the sum of squares for each of these. We then selected about 40 of the lowest values and used these as starting points as the Powell algorithm was chosen since it did not require us to evaluate the derivatives of the function.

Let us then discuss general features of the results before turning to a more detailed examination.

Perhaps the most important and most striking result is that we have in all cases confirmed the finding of Wales and Woodland that, by employing the non-endogenous procedure for handling the budget constraint, one obtains a higher estimate of the elasticity of substitution than is given using an endogenous treatment of the budget constraint.

However, the exact magnitude of the elasticity and the extent of the differences between the two techniques varies quite a lot depending on the functional form used. Here only two general conclusions seem to emerge. The CES function gives a lower estimate of elasticity of substitution than the GCES. So too does the quadratic approximation (in its strictly comparable form). Indeed for women the functional form shows up the endogeneity problem in its classic form. The majority of women work neither overtime nor a second job, and so have only two segments to their constraint with the boundary point occurring at the tax threshold. This implies that the level of associated non-employment income is higher on the second segment than on the first. Indeed when other sources of income are separated out from non-employment income, as they are in the Brown–Levin–Ulph procedure, then other things being equal, a higher level of non-employment income will go along with higher hours of work – which could well account for the positive income elasticity in the first column of Table 6.2. A further point worth mentioning is the finding of a positive price elasticity for women in all but the quadratic forms. This is in line with previous studies which have been made.

This suggests that the estimates of the elasticity of substitution obtained by Brown, Levin and Ulph differ from that obtained here by the GCES form for four reasons. Both their functional form and the endogenous nature of their procedure combined to reduce the elasticity. It also appears that the larger sample resulted in a lower elasticity, though our results suggest that separating other income from non-employment income probably led to a somewhat higher estimate than might otherwise have been the case for men. The difference is clearly much more marked for women than for men.

More specific conclusions are that having imposed the non-positivity restrictions on the GCES function for men, the additional restrictions of additivity and hometheticity seem to make little significant difference.

Finally, it should be noted that the non-endogenous GCES results for men and women are very similar in terms of their elasticity of substitution, though women have income elasticities which are somewhat greater in absolute magnitude, a positive price elasticity which is in line with previous studies and a substitution elasticity of much greater magnitude than for men.

CONCLUSIONS

In this chapter we have explored a procedure for removing the endogeneity problem which has beset labour supply estimation. Though similar in essentials, the procedure is more general than that recently developed by Wales and Woodland both in terms of the functional form it can handle and in terms of the types of piecewise linear budget constraint considered. We have applied the procedure to a sample of married male and married female workers in the UK, and have argued that previous UK estimates of the elasticity of substitution were too low both because of the endogeneity problem and because of the functional form adopted. Our estimates suggest a value of around 0.55 for the elasticity of substitution for both men and women. We have argued however that the procedure may not completely eliminate bias, because it essentially requires that the utility function be well behaved over the entire budget constraint, which it may be impossible to guarantee without placing restrictions on the range of permissible parameter values. This has led us to use a functional form which is more flexible than those previously proposed, but even then we cannot guarantee that this will eliminate the bias.

The strength of the procedure, which it shares with that of Wales and Woodland and Burtless and Hausman, is that it allows one to handle naturally and simultaneously those individuals whose equilibria occur at the standard tangency points, and those whose equilibria occur at kinks in the budget constraint. In particular it provides a way of estimating the underlying structure of preferences even when individuals may be constrained in some ways in their choice of hours of work – though in this chapter we have only considered the case in which individuals are constrained to work fewer hours than they desire.

The procedure will clearly generalise beyond labour supply to any case where the price an individual pays for a commodity depends on the amount he buys, for example, electricity tariff. On the other hand, as we point out in Chapter 9, it is not applicable to bargaining type models of household labour supply decisions.

Finally, it should be recalled that what we have tried to do is consistently estimate the underlying structure of preferences, and that the supply elasticities we have presented are those of the classical supply function derived for linear budget constraints. To predict the actual consequences for an individual's labour supply of, say, a change in the tax system, one has in principle to be able to construct in detail the individual's entire budget constraint before and after the tax change and to solve for his hours of work under the two constraints by a maximization procedure of the type outlined here. The resulting elasticities could well be very different from those suggested in this chapter.

NOTES : CHAPTER 6

1   See, for example, Greenhalgh (1976), Wales and Woodland (1979), Burtless and Hausman (1978), Heckman and Killingsworth (1979) among others.
2   This point can best be made by considering the following diagram, in which the individual faces the three-segment budget constraint ABCD

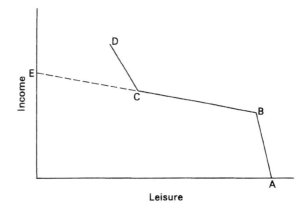

Leisure

Figure 6.1

If there were only two segments ABE then, as Burtless and Hausman show, it is straightforward to calculate the three intervals in the range of parameter values for which the utility maximum occurs on AB, at B, and on BE, respectively. When segment CD is present, however, then the range of parameter values for which the optimum occurs at B or on BC could both be affected. To determine whether or not this is the case one has to compare the maximum utility at B or on BC with that on CD and hence find the precise point at which the switch on to the DC segment occurs. In principle this is fairly straightforward, but as the number of segments increases, the computation involved in predetermining the interval ranges of the parameter space becomes similar to that employed in the method we propose.
3   Global in the sense that this is over the entire budget constraint defined by X.

4 Although we have defined this for interior solutions the same argument holds for the end points of the budget constraint, that is, for $H(p_1,q_1) < 0$ and $H(p_n,q_n) > 1$ for the lower and upper ends, respectively.

5 The procedure operates as follows. At a point $(c,\bar{H})$ we have wage rates W_L, W_{L+1} and levels of unearned income H_i, N_{i+1} which satisfy the conditions

$$W_{i+1} < W_i \qquad \bar{c} = W_j\bar{H} + N_j \qquad j = i, i+1$$
$$f(W_i,N_i) > \bar{H}$$
$$f(W_{i+1}, N_{i+1}) < \bar{H}$$

where $f(W,N)$ is the supply function $f(w,N) = H(1/W + N, W/W + N)$. In other words we have

$$W_{i+1} < W_i \tag{1}$$
$$\phi(W_i) > \bar{H} \tag{2}$$
$$\phi(W_{i+1}) < \bar{H} \tag{3}$$

where $\phi(W) = F(W, \bar{c} - W\bar{H})$. Find the value of λ such that

$$\lambda\phi(W_i) + (1 - \lambda)\phi(W_{i+1}) = \bar{H}$$

and compute

$$\hat{W} = \lambda W_i + (1 - \lambda)W_{i+1}$$

If $\phi(\hat{W}) = \bar{H}$ the procedure stops. If $\phi(\hat{W}) > \bar{H}$ set $W_i = \hat{W}$. Conditions (1), (2) (3) are once again satisfied and we repeat the process. If $\phi(\hat{W}) < H$ set $W_{i+1} = \hat{W}$ and repeat the process. By this procedure we continually contract the interval within which the desired value of W lies. After several iterations one has either found the solution exactly or contracted the interval so much that the mid-point gives a very accurate approximation.

6 Notice that by using this procedure it is not necessary, as has sometimes been thought to restrict the functional form of $V(\quad)$ to be self-dual so that one finds the appropriate prices $\bar{p}, \bar{q}$ by directly computing the marginal rate of substitution at C, H. This is important in that it enables us to maintain the advantage of starting from an indirect utility function, namely, that even with quite complex functional forms one can devise the supply function (2) by simple differentiation.

7 Put another way, the function ϕ will, in general, be a non-linear function, not just because of any non-linearities introduced by way of the ratio form of H in equation (2), but more importantly, because the derivation of the utility maximizing prices from X is an inherently non-linear process.

8 Of course this ignores the possibility of truncation bias arising from the restriction that to be included in the data set people had to be working at least eight hours a week. Since most people in our samples were actually working over twenty hours a week we have simply assured for the moment that this is likely to be a less important source of bias than endogeneity bias. We hope to investigate this in later work.

9 Theil (1971, p. 392).

10 It is worth noting that Wales and Woodland avoid this problem by confining attention to the case where the marginal wage is always falling with hours. Burtless and Hausman avoid the difficulty by having essentially a continuum of consumers with any given budget constraint. Since this problem only arises on a

set of measure zero, it can have no effect on the continuity and differentiability of the likelihood function.

11 The problem of possible discontinuity at the band point where the marginal wage rate is falling can be covered by reference to Holly again.

12 Though they do recognise that the other factors we mention can give rise to piecewise non-linearity.

13 We measure hours as percentage of the week (168 hours) the wage as the rate in £'s for 168 hours work and non-employment income in £'s.

14 The results have also been evaluated using an algorithm devised by Peckham (1970).

Chapter 7

Preferences

I INTRODUCTION

In this chapter we investigate to what extent the explanation of variation in hours worked can be improved by taking account of preferences, as compared with a simple model including only measures of the slope and position of the budget constraint as arguments of the labour supply function. The work extends the analysis of Chapter 5 in two directions: the treatment of preferences is more comprehensive; and samples of married women and single people are used, as well as of married men.

Our approach to the specification of preference patterns is to attempt as far as possible to define variables which offer an economic explanation of observed behaviour. Other studies (e.g. Greenhalgh, 1977, 1979; Cain and Watts, 1973) have typically included dummy variables for such characteristics as industry, race and region. While such a treatment is useful in identifying the variation to be explained, the explanation is only statistical. It also runs into a degrees of freedom problem: the number of regressors is very large if a dummy is included, for example, for each region, and reduction of the list by inferences from regression on subsets of the variables is likely to be seriously misleading in view of the fairly strong correlations between many of the variables. Our approach greatly reduces the number of variables needed to represent preferences. It also exposes numerous measurement and specification problems not previously discussed in the literature. A large part of this chapter will be spent in analysing these problems. As they cannot be adequately solved with present data, our results are of interest more for the light they throw on the significance of these problems than for the positive conclusions which can be drawn about the nature of preferences.

In previous work on preferences, the preference variables have always been included linearly, implying that their effect on hours worked is independent of the parameters of the budget constraint. It seems, however, *a priori* at least as likely that variations in preferences affect responsiveness to variation in these parameters as that they only cause independent changes in hours worked. If preferences are represented by a large number of dummies, testing this hypothesis would be impracticable as it increases the number of regressors almost threefold. We have been able to allow for both the wage and income responses to be functions of all the preference variables.

In order to be able to investigate more fully the specification of preference patterns, we have left aside several other specification problems: principally, the specification of the simultaneous relationship between hours worked and the wage rate arising from non-linearity of the budget constraint; also the specification of the error distribution for low values of hours worked, given that actual hours must be at least eight in our sample; and of the possible interdependence between the income-leisure choice of members of our sample and the choices of other members of their households.

The bias resulting from some specification errors may be small for some samples. Estimates of the size of simultaneity bias for our samples of married men and women are presented in Chapter 8. Such evidence as there is on the importance of other biases is discussed in Section VIII of that chapter. The possibility of significant bias means that final answers cannot be given to the questions ultimately of interest about the sensitivity of labour supply to variations in wage rates, income and preferences. Given the lack of hard evidence that any of the problems mentioned may safely be ignored, this qualification does of course apply to all studies of labour supply so far published, since all neglect either preferences or at least one of the other problems. The present analysis does enable difficulties to be identified and conclusions drawn about alternative formulations which will be useful when the quantity and quality of the data permit a more comprehensive analysis.

The basic model into which preferences have been incorporated is presented in Section II. The analysis of the sample of married women is set out in Sections III–V. Section III describes the selection of the sample. In Section IV we define the variables chosen to represent preference patterns, put forward hypotheses about their likely relationship to hours worked, discuss the associated measurement and identification problems, and analyse the possible consequences of measurement and specification errors. Section V gives the results of estimating the basic equation and of incorporating preferences in various ways. Sections VI–VIII set out the analysis of the sample of married men and Sections IX–XII the analysis of the sample of single people. As the form of analysis was essentially similar, Sections VI and IX describe only how the selection of these samples differed from the selection of the sample of married women described in

Section III, and likewise Sections VII and X discuss only the differences in the treatment of preferences. Section XII presents an analysis of subdivisions of the sample of single people designed to investigate whether differences of sex and status within the household, as judged by age and earnings as a fraction of household income, have a significant effect on supply responses. The conclusions are brought together in Section XIII.

II   THE BASIC MODEL

The following simplifying assumptions are made:

(1) The decision-making unit is an individual. (For brevity this individual is referred to as 'she', but the same model will be used for male and female workers.)

(2) This individual faces a choice between two homogeneous commodities, income and leisure.

(3) She has a predetermined endowment of non-employment income, which includes any state transfers not related to employment income.

(4) She makes the choice independently of other members of the household, except that their income net of tax is part of her non-employment income.

(5) She has a preference ordering over combinations of income and leisure which satisfies the usual conditions.

(6) All respondents in a given sample have the same preference ordering except for random variations which may be represented by an additive error in the supply equation.

(7) Her employment income is related only to the hours she works, and not to the effort put in.

(8) She faces a budget constraint which is linear over the entire range of hours, from 0 to 168 per week.

(9) She maximises utility, a function of income and leisure, subject to this budget constraint.

Desired hours of work may then be expressed simply as a function of the two parameters of the budget constraint: its slope, the marginal wage rate (W), and the hypothetical income at zero hours of work which we shall term the intercept (I).

The form of the function is postulated to be the simplest consistent with both the price and income effects being dependent on both the wage rate and the intercept.

Making the additional assumption:

(10)   The individual's actual hours of work (H) equal her desired hours or differ from them only by a random disturbance.

The basic equation becomes

$$H = \beta_1 + \beta_2 W + \beta_3 W^2 + \beta_4 WI + \beta_5 I + \beta_6 I^2 + \epsilon \tag{1}$$

where $\beta_1, \ldots, \beta_6$ are the parameters to be estimated, and ϵ is a random error assumed to be independently Normally distributed.

The dependent variable, H, is actual hours worked in all jobs during the week before the respondent's interview.

The values of W and I were derived from the computation of the individual's actual (non-linear) budget constraint, described in Chapter 8. The wage rate W is the actual rate net of tax and inclusive of any overtime premium at her actual hours of work. If actual hours were at a kink in the budget constraint, an average was used of the wage rate for the last hour worked (w_{k-1}) and the rate for an extra hour (w_k), defined by

$$\arctan \left[\tfrac{1}{2}(\tan w_k + \tan w_{k-1}) \right] \tag{2}$$

Some results showing the effect of varying the value used for those on a kink are given in Chapter 8.

The intercept I was calculated assuming that the wage rate for the actual hours applied over the whole range of hours down to zero. It is thus a sum of three components: the individual's own actual non-employment income net of tax, the actual net income of other members of the household, and an adjustment for non-linearity. It is implicit in this treatment of non-linearity that the individual's own actual non-employment income and the adjustment, or hypothetical non-employment income, have the same coefficients in the supply function. In reality an individual may respond differently to changes in the income of other members of the household. We have preferred, however, not to separate out this term, but to make an *ad hoc* adjustment to model one aspect of the complexity of household decision-making which is not otherwise taken into account in our analysis.

Reference should be made to Chapter 5 for further discussion of the definition of, and problems of measuring, H, W and I.

III   MARRIED WOMEN – SELECTION OF THE SAMPLE

The respondents in the 1971 survey include 505 married women. The data available on them enables us to identify characteristics which, if used as selection criteria, will lead to a sub-sample whose members are closer to satisfying the assumptions listed in the previous section than those omitted. Application of some of these criteria reduces the sample size appreciably, so that striking a balance between retaining adequate degrees of freedom and refinement of the sample is difficult. The analysis reported in Chapter 5 on married men and preliminary experimentation on the present sample showed that results are quite sensitive to the selection criteria. It is presumed that the results for the most refined samples are closest to reflecting the behaviour of those to whom the model is closest to being applicable. This has inclined us as far as possible towards refinement of the sample at the expense of sample size. Hence individuals were excluded:

(1) if they were past retirement age, on the grounds that their behaviour was likely to be different in a way that would be difficult to model because of, for example, pension earning rules;
(2) if they had been off sick so that their observed hours probably diverged from the equilibrium figure;
(3) if there was at least one other worker in the household other than a spouse, on the grounds that the independence assumption was likely to be violated in such households. The sample could not be restricted to single worker households as all but eight had working husbands and the remainder were almost certainly not normally single worker households;
(4) if they actually worked fewer than eight hours or earned less than £2 in the week. These are abitrary limits to exclude those whose hours were low enough to suggest that their motives for working were different from the rest of the sample or they were out of equilibrium for reasons not identified by the survey.
(5) if they received some payment for effort such as a bonus, incentive payments or piece-rates;
(6) if their hours were constrained both ways. There are both conceptual and interpretative problems with questions about constraints. But as far as can be judged from answers about possibilities in the week to which data on an individual refers, no one in the sub-sample was prevented from working as few hours as they would have liked, but free to work as many more hours as they would have liked. Those who said they were prevented from working as many hours as they would have liked were included in the sample, their budget constraint being constructed as described in Section II, using $w_k = 0$ in equation (2);
(7) if incomplete answers prevented calculation of their actual hours or

budget constraint. Applying this meant that some were excluded for whom the missing information would not have prevented calculation of all the variables required for this analysis, since it does not use information on the whole budget constraint. The criterion was applied, however, so that the same sample could be used with the full information approach of Chapter 8 to give comparable results.

Table 7.1   *Selection of the sample of married women*

Total no. from which selection made		505
Reason for exclusion	*No. excluded*	
	Gross[a]	*Net[a]*
Past retirement age	33	33
Ill	83	76
Worker other than spouse	148	117
Hours worked $<$ 8 or pay $<$ £2	30	8
On bonus, piece-rate or incentive scheme	115	71
Hours constrained both ways	8	2
Hours, standard working week or		
basic wage rate unknown	154	69
No. selected		129

a The gross figure is the number who would be excluded if the reason given against it were the only one applied; the net figure is the additional number excluded after individuals have been excluded for all the reasons given higher on the list.

The impact of these criteria on sample size is shown in Table 7.1. They give a sub-sample of 129 married women on which all the analysis in the next two sections is carried out. All of them had non-linear budget constraints, details of which are given in Chapter 8, Section II.

IV   MARRIED WOMEN – PREFERENCES

Our approach to the specification of preference patterns was to attempt, as far as the data allow, to define variables which would offer an economic explanation of behaviour and to eschew the inclusion of dummy variables for such attributes as race, region and occupation which might well achieve a better statistical fit but afford little clue to causation.

Eight major determinants of preferences on which we have some data may be distinguished:

(1)   the presence of dependants and in particular children;

(2)   demands on 'leisure' time, in particular doing chores and travelling to and from work;

(3)   the desire to acquire wealth;

(4)   unemployment of the main earner in the household, if not the respondent;

(5)   job satisfaction;

(6)   energy in relation to the demands of the job;

(7)   education;

(8)   age.

Another major determinant which has been mentioned in the literature (e.g. Hill, 1973) is the health of members of the household. We have insufficient data to include this separately. If the respondent herself was so ill that she worked less than eight hours or earned less than £2 in the week, she would have been excluded from the sample. If the illness was such that she went to work for more than eight hours, had not taken time off as sick leave but had to work fewer hours than usual because of lack of energy this is covered by the eighth determinant, energy. If illness of the main earner kept her at home, this is covered by the fourth determinant, unemployment of the main earner. But there are obviously other possibilities that will give rise to an error in the equation.

A survey of the literature (e.g. Cain and Watts, 1973; Bowen and Finegan, 1969; Mahoney, 1967; Rosen, 1976; Watts and Rees, 1977; Greenhalgh, 1977, 1979; Cohen *et al.*, 1970) reveals many variables not included explicitly on the above list such as region and occupation. Our hypothesis is that where a significant effect has been found which might also be expected in our sample, a major part of it is due to some combination of the determinants listed, the remainder being sociological and other influences which have been relegated to the disturbance term.

In the rest of this section, taking each determinant in turn, we elaborate the hypothesis underlying its inclusion, and give the definitions of the variables used to measure it. The causes and likely consequences of biases arising from unavoidable measurement and specification errors are discussed in some detail both as a prelude to analysis of the results and as a pointer to the areas in which in future data will have to be improved and the model extended. Summary statistics on each variable are given in Table 7.3.

Dependants

There are two opposing effects of having children: on the one hand, a mother may want to be at home with her children, or, if no other childminder is available, may need to stay at home. We call this the 'preference effect'. On the other hand, the more children there are, and the older they are, the more income will be needed to maintain the family's standard of living: given the income of other earners, other non-employment income and the woman's wage rate, the longer the hours she will have to work. We call this the 'income effect'.

The degrees of freedom problem prevents us from attempting to discriminate between the effects of children of different ages. We have no information on the strength of a woman's desire to be with her children, nor adequate information on the myriad circumstances which affect whether a woman needs to stay at home simply to look after the children when she would prefer to be working. It seems likely that the preference effect will not vary with variation in the number of children above one and will be small once children reach secondary school age. If it is further assumed that the preference effect is important for children up to this age, it may be measured by

$$\text{YINF} = 1 \text{ if there are any children under 11}$$
$$= 0 \text{ otherwise}$$

The amount deemed necessary to compensate for the effect of a given child on the family's standard of living may of course differ from family to family. On this assessment we have no data. Instead, as one assessment of the cost of 'necessities', we have used the state supplementary benefit per child, which was an increasing step function of age, the steps being under 5, 5-10, 11-12, and 13-15 years of age. Thus our variable to measure the income effect, XINF, is the sum of the state benefits which would be payable to the family.

We would expect the preference effect to be clearly negative for married women and the income effect positive. A plausible alternative to our hypothesis about the preference effect is that it becomes negligible from primary, rather than secondary, school age onwards. If this is so, the coefficient on YINF may be very small. If the presence of children past secondary school age necessitates the woman curtailing her hours of work, perhaps because they make more housework to be done or because the additional hours she would like to work are outside their school hours, this effect is likely to be picked up by the coefficient on XINF. If the income effect is small, say, because the woman relies on an increase in other family income to cover the cost of a child or a lower standard of living is accepted, the coefficient on XINF might then be negative.

The presence of other dependants might also be expected to have a negative preference effect and positive income effect. Although we know the composition of a household by age we do not know whether, for example, an elderly person is dependent or not. We have therefore had to omit any variables designed to measure these effects.

Demands on 'leisure' time
One assumption of the theory set out in Section II was that a worker makes a choice simply between two homogenous alternatives - income and leisure. It is more realistic to break down 'leisure' into the different ways in which non-working time might be spent. Some of the 'leisure' time will be spent engaged in activities which are necessary and possibly to which no positive utility is attached - washing, shopping, preparing meals and travelling to work for example. Now a woman's preference function may be such that within the usual range the time spent on these activities does not affect hours worked. But it is plausible that they usually do have some effect - that those who have to spend more time on chores, or travelling to work, work less.

On many of the determinants of how long needs to be spent on chores such as the closeness of shops and size of the house, we have no data but we do know whether the family owned a refrigerator or washing machine. On the assumption that ownership of a refrigerator will save time on shopping and preparation of meals and of a washing machine on laundry, we have defined a variable TASS to measure the ownership of these time-saving assets:

TASS = 2 if both a refrigerator and a washing machine are owned
 = 1 if only one is owned
 = 0 if neither

Respondents were asked directly about the time they spent travelling to work. We are therefore able to define a variable TIME to measure the effect of this separately.

TIME is the time taken by a single journey to work.

Although the above argument implies a negative coefficient on this variable, one reason why some women may travel further is in order to get a job in which they can earn more by working longer hours. This negative demand effect may cancel out the positive preference effect.

Wealth
Individuals may save for the specific purpose of acquiring durable consumer goods or other assets. This earning may be done in advance of

acquisition or afterwards through, for example, a hire purchase agreement. They may also enter into contracts for the hire of certain goods, notably housing, which commit them to a certain weekly outlay. Both sorts of 'committed' income may be taken as given when making the choice between income and leisure. If this is so, then one might expect that the higher is committed income, the higher will be hours worked given the budget constraint.

From the survey we can identify rent, mortgage payments, savings to buy specific durables and HP instalments. A variable (COMY) has been included which is the sum of these. It does not include planned savings which were not committed to the purchase of a particular durable. If there is a low correlation between actual and planned wealth, actual wealth will be negatively correlated with net saving. If also ownership of assets not included in the survey is positively correlated with those included, then measured wealth may be included as a proxy for these other planned net savings. Given that the survey gives only ownership levels of some major durables, our variable (WLTH) has been calculated as an average of the ownership levels weighted by estimated replacement values:

$$
\begin{aligned}
\text{WLTH} = {} & 5000 \text{ if the family owns a house} \\
& + 1000 \text{ if a car} \\
& + 50 \text{ if a refrigerator} \\
& + 60 \text{ if a television set} \\
& + 80 \text{ if a washing machine}
\end{aligned}
$$

Given the negative correlation between actual wealth and net saving and the other assumptions made, and no relationship between measured wealth and saving for replacement, a negative coefficient on WLTH would be expected. An individual with a high value of actual wealth may, however, be no nearer to her desired wealth than one with a lower figure. In this case higher wealth will not imply lower net savings. If across the sample there is a positive correlation between actual and desired wealth then the coefficient on WLTH will be biased towards zero. If relatively wealthy individuals undertake more saving to replace depreciating assets or spend more on complementary goods such as petrol for a car, and these expenditures are determined before deciding on hours or work, then the WLTH coefficient will be biased upwards and may be positive.

The implication of the argument in the first paragraph of this section is that the coefficient on COMY will be positive. If at least some of the components were not treated as predetermined by many individuals then the coefficient could be very close to zero. Relatively high expenditure on such goods as cars and television sets may be associated with a relatively strong preference for spending time on leisure activities, a preference which may not be measured by any of the other variables included. If so, the resulting bias could result in a negative coefficient on COMY.

Unemployment of the main earner

The intercept term of the basic model includes *actual* non-employment income. Although workers may be prevented from relating their hours of work to their permanent non-employment income by imperfections in capital markets, many relate their hours to some longer run average non-employment income. The intercept coefficients will measure the effect of the average change in this determinant of hours corresponding to a given change in actual non-employment income. Some changes in actual income may not have this average effect.

In most, if not all, households in our sample it would not be the married woman but her husband who was normally the main earner. It is plausible that if he was involuntarily unemployed without immediate prospect of further employment, the fall in his wife's actual non-employment income would be associated with a larger fall in her long-run income than other equal changes in her actual income. Hence there would be a positive effect on her hours of work in addition to that measured by the intercept terms. This effect may be strengthened if greater uncertainty about future non-employment income increases the preference for current income for precautionary reasons.

The closest we can get to measuring this effect of unemployment of the main earner is to include a dummy variable UME where

UME = 1 if the spouse was not working in the week to which the data refer
= 0 otherwise

There are several deficiencies of this measure: 'not working' does not mean involuntarily unemployed; if he was unemployed, it may have temporary, or part of an accepted work pattern. If he was only temporarily out of work, the change in actual income may have corresponded to a much smaller than average change in the relevant long-run measure, so that the coefficient on UME would be negative. If the reason for not being at work was illness, then the husband could have the same negative preference effect as other dependants. As we have not been able to include any variable to measure this, the coefficient on UME could be biased downwards.

Job satisfaction

Since *ceteris paribus* someone who likes a job will probably work longer at it than someone who dislikes it, we would expect hours worked to depend positively on job satisfaction. Job satisfaction is, however, difficult to measure. In the survey, it was measured on five scales relating to the job itself, pay, promotion, people at work and supervisors (see Chapter 5). We have taken as our variable (SAT) the figure on the scale relating to the job itself. There is also an identification problem. How satisfied a woman is with her job may depend on how many hours she works. If satisfaction dwindles as hours increase, the coefficient on SAT measures a composite effect which may be negative.

Energy

Workers vary in their physical and psychological stamina for any particular job. Those who have more energy of the type required for a given job might be expected to work longer hours at it, other things (including age) being the same. Similarly comparing the hours a given person might work in different jobs, one might expect fewer hours to be worked in jobs which require more energy per hour in relation to the person's endowment of energy specific to those jobs. Thus if we could measure how much more a woman felt able to work at a fixed number of hours - that is, her excess energy supply - we would expect this variable to have a positive coefficient.

The closest we can get to this concept from the survey is a variable ENER defined such that

> ENER = 1 if the respondent said she could work harder without being ill
> = -1 if she said she could not do so
> = 0 otherwise

This relates to the number of hours actually worked. Since the excess energy supply will tend to fall as hours worked increase, there is an identification problem. The less variation there is in women's excess energy supplies at fixed hours and the more there is in hours worked due to variation in other determinants, the lower the estimated coefficient will be.

Education

Education is usually assigned an important role in the determination of a person's wage rate and income, and there is a clear expectation that both will be positively related to education. It is not clear, however, in which direction education can be expected to influence hours worked. There will be a positive relationship, holding gross hourly earnings and other determinants of hours worked constant, if education is viewed solely as investment in human capital. On the other hand, education may incline people to wanting more leisure time, hence producing a negative effect.

If education increases one's enjoyment of work or enables a person to engage in more interesting work, this effect should be captured by the job satisfaction variable (SAT). If as a result of education a person aspires to a higher material standard of living, there will be a positive effect on hours worked if the education has not earned the person a sufficiently high hourly wage. To the extent that this aspiration increases expenditure on items covered by our committed income variable (COMY) – see above – its coefficient will measure this effect.

Our education variable (EDUC) is defined as years of full-time schooling after the school-leaving age applicable to the particular respondent. It thus ignores variations in the quality and relevance of the education received and excludes some forms of education such as training on the job.

Age

The simple association between age and hours worked is one of the most obvious, and is undoubtedly negative. This can, however, largely be accounted for by the correlation of age with other determinants of hours worked, identified separately here, notably the presence of children, committed income and energy. Age is included as a variable to test whether there is any remaining effect, and which direction it takes. *A priori* the direction is not clear. It may be argued that for some workers at least the marginal cost of leisure falls with age: the taking of leisure forfeits not only current income but for some a future-income-enhancing experience. Thus the cost of leisure will be lower for those with few earning years ahead of them than those with many. Hence a negative association between age and hours of work might be expected. On the other hand, comparing workers differing only in age, in a growing economy the older workers will have consumption related to lower expected lifetime income than the younger if they work the same hours. If they wish to make at least a partial adjustment to the current consumption standards of the younger workers, they will need to work longer hours; hence age and hours of work would be positively associated.

Measurement error in the variable itself (AGE) should be relatively small as the figure was provided by the respondent. The coefficient will, however, be particularly sensitive to errors in the associated variables and, as health of the respondent has not been included as a separate variable, may take up the negative effect of ill health if this is correlated across the sample with age.

V   MARRIED WOMEN – RESULTS

As a basis for comparison with the equations including preference variables, the basic equation (1) (p. 72) was estimated. The results are reported in Table 7.2.

Table 7.2   *Married women: the basic model without preference variables*

Variable	Coefficient	Std. error	t	Joint F
Constant	27.3	—	—	
W	2.77	33.6	0.08 ⎫	
W^2	34.6	32.3	1.08 ⎬	2.13
$W.I$	−0.943	0.878	−1.07 ⎭	
I	0.109	0.321	0.34 ⎱	1.05
I^2	−0.000391	0.00219	−0.18 ⎰	

$R^2 = 0.07$ $F(5,123) = 1.89$
$\bar{R}^2 = 0.03$

Elasticities at the sample mean
(W = £0.249 per hour, I = £21.3 per week, H = 28.1 hours)
Price	−0.00
Income	−0.11
Substitution	0.04
Elasticity of substitution	0.02

There is little prior information or theory which offers any guidance on the functional form of the relationship between hours worked and the preference variables. We have experimented with several forms of increasing complexity. First, the preference variables were included simply as 'control' variables, that is, without interactions with the wage and intercept, as has typically been done in earlier studies. The results are given in Table 7.3.

It seems *a priori* at least as likely that changes in preferences will affect responsiveness to changes in the wage and intercept as that they will only cause independent shifts in hours worked. Accordingly, interactions between all the preference variables and the wage and intercept variables were added to the previously estimated equation. The results are given in Table 7.4.

Table 7.3 *Married women: preference variables included without interactions*

Name	Variable Units	Mean	s.d.	Coefficient	Std. error	t	Joint F
Constant	—			29.6	—		
W	£ per hour	0.249	0.137	16.1	33.3	0.48	
W²	—			38.2	32.2	1.18	
W.I	—			−1.95	0.894	−2.18[a]	
I	£ per week	21.3	10.9	0.486	0.346	1.40	
I²	—			−0.00120	0.00239	−0.50	
YINF	—	0.426	0.495	−5.79	2.56	−2.26[a]	
XINF	£ per week	11.8	2.96	−0.318	0.390	−0.82	
TASS	—	1.55	0.682	−1.28	1.39	−0.92	
TIME	minutes	17.2	14.2	0.0679	0.0676	1.00	
COMY	£ per week	25.7	11.3	−0.0335	0.0843	−0.40	
WLTH	£000	3.44	2.59	0.545	0.370	1.47	2.04[a]
UME	—	0.0543	0.227	3.545	4.34	0.82	
SAT	index	31.9	9.65	0.0335	0.0954	0.35	
ENER	—	−0.279	0.853	0.946	1.03	0.91	
EDUC	years	0.326	0.759	−2.74	1.34	−2.05[a]	
AGE	years	39.6	11.0	−0.0625	0.0996	−0.63	
H	hours per week	28.1	10.1	(dependent)			

$R^2 = 0.23$ $F(16,112) = 2.05[a]$
$\bar{R}^2 = 0.12$

Preference variables – see Section IV:

YINF	presence of young children	COMY	committed income
XINF	expenditure on children	WLTH	wealth
TASS	ownership of time-saving assets	UME	unemployment of main earner
TIME	time travelling to work	SAT	job satisfaction
EDUC	education	ENER	energy
AGE	age		

[a]Significant at the 5 per cent level in a test of the hypothesis that the co-efficient(s) are zero against the alternative that they are not all zero.

It also seems likely that there are interdependencies between the preference variables themselves. For example, the effect of owning time-saving assets may be greater if young children are present. Given only 129 observations it was impossible to include all possible combinations of the eleven variables and yet very difficult to decide *a priori* which could be omitted. Experimentation with subsets of possible combinations and results with the less complex equations indicated that the present data are inadequate for the investigation of this further complexity. No results are reported.

Referring to Table 7.2, it will be noted that while all the elasticities are

Table 7.4   *Married women: preference variables included with interactions*

Variable	Coefficient	Std error	t	Joint F
Constant	31.4			
W	101.0	99.1	1.02	
W^2	18.1	50.5	0.36	
$W.I.$	−4.01	1.57	−2.56[a]	
I	0.258	1.36	0.19	
I^2	−0.00923	0.0110	−0.84	
YINF	12.8	12.4	1.03	
XINF	−2.73	2.30	−1.19	
TASS	0.896	6.49	0.14	
TIME	0.0477	0.253	0.19	
COMY	0.409	0.393	1.04	
WLTH	1.93	1.57	1.23	
UME	57.5	32.8	1.75	
SAT	−0.315	0.505	−0.62	
ENER	2.34	4.77	0.49	
EDUC	−9.87	7.80	−1.27	
AGE	−0.114	0.457	−0.25	
W.YINF	−30.8	24.7	−1.25	
W.XINF	−0.291	3.78	−0.08	
W.TASS	11.4	14.2	0.81	
W.TIME	0.541	0.505	1.07	
W.COMY	−2.43	1.12	−2.17[a]	
W.WLTH	−0.752	3.57	−0.21	0.95
W.UME	−139.0	84.0	−1.65	
W.SAT	−0.0607	1.23	−0.05	
W.ENER	5.24	11.8	0.44	
W.EDUC	2.33	15.4	0.15	
W.AGE	0.739	1.12	0.66	
I.YINF	−0.489	0.412	−1.19	
I.XINF	0.103	0.0738	1.40	
I.TASS	−0.205	0.240	−0.85	
I.TIME	−0.00325	0.00955	−0.34	
I.COMY	0.00273	0.0129	0.21	
I.WLTH	−0.0656	0.0566	−1.16	0.92
I.UME	−2.52	1.78	−1.42	
I.SAT	0.0202	0.0153	1.32	
I.ENER	−0.107	0.163	−0.66	
I.EDUC	0.272	0.225	1.21	
I.AGE	−0.00510	0.0152	−0.34	

Additional joint F brackets spanning groups: 0.90 and 1.26.

$R^2 = 0.37$ $F(38,90) = 1.36$
$\bar{R}^2 = 0.10$

Elasticities	F[b]	*Elasticity*[c]
Variable		
W (price)	1.55	0.09
I (income)	1.21	0.01
YINF[d]	2.23	−0.19
XINF	1.00	−0.25
TASS[d]	0.55	−0.04
TIME	1.09	0.07
COMY	1.69	−0.13
WLTH	0.89	0.04
UME[d]	1.21	−1.10
SAT	0.85	0.11
ENER[d]	0.66	0.05
EDUC[d]	1.94	−0.12
AGE	0.26	0.05
Substitution Elasticity		0.09
Elasticity of Substitution		0.04

[a] As Table 7.3.

[b] Joint F statistic for all the terms involving the particular variable.

[c] Computed at the following values of the variables marked d: YINF = 0, TASS = 2, UME = 0, ENER = −1, EDUC = 0 (except that YINF = 1 was used to compute the elasticity with respect to YINF, UME = 1 the elasticity with respect to UME, and EDUC = 1 the elasticity with respect to EDUC). These values were in every case the mode, and the nearest integer to the mean – except for ENER which had a mean of 0 to the nearest integer. The mean was used for all other variables. The sign reported on the elasticity for ENER has been changed to make it the same as the sign on the effect.

[d] A dummy variable or a variable that takes only very few integer values.

consistent with theory, they are very low, suggesting substantial bias. We shall not analyse this feature of the results further here. It is discussed in Chapter 8. For the present purpose it is sufficient to note that the explanatory power of the basic equation is low. There is obvious scope for improvement by the inclusion of other variables.

Referring to Table 7.3, the coefficients on the preference variables when included without interactions are jointly significant though only two, education and the presence of young children, are individually significant: that on the presence of young children (YINF) has the expected negative sign. (By 'significant' we mean throughout significant at the 5 per cent level in a test of the hypothesis that the coefficients are zero against the alternative that they are not all zero.) As the sign on the coefficient of XINF, expenditure on children, is also negative, it would appear that not all the negative preference effect of children has been captured by YINF and that it dominates the positive income effect for married women. The coefficient on education, EDUC, is also negative, suggesting that on balance education inclines women towards wanting more leisure. It must be noted, however, that a narrow definition of education has been used and very few women in the sample had a positive value of EDUC.

Augmenting the equation with the interaction terms failed to confirm the importance of these variables. In view of the relatively low degrees of freedom and the high correlations between regressors inherent in this functional form, it is not surprising that, as Table 7.4 shows, only one preference term, the interaction of the wage and committed income, proved individually significant. What is more noteworthy is that all the terms involving the preference variables together are not jointly significant. Similarly, in no case are all the terms involving a particular preference variable jointly significant. Looking at signs, the evidence still favours the hypothesis that the effects of increases in YINF and EDUC are both negative.

The magnitudes of the price, income and substitution elasticities were very little affected by the inclusion of the preference variables.

We shall discuss what conclusions may be drawn from these results in Section XIII when we have looked at the results for married men and single people.

VI   MARRIED MEN – SELECTION OF THE SAMPLE

The sample of married men was selected using the same criteria as applied in the selection of married women described in Section III. From the 928 married male respondents in the survey, 213 were selected. Figures showing the impact of sample size of each of the selection criteria are given in Table 7.5. The effect of criterion (3) in Section III concerning other workers was that just half of the 213 men had a working wife and the remainder were the only worker in the household.

VII   MARRIED MEN – PREFERENCES

In Section IV we distinguished the major determinants of the preferences of married women. As there would appear to be no major déterminant of the preferences of married men missing from the list given there, we do not need to consider here the inclusion of any extra variables.

One of the determinants distinguished was 'unemployment of the main earner, if not the respondent'. The survey data does not enable us

Table 7.5   *Selection of the sample of married men*

Total no. from which selection made		928
Reason for exclusion	No. excluded	
	Gross [a]	Net [a]
Past retirement age	23	23
Ill	76	74
Worker other than spouse	246	229
Hours worked < 8 or pay < £2	10	5
On bonus, piece-rate or inventive scheme	437	296
Hours constrained both ways	42	18
Hours, standard working week or basic wage rate unknown	226	70
No. selected		213

[a]As Table 7.1.

to identify reliably who was the main earner in a household. It would seem reasonable to suppose, as we did in the analysis of married women, that in most if not all of the households to which the members of the sample belong the married man was the main earner. Thus the same argument which led to the inclusion of the dummy variable UME, indicating whether or not the spouse was working, in the analysis of married women, leads us to omit this variable from the present analysis. Since it is likely that there were very few households in this sample in which not only was the main earner not the married male respondent but the main earner was suffering the sort of involuntary unemployment which might lead to adjustment of the married man's hours of work, omission of any variable measuring this determinant is unlikely to cause any serious bias.

The variable included in the analysis of married women to measure the ownership of time-saving assets (TASS) was a function only of the ownership of a refrigerator and of a washing machine. Given that these assets save time, if at all, on activities usually performed by the wife, its coefficient can be expected to be very small for married men. The variable has nevertheless been included for comparative purposes. The survey data does not enable us to obtain any useful measures of other determinants of the time a married man needs to spend on chores.

Other determinants may differ in importance between married men and married women. In particular, one might expect the negative preference effect of dependants to be smaller for men nd the positive income effect possibly larger if the husband is seen as the one who provides for, and the wife as the one who cares for, dependants. But there are none which *a priori* appear completely unimportant for men.

Thus with the exception of UME noted above the same set of preference variables has been used for married men. The reader is referred back to Section IV for a full discussion of each of these variables.

VIII   MARRIED MEN – RESULTS

Our analysis of the effect of including the preference variables followed the pattern described in Section V – starting from the basic equation, preference variables were first included linearly, then interactions with the wage and intercept were introduced. The results are reported in Tables 7.6 – 7.8.

Estimation of the basic equation yielded price, income and substitution elasticities consistent with theory. Whether the fairly low values obtained are a consequence of bias will be discussed in Chapter 8. For the present purpose, it is sufficient to note that the scope for improvement of the equation's explanatory power by including more variables is great.

As Table 7.7 shows, the coefficients on the preference variables when included without interactions were jointly significant, though only two coefficients, on expenditure on children and wealth, were individually so, and the improvement in fit was quite small.

The coefficients on the additional terms added at the third stage, the

Table 7.6   *Married men: the basic model without preference variables*

Variable	Coefficient	Std. error	t	Joint F	
Constant	62.2	–	–		
W	−33.5	16.1	−2.08[a]		
W^2	19.5	9.99	1.95		1.46
$W.I$	1.04	0.639	1.63		
I	−0.958	0.440	−2.18[a]	5.07[a]	
I^2	0.00775	0.00749	1.03		

$R^2 = 0.07$ $F(5,207) = 3.27$[a]
$\bar{R}^2 = 0.05$

Elasticities computed at the sample mean
(W = £0.50 per hour, I = £7.17 per week, H = 48.1 hours per week)
Price   −0.07
Income   −0.05
Substitution   0.09
Elasticity of Substitution   0.11

[a] As Table 7.3.

Table 7.7 *Married men: preference variables included without interactions*

Name	Variable Units	Mean	s.d.	Coefficient	Std error	t	Joint F
Constant	–			51.2			
W	£ per hour	0.502	0.196	−32.6	16.9	−1.94	
W^2	–			17.0	10.4	1.63	
W.I	–			1.28	0.645	1.98[a]	
I	£ per week	7.17	8.33	−1.15	0.448	−2.56[a]	
I^2	–			0.0118	0.00769	1.53	
YINF	–	0.498	0.500	−2.59	2.01	−1.29	⎫
XINF	£ per week	11.9	3.14	0.669	0.274	2.44[a]	⎪
TASS	–	1.53	0.654	1.40	1.01	1.39	⎪
TIME	minutes	20.2	15.8	0.00653	0.0401	0.16	⎪
COMY	£ per week	25.4	10.7	−0.0158	0.0588	−0.27	⎬ 2.16*
WLTH	£000	3.26	2.64	−0.655	0.264	−2.49[a]	⎪
SAT	index	31.9	9.46	0.129	0.0664	1.95	⎪
ENER	–	0.00	0.939	−0.458	0.685	−0.67	⎪
EDUC	years	0.282	0.722	0.625	0.907	0.69	⎪
AGE	years	41.0	12.1	0.0174	0.0660	0.26	⎭
H	hours per week	48.1	9.45	(dependent)	–	–	

$R^2 = 0.16$ $F(15,197) = 2.59^a$
$\bar{R}^2 = 0.16$

Preference variables – see section IV:

YINF	presence of young children	WLTH	wealth
XINF	expenditure on children	SAT	job satisfaction
TASS	ownership of time-saving assets	ENER	energy
TIME	time travelling to work	EDUC	education
COMY	committed income	AGE	age

[a]As Table 7.3.

interactions with the wage and intercept, proved to be jointly significant. This was largely accounted for by the interactions with the wage, three of which – with committed income, wealth and job satisfaction – were individually significant. The joint F statistics for the three terms involving a particular preference variable given in Table 7.8 give a different impression of the importance of the variables from the t statistics in Table 7.7 for the simpler equation. The coefficients on expenditure on children (XINF) are not jointly significant when the interaction terms are included but the one coefficient in the simpler equation was significantly different from zero. The converse is true of job satisfaction (SAT) which has the expected positive elasticity in the more complex equation. The elasticity

Table 7.8   *Married men: preference variables included with interactions*

Variable	Coefficient	Std error	t	Joint F
Constant	88.0	18.9	—	
W	−75.8	34.9	−2.17[a]	
W	−10.5	13.3	−0.79	
W.I	0.584	0.725	0.81	
I	−1.68	0.842	−1.99[a]	
I	0.00194	0.0112	0.17	
YINF	−1.14	7.19	−0.16	
XINF	−1.15	1.11	−1.03	
TASS	−1.58	4.03	−0.39	
TIME	−0.125	0.157	0.80	
COMY	−0.609	0.221	−2.76	
WLTH	1.53	0.996	1.53	
SAT	−0.291	0.233	−1.25	
ENER	−1.73	2.67	−0.65	
EDUC	3.83	3.72	1.03	
AGE	−0.0701	0.220	−0.32	
W.YINF	1.14	11.8	0.10	
W.XINF	2.34	1.70	1.38	
W.TASS	3.69	7.10	0.52	
W.TIME	−0.269	0.278	−0.97	
W.COMY	1.14	0.363	3.13[a]	3.05[a]
W.WLTH	−4.03	1.66	−2.43[a]	
W.SAT	0.913	0.399	2.29[a]	
W.ENER	0.105	4.48	0.02	
W.EDUC	−5.72	6.10	−0.94	
W.AGE	−0.140	0.367	0.38	1.90[a]
I.YINF	−0.198	0.317	−0.62	
I.XINF	0.0693	0.0502	1.38	
I.TASS	0.110	0.146	0.76	
I.TIME	0.00497	0.00528	0.94	
I.COMY	0.00135	0.00891	0.15	0.76
I.WLTH	−0.0308	0.0447	−0.69	
I.SAT	−0.000939	0.0106	−0.09	
I.ENER	0.195	0.117	1.66	
I.EDUC	0.0285	0.110	0.26	
I.AGE	0.00484	0.00902	0.54	

(The overall Joint F for the interaction block = 2.05[a])

$R^2 = 0.31$ $F(35,177) = 2.30^a$
$\bar{R}^2 = 0.18$

Elasticities

Variable	F^b	Elasticity^c
W (price)	2.58	−0.02
I (income)	1.37	0.01
YINF^d	0.37	−0.04
XINF	2.28	0.13
TASS^d	0.53	0.04
TIME	0.70	0.01
COMY	3.85^a	−0.02
WLTH	3.92^a	−0.05
SAT	3.52^a	0.11
ENER^d	1.18	−0.01
EDUC^d	0.79	0.02
AGE	0.21	0.03
Substitution elasticity		−0.06
Elasticity of substitution		−0.07

^{a} As Table 7.3.
^{b} Joint F statistic for all the terms involving the particular variable.
^{c} Computed at the following values of the variables marked d: YINF = 0, TASS = 2, ENER = 1, EDUC = 0 (except that YINF = 1 was used to compute the elasticity with respect to YINF, and EDUC = 1 that with respect to EDUC). These values were in every case the mode and, except for ENER, the nearest integer to the mean. The mean was used for all other variables.
^{d} A dummy variable or a variable that takes only very few integer values.

with respect to committed income (COMY) remains negative when inter-actions are included and the coefficients are jointly significant. While this is contrary to the predicted sign in the absence of measurement and specification errors, one explanation of this sign has been given in Section IV. The related variable wealth (WLTH) has the expected negative sign and significant coefficients in both regressions. The values of the price, income and substitution elasticities were very little affected by the inclusion of the preference variables.

IX   SINGLE PEOPLE – SELECTION OF THE SAMPLE

The 555 single people in the total sample are, taken together, a more heterogeneous sample than either of the sub-samples of married people already analysed. There may well be a greater variety of responses to changes in the measured determinants of labour supply and of characteris-tics not directly measured by the preference variables such as expected lifetime earnings patterns because (1) both sexes are included and (2) the economic status of respondents varies from that of an 18-year-old living with working parents who earn most of the household income to, say, a divorced woman who is the sole earner. In order to be able to test whether there are any significant differences between the supply responses of sub-samples classified by sex and economic status, as well as to perform an analysis of all single people similar to that of married men and women, larger numbers were needed in each of the sub-samples than would have been achieved if all the criteria listed in Section III had been used to exclude respondents. For this reason two of the criteria which have the biggest impact on sample size were not applied.

Those earning a bonus, piece-rates or incentive payments were not excluded. While a relationship between earnings and effort is not consistent with the model being used, many of those earning such payments may not have seen them as at all closely related to their effort during the week in question, so that one is then justified in treating the payment as predetermined and including it in the intercept term, as we have done.

Secondly, respondents have been included in the sample irrespective of the number of other workers in the household. This means that, as in the other samples, there will be respondents included for whom the assumption that they respond to changes in the income of other members of the household and take it as predetermined is invalid. It should be noted that there may be members of the present sample, such as the young person still living with his or her working parents, who do not take into account the income of other members of the household as defined in the survey when deciding on their hours of work. They may then be viewed as a single worker household in the theoretical sense. Thus the recorded number of other workers does not imply that the model is inappropriate

Table 7.9 *Selection of the sample of single people*

Total no. from which selection made		555
Reason for exclusion	*No. excluded*	
	Gross [a]	*Net* [a]
Past retirement age	28	28
Ill	59	58
Hours worked < 8 or pay $< £2$	13	9
Hours constrained both ways	15	13
Hours, standard working week or basic wage rate unknown	179	141
No. selected		306

[a]As Table 7.1.

for them but there will be a larger error in the 'other income' component of the intercept unless, as may have happened sometimes owing to ignorance, the respondent ignored or grossly underestimated the income of the other workers.

All the other criteria of Section III were applied, and their impact on the size of the sample of all single people is shown in Table 7.9. The next two sections refer to the analysis of this sample, while the analysis of the sub-samples is reported in Section XII.

X SINGLE PEOPLE – PREFERENCES

One of the determinants of the preferences of married women distinguished in Section IV was the presence of dependants and, in particular, children. This is also a possible determinant of the preferences of single people. The different characteristics of the present sample mean that the measurement of this determinant must be reconsidered. An assumption implicit in our earlier treatment was that all children of a given age were equally dependent in the sense of giving rise to the same preference and income effects. Given that in most households the married respondent would have been the parent of all the children present this assumption is more nearly valid than it would be for the present sample of which some members, for example, the widowed and divorced, were a parent of at least some of the children present but others were not a parent, but, instead, brother, sister, uncle or aunt, for example. In the present analysis children who are offspring of the respondent will be distinguished from other children. No attempt will be made to measure separately the preference and income effects of each group. As before the data is inadequate to allow measurement of the effect of other dependants. Accordingly the variables YINF and XINF have been replaced by two new variables: NCH, the number of offspring, or natural children, of the respondent present, and OCH, the number of other children present.

One problem of measuring the effect of unemployment of the main earner in a household as in the earlier analysis is to identify who was the main earner. The solution adopted here is to define UME=1 if either the respondent's father was present, aged under 65 and not working, or the father was absent and the mother present, aged under 50 and not working; and UME=0 otherwise. This variable has the deficiencies noted in Section IV.

With the exceptions noted, the set of preference variables used was the same as in the analysis of married women. The reader is referred to Section IV for a full discussion of these variables.

XI   SINGLE PEOPLE - RESULTS

The analysis of the sample of all single people followed the pattern described in Section V: starting from the basic equation, preference variables were first included linearly, then interactions with the wage and intercept were introduced. The results are reported in Tables 7.10 – 7.12.

Estimation of the basic equation yielded a substitution elasticity of the expected positive sign. The income elasticity was positive but very small and the three intercept terms were not jointly significant. Evidence on the possible sources of bias will be discussed in Chapter 8. It is sufficient for our present purpose of analysing preferences to note that there is considerable scope for improving the explanatory power of the equation by including more variables.

As shown in Table 7.11, inclusion of the preference variables linearly produced only two significant coefficients on them - on job satisfaction and education. The coefficients on the preference terms were not jointly significant. The further inclusion of the interaction terms gave the results in Table 7.12. The coefficients on the additional terms are jointly significant. Three of the interactions with the intercept - those involving travelling time, wealth and education - are individually significant, but only one interaction with the wage rate - that involving age. The evidence of these results still favours the hypothesis that job satisfaction has a

Table 7.10   *Single people: the basic model without preference variables*

Variable	Coefficient	Std error	t	Joint F
Constant	30.8	—	—	—
W	42.3	9.30	4.55[a]	
W^2	−29.7	7.93	−3.75[a]	10.26[a]
$W.I$	−0.192	0.169	−1.14	
I	0.119	0.0989	1.20	
I^2	−0.000464	0.000831	−0.56	0.61

$R^2 = 0.09$ $F(5,300) = 6.25^a$
$\bar{R}^2 = 0.07$

Elasticities computed at the sample mean
(W = £0.326 per hour, I = £26.7 per week, H = 41.5 hours per week)

Price	0.14
Income	0.02
Substitution	0.13
Of substitution	0.08

[a]As Table 7.3.

Table 7.11 *Single people: preference variables
included without interactions*

Name	Units	Mean	s.d.	Coefficient	Std error	t	Joint F
Constant	–				4.01	7.35[a]	
W	£ per hour	0.326	0.181	43.6	9.52	4.58[a]	
W^2	–			−30.9	8.25	−3.74[a]	
$W.I$	–			−0.146	0.170	−0.86	
I	£ per week	26.7	19.4	0.0730	0.103	0.71	
I^2	–			−0.0000900	0.000863	−0.10	
NCH	–	0.0882	0.422	−0.78	1.21	−0.64	
OCH	–	0.810	1.25	0.131	0.428	0.31	
TASS	–	1.50	0.648	0.148	0.819	0.18	
TIME	minutes	21.0	16.1	0.0338	0.0306	1.11	
COMY	£ per week	27.6	10.5	−0.0288	0.0473	−0.61	
WLTH	£ ,000	2.56	2.62	0.126	0.207	0.61	1.57
UME	–	0.108	0.310	0.893	1.70	0.53	
SAT	index	30.6	11.3	0.0914	0.0449	2.03[a]	
ENER	–	0.284	0.901	0.169	0.567	0.30	
EDUC	years	0.431	0.807	−1.76	0.635	−2.78[a]	
AGE	years	25.7	11.4	−0.0443	0.0496	−0.89	
H	hours per week	41.5	8.86	(dependent)			

$R^2 = 0.15 \quad F(16,289) = 3.07a$
$\bar{R}^2 = 0.10$

[a] As Table 7.3.

positive effect on hours worked but the interaction terms involving it are
not significant. Education is confirmed as having a significant effect but,
in contrast to the earlier result in Table 7.11, has a positive elasticity.
Introduction of the interaction terms makes the terms including time
travelling jointly significant, and the elasticity has the expected negative
sign but is very small.

The magnitudes of the price, income and substitution elasticities are
hardly affected by the inclusion of the preference variables. The income
elasticity remains positive.

XII SINGLE PEOPLE – SUBDIVISION OF THE SAMPLE

As discussed earlier (Section IX), there are reasons for believing that subdivision of the sample of single people by sex and economic status within
the household might reveal significant differences in supply responses.
Although the criteria for inclusion in the sample were relaxed as compared

Table 7.12   *Single people: preference variables included with interactions*

Variable	Coefficient	Std error	t	Joint F
Constant	34.3	–		
W	45.0	22.2	2.03[a]	
W^2	–35.5	12.5	–2.84[a]	
$W.I$	–0.0998	0.202	–0.49	
I	–0.132	0.204	–0.65	
I^2	–0.000437	0.00104	–0.42	
NCH	–6.07	3.75	–1.62	
OCH	–1.53	1.29	–1.19	
TASS	–0.349	2.30	–0.15	
TIME	–0.00636	0.0814	–0.08	
COMY	–0.000603	0.120	–0.01	
WLTH	–1.00	0.623	–1.61	
UME	5.35	4.07	1.32	
SAT	0.272	0.126	2.16[a]	
ENER	–1.41	1.57	–0.90	
EDUC	0.968	1.90	0.51	
AGE	–0.325	0.146	–2.22[a]	
W.NCH	6.40	5.02	1.27	
W.OCH	1.27	2.86	0.45	
W.TASS	1.17	5.12	0.23	
W.TIME	–0.301	0.216	–1.39	
W.COMY	–0.281	0.270	–1.04	1.39
W.WLTH	1.11	1.39	0.80	
W.UME	–8.62	9.13	–0.94	
W.SAT	–0.353	0.266	–1.32	
W.ENER	2.15	3.45	0.62	
W.EDUC	0.137	4.77	0.03	
W.AGE	0.766	0.351	2.18[a]	1.72[a]
I.NCH	0.0987	0.112	0.88	
I.OCH	0.0475	0.0297	1.60	
I.TASS	0.0215	0.0456	0.47	
I.TIME	0.00379	0.00141	2.69[a]	
I.COMY	0.00181	0.00268	0.68	1.93[a]
I.WLTH	0.0281	0.0127	2.21[a]	
I.UME	–0.0707	0.0101	–0.70	
I.SAT	–0.00295	0.00243	–1.22	
I.ENER	0.0278	0.0328	0.85	
I.EDUC	–0.0835	0.0260	–3.22	
I.AGE	0.00315	0.00407	0.77	

The Joint F braces span: the block NCH through AGE together with the interaction blocks gives an overall Joint F of 1.70[a].

$R^2 = 0.25$ $F(38,267) = 2.36[a]$
$\bar{R}^2 = 0.14$

Elasticities

Variable	F^b	Elasticity[c]
W (price)	2.84[a]	0.15
I (income)	0.48	0.05
NCH	1.00	-0.00
OCH	0.90	0.00
TASS[d]	0.21	0.01
TIME	3.26[a]	-0.00
COMY	0.75	-0.03
WLTH	1.78	0.01
UME[d]	0.59	0.13
SAT	1.87	0.06
ENER[d]	0.34	0.00
EDUC[d]	5.40[a]	0.02
AGE	1.91	0.01
Substitution	—	0.13
El. of Substitution	—	0.08

[a] As Table 7.3.

[b] Joint F statistic for all terms involving the particular variable.

[c] Computed at the following values of the variables marked d: TASS = 1, UME = 0, ENER = 1, EDUC = 0 (except that UME = 1 was used to compute the elasticity with respect to UME, and EDUC = 1 that with respect to EDUC). These values were in all cases the mode and the nearest integer to the mean. The mean was used for all other variables.

[d] A dummy variable or a variable that takes only very few integer values.

with those used to select the samples of married people, there are still not enough observations in each of the subdivisions to repeat the analysis of preferences for each subdivision, but comparisons can be made using the basic equation.

The economic status of a single person in a household may of course vary greatly from one who is head of the household and earns most of the household's income to, for example, a young person who plays little or no part in the decision-making of the rest of the household and whose income is a small part of the total. The survey data do not allow us to identify the gradation between these extremes. What we have done is to identify two groups, called 'primary' and 'secondary' workers, whose behaviour is likely to differ most sharply, and to leave other single people out of the analysis. A 'primary' worker is defined as someone aged 21 or over whose earnings represent at least half of total household income. A 'secondary' worker is someone aged under 21 whose earnings represent less than half of total household income.

Results for the four subdivisions - male primary, male secondary,

Table 7.13 Single People: Subdivisions of the Sample

Variable	Coefficients (standard errors in brackets)							
	Primary Men	Primary Women	Secondary Men	Secondary Women	All Primary	All Secondary	All Primary All Secondary	All
Constant	33.2	42.8	26.3	41.3	38.4	35.1	35.8	30.8
W	39.2a	32.0	10.3	2.64	29.1	3.18	32.0a	42.3a
	(17.7)	(44.2)	(34.8)	(17.2)	(17.6)	(18.1)	(11.1)	(9.30)
W^2	-25.3a	-40.6	55.2	21.8	-23.3	36.4	-23.6a	-29.7a
	(10.8)	(44.5)	(41.6)	(21.9)	(13.4)	(22.9)	(9.85)	(7.93)
$W.I$	-0.678	-0.587	-0.742	-0.139	-0.612	-0.329	-0.158	-0.192
	(0.739)	(1.05)	(0.734)	(0.221)	(0.652)	(0.279)	(0.196)	(0.169)
I	-0.347	-0.156	0.533a	-0.0784	-0.0515	0.193	0.0119	0.119
	(0.569)	(0.634)	(0.216)	(0.137)	(0.394)	(0.124)	(0.108)	(0.0989)
I^2	0.0260	0.0104	-0.00218	0.000900	0.00920a	-0.000694	0.000513	-0.000464
	(0.0202)	(0.00532)	(0.00206)	(0.00141)	(0.00389)	(0.00117)	(0.000886)	(0.000831)
No. in sample	22	43	56	62	72	118	190	306
R^2	0.26	0.12	0.25	0.15	0.14	0.14	0.09	0.09
$\bar{R}^2$	0.10	0.01	0.18	0.07	0.08	0.10	0.06	0.07
F	1.63	1.04	3.36a	1.95	2.17	3.65a	3.59a	6.25a
Elasticities[b]								
Price	0.04	-0.08	0.21	0.10	-0.02	0.14	0.10	0.14
Income	0.52	0.13	0.11	-0.05	0.16	0.03	-0.01	0.02
Substitution	-0.23	-0.15	0.15	0.13	-0.10	0.12	0.10	0.13
Of substitution	-0.15	-0.10	0.10	0.09	-0.06	0.08	0.06	0.08

Regressions compared	F
Primary men – primary women	1.29
Secondary men – secondary women	1.91
Primary – secondary	3.16c

[a] As Table 7.3.
[b] All elasticities were computed at the mean of the sample of all single people.
[c] Regressions significantly different at the 5 per cent level.

female primary and female secondary – are shown in Table 7.13. As nearly all the test statistics for individual regressions favour the hypothesis of zero coefficients, little can be inferred from differences between coefficients or implied elasticities. It does appear, however, that heterogeneity of the sample was not the cause of the positive income elasticity for all single people: the point estimate of the income elasticity is also positive for three of the subdivisions.

To compare the regressions, we have computed Chow's F test (see Chow, 1960). If the conventional 5 per cent significance level is used and the assumptions underlying the test are strictly valid, then the hypothesis that primary and secondary workers behave differently is accepted but the hypothesis of intersexual differences among primary and secondary workers is rejected. In all cases, however, the test statistic is close to the critical value and the assumptions that the model is correctly specified and that the errors are Normally distributed are unlikely to be very close to the truth. The only safe conclusion must then be a much more tentative one: the tests have not shown strong evidence that heterogeneity of the sort investigated is a major explanation of the poor fit of the model but they do suggest that in a future analysis variations in an individual's role in the household should be taken into account.

The definitions of primary and secondary workers adopted make the allocation of individuals to a particular category depend critically on the estimate of total household income. This is a particularly unreliable figure: in some cases the respondent's estimate was less than his or her own earnings. In this case the respondent's estimate was replaced by our own estimate related to the number of workers in the household. Experiments with alternative assumptions showed that the sample sizes and individual regression results varied widely but do not lead us to alter the above conclusion based on the Chow tests.

XIII CONCLUSIONS

In order to facilitate the exploration of preference patterns, which has been our objective in this chapter, a very simple basic model was used. Various specification errors in the basic model have been pointed out in the course of our analysis, and are discussed at greater length in Chapter 8 and elsewhere in this volume. Until the resulting bias has been quantified, it would be wrong to draw any conclusions from such a partial analysis about the true price and income elasticities for any of the demographic groups analysed here. As to the effect of including preference variables on the estimates of these elasticities, we have found scarcely any effect.

We have presented separate results for each of three sub-samples – married women, married men and single people. All three sets of results lead to the same, negative conclusion: if one believes that there are systematic variations in preferences, then the biases resulting from the measurement and specification errors identified in Section IV are quantitatively important. While the set of all regressors involving a preference variable were jointly significant for married men and single people, this was not so for married women; taking into account the number of regressors added to the basic equation, the improvement in fit was small for all the sub-samples. Few individuals coefficients were significant.

Broadly similar conclusions also may be drawn from the three analyses on the sensitivity of the results to changes in the criteria for selecting the samples, changes in the definitions of variables and omission of variables. In the course of our work we have found ways of reducing the likely error where there are deficiencies of the raw data, for example, where there is a 'don't know' answer or answers are inconsistent. In earlier work other selection criteria were used generally resulting in larger samples. Comparison with these earlier results (McGlone and Ruffell, 1978a, 1978b, 1979; Glaister and Ruffell, 1979a, 1979b) shows that improvements in the data and narrowing of samples to approximate more closely the theoretical assumptions (given in Section II) has led to markedly different inferences about preference patterns, and generally to fewer coefficients being individually or jointly significant. Experimentation has also confirmed the result which could be expected from the high correlations between some of the preference variables, and especially between interaction terms: use of a less comprehensive set of preference variables or of a functional form including them only linearly carries a high risk of false inferences being made about which are the most important determinants and the direction of their effect.

Chapter 8

Endogeneity II
Direct Estimation of Labour Supply Functions with Piecewise Linear Budget Constraints

I INTRODUCTION

In Britain and the United States workers typically face a budget constraint which is not linear as in the simple textbook analysis but piecewise linear because of the band structure of income taxation, overtime premiums and constraints on the number of hours that can be worked in any one job. Much of the work on labour supply has used a linear approximation to this budget constraint, treating it as if the net marginal wage rate at the hours actually worked applied over the whole range of possible hours of work. Given the present state of the subject, and present data sets, it is impracticable to study simultaneously all the problems connected with models of labour supply. As the linear approximation procedure greatly simplifies estimation, its use has facilitated a fuller investigation of other problems. In Chapter 7 we used the linear approximation approach in order to be able to undertake a fuller investigation of the preference patterns of married women and married men. Use of this approach does, however, give rise to the possibility of bias, the so-called 'endogeneity' or 'simultaneity' bias. Ashworth and and Ulph (Chapter 6) and Wales and Woodland (1979) have demonstrated the existence of such bias for other samples and other implied specifications of the supply function. The first objective of this paper is to assess the size of the endogeneity bias in the results reported in Chapter 7 for married men and married women by comparing them with the results of using a procedure which recognizes the piecewise linearity and uses the same quadratic form of supply function.

The recent work on piecewise linearity by Ashworth and Ulph (Chapter 6), Burtless and Hausman (1978), and Wales and Woodland (1979) all makes use of indirect or direct utility functions. In this chapter the supply function is estimated directly without making use of a utility function. One advantage of this approach is that a quadratic form can be used so that results can be compared with those in Chapter 7.

The second objective of this chapter is to attempt to handle preferences while at the same time recognising the piecewise linearity of the budget constraints. Another advantage of the functional form chosen is that it allows preference variables to be added relatively easily. Of the other three papers cited on the endogeneity problem, only Burtless and Hausman (1978) attempts to handle preferences. They postulated a random effect on the income response. In this paper it is postulated that several measurable determinants of preference patterns have a systematic effect on both the income and the wage response and, independently, on hours worked.

A consequence of the piecewise linearity of the budget constraint is that for some individuals small supply disturbances cause a change in hours worked but no change in their actual marginal wage, whereas for other individuals the same disturbances cause no change in either hours worked or in the (different) marginal rates they would get for an extra hour's work and the last hour they worked, but only in the marginal rate of substitution between income and leisure. This has implications for the choice of estimation procedure. The final objective of this chapter is to assess the effect on estimates of the supply function of using an estimation procedure which recognizes the variable effect of a given disturbance as compared with the more orthodox procedure used in the earlier part of this paper.

The plan of the chapter is as follows. In Section II, the construction of the data sets is described. Section III sets out the model and details the estimation procedures. Section IV reports the results on endogeneity bias and the effects of including preference variables. Section V presents the argument in favour of modifying the estimation procedure, and Section VI the results of using a modified procedure. In Section VII, the reasons for differences in endogeneity bias between samples are set out. Section VIII discusses other specification errors, while Section IX brings together some conclusions on methodology and the labour supply elasticities of married women and married men.

There is unfortunately no generally agreed terminology for several concepts that are used in this chapter. I have followed the practice of Wales and Woodland in referring to use of information on the whole budget constraint as the 'full information' approach, and in referring to the simpler approach as the 'linear approximation' approach. The hypothetical (non-employment) income at zero hours implied by a particular linear approximation to the budget constraint is termed the 'intercept', as in Chapter 7. This is Burtless and Hausman's 'virtual income'.

II THE DATA

This analysis used the samples of 129 married women and 213 married men whose selection was fully described in Chapter 7.

Three variables entered the basic equation of Chapter 7: the actual hours worked in all jobs during the week before the respondent's interview (H); the actual marginal wage rate net of tax and inclusive of any overtime premium (W); and the value of the intercept corresponding to this wage rate (I). In addition to these variables, the whole budget constraint of each respondent is needed for the present analysis.

For someone whose hours of work were unconstrained and had no second job, the budget constraint was computed from the person's non-employment income, basic wage rate, standard working week, over-time premium, and tax free income and the basic tax rate. The effect, at the bottom of the income range, of income-related benefits in introducing kinks was ignored owing to lack of data. For the same reason the possibility that different overtime premia applied to some hours of work had to be ignored. The effect of higher rates of tax in introducing kinks at the top of the income range was not allowed for as the kinks were considered to be far enough from observed income to be irrelevant. The resulting budget constraint had three segments (two, if the overtime premium was unity) with kinks at the tax threshold and standard working week in the appropriate order. Seventy-nine of the 129 women and 180 of the 213 men had this type of budget constraint.

There are both conceptual and interpretative problems associated with questions about demand constraints. As far as can be judged from the questions asked about possibilities in the week to which data on any individual refer, a few respondents were unable to vary their hours in either direction. They were excluded from the sample – see Chapter 7, Sections II and VI. No one in the samples selected was only constrained upwards, that is, able to work more hours than they actually did but not less. Some were constrained downwards, that is, prevented from working as many hours as they would have liked. Forty-nine women and eight men were so constrained and had no second job. Their budget constraints were constructed with a wage rate of zero beyond their actual hours of work.

One woman and eight men had second jobs. The only additional information used here was the gross second job wage rate (GSJWR) and second job hours. If GSJWR exceeded the main job overtime rate, the 'second job' was taken to be the first segment of the budget constraint; that is, it was assumed that a constraint on the second job rather than preference led to the individual to work in the 'main' job. If GSJWR was less than the overtime rate, it was assumed that the second job had been taken because of a constraint in the main job. (It will be noted that this is slightly different from Ashworth and Ulph's treatment of second jobs in Chapter 6.)

In general the budget constraint may be written as

$$W = w_k, \qquad h_k < H < h_{k+1} \qquad k = 1, 2, \ldots, n \qquad (1)$$

where w_k is the marginal wage rate on segment k net of tax but not of income-related state benefits, h_k is the lower limit of hours worked on segment $k(h_1 = 0, h_{n+1} = 168)$, and n is the number of segments, which ranged from 2 to 4 in the samples selected.

The corresponding intercept is written as

$$I = i_k, \qquad h_k < H < h_{k+1} \qquad k = 1, 2, \ldots, n \qquad (2)$$

where i_1 is actual net non-employment income computed as the total income of the household net of tax and including income-related state benefits, less the respondent's net earnings and

$$i_k = i_{k-1} + h_k (w_{k-1} - w_k) \qquad k = 2, \ldots, n \qquad (3)$$

that is, non-employment income plus an adjustment for each kink.

III   THE MODEL AND ESTIMATION

The supply function is postulated to be

$$H^s = \beta_1 + \beta_2 W^s + \beta_3 (W^s)^2 + \beta_4 I^s + \beta_5 (I^s)^2 + \beta_6 W^s \cdot I^s + \epsilon \qquad (4)$$

where H^s is hours of work supplied, W^s, I^s the corresponding 'supply' marginal wage rate and intercept, $\beta = (\beta_1 \ldots \beta_6)'$ is the vector of parameters to be estimated and ϵ a random error which will be assumed to be independently normally distributed with constant variance across a sample. (The truncation problem will be ignored – see Section VIII).

This functional form is the same as used in Chapter 7. It has the advantage of being simple yet allowing both the price and the income effect to depend on both the wage and the intercept

To complete the model, the following equilibrium conditions are added:

$$H^s = H$$
$$W^s = W$$
$$I^s = I \tag{5}$$

Equations (1) to (5) constitute the full information model.

In the linear approximation version of the model equations (1) and (2) are replaced by

$$W = w_a$$
$$I = i_a$$

where a is the number of the segment on which actual hours H lies. Writing predicted hours given an estimate $\hat{\beta}$ of β as $\hat{H}^\ell$, the linear approximation procedure simply involves finding the OLS estimator $\hat{\beta}$ which minimises $\Sigma(\hat{H}^\ell - H)^2$. There is only one problem in making this procedure operational: 53 (25 per cent) of the men and 61 (47 per cent) of the women in the samples are actually on a kink so that in the model so far specified W and I are undefined.

Three alternatives have been tried:

$$\left. \begin{aligned} w_k^* &= w_k \\ &= w_{k-1} \\ &= \bar{w}_k \equiv \arctan\left\{ \tfrac{1}{2}(\tan w_k + \tan w_{k-1}) \right\} \end{aligned} \right\} \quad H = h_k \tag{5}$$

With this approach, it is not required that predicted hours to consistent with the wage and intercept, that is, the condition

$$h_a < \hat{H}^\ell < h_{a+1}$$

may not be satisfied.

The essential feature of the full information approach is that consistency is imposed. Because the reduced form cannot now be written explicitly the estimation procedure is much more complicated.

Substituting the equilibrium conditions (5) into the supply function (4), the predicted hours given an estimate $\hat{\beta}$ may be written as

$$\hat{H} = \hat{\beta}_1 + \hat{\beta}_2 W + \hat{\beta}_3 W^2 + \hat{\beta}_4 I + \hat{\beta}_5 I^2 + \hat{\beta}_6 WI \tag{6}$$

Equations (1), (2) and (6) then have to be solved for each individual. If there is no solution $\hat{H}^*$ in the interval (0,168) and $\hat{H} < 0$ for $W = w_1$, $\hat{H}^* = 0$ is used. Similarly if there is no solution and $\hat{H} > 168$ for $W = w_n$, $\hat{H}^* = 168$ is used. This ensures that there is always a solution. There may be more than one. (Given the quadratic form of the supply function there may be two solutions $\hat{H} = h_k$ on a kink.) Two criteria have been used when deciding which solution to take. First, any unstable equilibria occurring on steps in the budget function have been rejected, that is,

$$(\hat{W}^* - w_k) \frac{\partial \hat{H}}{\partial W} > 0$$

is required where $\hat{W}^*$ is the predicted wage at a solution with $\hat{H} = h_k$. Secondly, when there is a disturbance to an individual's behaviour he or she may well in the short run ignore a utility maximising position far from actual hours or may not be able to adjust that far very quickly. The solution closest to actual hours has therefore been used. (This is an important distinction from studies which use direct or indirect utility functions, since they use the utility maximising solution, which may not be the closest to actual hours.)

Hence $\Sigma h^2 \equiv \Sigma(\hat{H}^* - H)^2$ may be calculated for any $\hat{\beta}$, and minimization over $\hat{\beta}$ carried out using a non-linear least squares algorithm. The algorithm by Peckham (1970) was used as this is particularly economical in calls of the subroutine which computes $(\hat{H}^* - H)$; given that up to nine segments and kinks have to be checked for solutions this is very time consuming. Some solutions were checked using the general function minimization algorithm by Gill and Murray (1973).

IV   RESULTS I

The results of estimating by the linear approximation and full information methods are given in the first four columns of Table 8.1. Column 2 summarises results given in Tables 7.2 and 7.6.

Looking first at the results for married women: although the three sets of linear approximation results vary considerably, comparing any one set with the full information results indicates the presence of significant bias. For regression 2, thirty-two women (25 per cent) had predicted hours inconsistent with the wage and intercept used. Both the income and substitution elasticities obtained by the full information approach have the expected sign. The standard errors quoted are approximate since they are derived from a linear approximation to the residuals $h(\hat{\beta})$ in the neighbourhood of the solution (see Wolberg, 1967), but suggest a significantly positive price elasticity.

For married men the differences between the four results are much smaller. As only twelve men (6 per cent) had predicted hours inconsistent

Table 8.1   *Direct estimates of labour supply*

$$H = \beta_1 + \beta_2 W + \beta_3 W^2 + \beta_4 I + \beta_5 I^2 + \beta_6 WI + \epsilon$$

Column	1	2	3	4	5	6	7
Actual wage used for individuals on a kink[a]	w_{k-1}	$\overline{w}$	w_k	—	w_{k-1}	$\overline{w}_k$	w_k
Minimand[b]		VD	VD	VD	VD	MD	MD	MD
Estimation procedure[c]	LA	LA	LA	FI	FI	FI	FI

Married Women (Sample size n = 129)

Elasticities[d]

	1	2	3	4	5	6	7
Price	−0.59	−0.00	0.08	0.43	1.37	0.72	−0.12
	(0.15)	(0.09)	(0.04)	(0.10)	(0.11)	(0.03)	(0.04)
Income	−0.09	−0.11	−0.11	−0.25	−0.43	−0.16	−0.28
	(0.09)	(0.09)	(0.09)	(0.10)	(0.07)	(0.03)	(0.06)
Substitution	−0.57	0.04	0.12	0.51	1.51	0.77	−0.02
	(0.15)	(0.09)	(0.05)	(0.11)	(0.11)	(0.03)	(0.04)
Of substitution	−0.25	0.02	0.05	0.23	0.68	0.35	−0.01
	(0.07)	(0.04)	(0.02)	(0.05)	(0.05)	(0.01)	(0.02)
$\Sigma h^2/n$ [e]	85.56	95.61	94.48	69.93	96.39	91.31	229.85
$\Sigma r' M^{-1} r$ [f]	—	—	—	—	30.63	25.12	49.59

Married Men (Sample size n = 213)

Elasticities[g]

	1	2	3	4	5	6	7
Price	−0.11	−0.07	−0.04	−0.07	0.02	−0.05	−0.17
	(0.05)	(0.05)	(0.04)	(0.04)	(0.03)	(0.01)	(0.02)
Income	−0.04	−0.05	−0.04	−0.03	−0.07	−0.02	−0.01
	(0.01)	(0.02)	(0.02)	(0.02)	(0.01)	(0.01)	(0.01)
Substitution	0.04	0.09	0.10	0.04	0.26	0.03	−0.15
	(0.06)	(0.05)	(0.05)	(0.04)	(0.04)	(0.01)	(0.02)
Of substitution	.05	0.11	0.12	0.04	0.30	0.03	−0.18
	(0.07)	(0.06)	(0.06)	(0.05)	(0.05)	(0.02)	(0.02)
$\Sigma h^2/n$	83.27	82.75	82.14	81.61	99.98	93.52	91.96
$r' M^{-1} r$	—	—	—	—	57.62	26.48	43.54

[a] w_{k-1} = the wage rate on the segment before the kink (hours of work less than at the kink).
w_k = the wage rate on the segment after the kink (hours greater than at the kink).
$\overline{w}$ = arctan ($\frac{1}{2}$ tan w_{k-1} + tan w_k).
[b] VD = sum of squared vertical (hours) residuals.
MD = sum of squared minimum distance residuals.
[c] LA = linear approximation.
FI = full information.
[d] Computed at the sample mean H = 28.1 hours, W = £0.25 per hour, I = £21.3 per week.
[e] Mean squared vertical residual.
[f] Value of minimum distance minimand.
[g] Computed at the sample mean H = 48.1 hours, W = £0.50 per hour, I = £7.17 per week.
The figures in parentheses are standard errors, calculated taking the values of W, I and H as given. They are approximations for full information estimates.

with the wage used in regression 2, it is not surprising that comparison with the full information results indicates very little bias. All the full information elasticities are very small (at the sample mean). The price elasticity, although negative, does not differ significantly from very small positive values.

The second objective of this study was to attempt to combine a treatment of preferences with the full information approach. In the analysis using the linear approximation approach in Chapter 7, eleven variables were defined to measure possible major determinants of preferences, and it was argued that the price and income effects were both likely to be functions of all these variables. This led to thirty-three variables (thirty for men) being added to the basic equation. It was not feasible to include so many variables given the number of observations when using a non-linear minimization algorithm. Judged by the results and *a priori* arguments, the most promising subset of variables for married women was education (EDUC), the presence of young children (YINF) and expenditure on children (XINF). As pointed out in Chapter 7, results with such subsets indicate that omission of the other, quite highly correlated variables is likely to lead to false inferences about magnitudes and signs of effects, but the analysis was pursued with the limited objective of attempting to discover whether inclusion of preferences had any effect on the estimates of elasticities reported in this chapter. Using a supply function augmented only by these three variables and their associated six interaction terms and the full information approach, the algorithms still proved unable to identify a solution which could be treated as the global minimum with any confidence.

For married men the most promising subset of variables was committed income (COMY), wealth (WLTH) and job satisfaction (SAT). Despite the better prospect of a well-defined solution given the greater number of observations and the greater explanatory power of the chosen variables in the earlier analysis, the problem again proved too ill-conditioned for the algorithms to cope with when the nine additional terms were added to the basic equation.

V   ECONOMETRIC PROBLEMS

Wales and Woodland (1979) in their analysis using direct utility functions noted that if, for a particular parameter vector, the highest attainable indifference curve for some individual is tangential to a segment of the budget constraint precisely at a kink then their sum of squared shares residuals is not differentiable. There is an exactly analogous problem with the minimand Σh^2 in the above analysis. To repeat their argument, this problem can be ignored because the nondifferentiability only occurs at a finite number of points in the parameter space so that it is likely that there exists an interval around the true vector in which the function is continuously differentiable. This is sufficient to leave the properties of the estimator unaffected (see Wales and Woodland, 1979, pp. 87–8).

There are, however, three other problems which arise when using the full information approach. The exposition which follows will be in terms of direct estimation of supply function but the same argument applies to the methods using direct or indirect utility functions employed by Ashworth and Ulph (Chapter 6), Burtless and Hausman (1978) and Wales and Woodland (1979).

To remove unnecessary complications, let the supply function be

$$H^s = \beta_1 + \beta_2 W^s + \epsilon$$

and consider an individual who has a budget function with a single step

$$
\begin{aligned}
W &= w_1 \quad H < h_2 \\
&= w_2 \quad H > h_2
\end{aligned}
$$

and for whom $\epsilon = 0$.

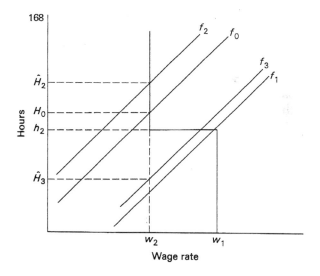

Fig 8.1   *Comparison of alternative supply estimates*

Suppose that β is such that the supply function is given by line f_0 in Figure 8.1. Then observed hours will be H_0 and the observed marginal wage w_2.

Now consider several alternative estimates of the true function

$$\hat{H}s = \hat{\beta}_1^j + \hat{\beta}_2^j Ws \qquad j = 1, 2, 3$$

and for simplicity take $\hat{\beta}_2^j = \beta_2$ all j.

Three problems can now be identified:

(1) Estimates f_1 and f_3 give the same predicted hours $\hat{H}_k = h_2$. Hence there is an interval in which the residual $(\hat{H}^* - H)$ is a constant. In principle, then, if all individuals in the sample were simultaneously on a kink there could be a range of $\hat{\beta}_1$ over which all derivatives of $\Sigma(\hat{H}^*-H)^2$ would be zero. If the minimand attains its lowest value over this range, the method fails to identify a unique solution. With many data sets this extreme possibility is unlikely to occur. Even for the sample of married women used here, many of whom had pronounced kinks in their budget constraints and were actually on a kink, the lowest value of the minimand was not in such an interval. The computation of a solution, however, necessarily involves the use of algorithms which explicitly or implicitly approximate gradients. It may be difficult to achieve convergence if there is such an interval in the search area or if the minimum lies in an interval in which a large proportion of the sample are on a kink so that gradients are very close to zero.

(2) Related to (1), while f_1 and f_3 give the same value of the residual $(\hat{H}^* -H) = (h_2-H_0)$, clearly whatever measure of distance is used f_3 is closer to the true line f_0.

(3) By construction $(h_2-H_0)^2 < (\hat{H}_2-H_0)^2 < (\hat{H}_3-H_0)^2$. Thus f_3 gives a lower residual than f_2 but again is clearly farther from f_0.

As the cause of these problems is the relationship between the disturbance ϵ and the observed values of W, this suggests that a solution is to use an errors-in-variables procedure, though obviously the 'error' in W is not the usually envisaged measurement error.

One such procedure is minimum distance estimation, in the sense of Malinvaud (1966). Let the 'errors' in H and W be denoted respectively as

$$\eta \equiv W-\bar{W}$$
$$\nu \equiv \epsilon-\beta_2\eta$$

where $\tilde{W} \equiv (W|\beta_1, \beta_2; \epsilon = 0)$

Then the minimand is

$$\sum_i r_i' \Omega_i^{-1} r_i$$

where summation is over individuals i.

Ω_i is the covariance matrix of η and ν of the ith individual
$r_i' = (r_{1i} \, r_{2i})$
$r_{1i} = \hat{W}^* - W_i$,   The difference between the predicted wage $\hat{W}^*$ and the actual W_i of the ith individual
$r_{2i} = \hat{H}^* - H_i$, the corresponding hours residual

There are two major difficulties with this estimator. Firstly, Ω_i has to be known. As the distribution of η is dependent on β_1 and β_2 this condition cannot be satisfied. One way of proceeding might be as follows. For any given β_1, β_2, obtain the distribution of η conditional on ϵ. This is easily done. For example, given the supply and budget functions represented in Figure 8.1

$$\eta = 0 \qquad 168 - H_0 > \epsilon > h_2 - H_0$$
$$= w_1 - w_2 \qquad h_2 - H_0 > \epsilon > -H_0$$

and the rest of the distribution can be derived from the restriction $0 \leqslant H \leqslant 168$. If ϵ is assumed to be distributed $N(0, \sigma^2)$ for all i, all the Ω_i can be obtained up to a scaler, σ^2. Hence for any estimates of β_1 and β_2, the minimand could be computed using the estimates of Ω_i corresponding to these estimates of β_1 and β_2. This procedure has not been tried as it would be greatly more expensive in computing time than the already time-consuming full information procedure described in Section III.

Instead, Ω_i has been replaced by the sample covariance matrix of the actual values of hours and the wage rate (**M**). If all budget constraints were linear with different wage rates, then the sample wage variance would not reflect the presence of kinks and this estimate would give too much weight to the wage residual since $\text{var}(\eta) = 0$ for all individuals. If, on the other hand, everyone was on a pronounced kink the sample variance of hours would be much greater than $\text{var}(\nu)$ so that too much weight would be given to the hours residual. As in the actual samples, the situation lies between these two extremes, it is not obvious that there is any gross error in **M** as an estimate of the *average* Ω_i.

The second difficulty is one that arose in the linear approximation procedure: an actual wage W_i, is needed for all individuals including those on kinks. The three alternatives (5) were tried as before.

Generalising the above to the six-parameter supply function actually estimated, the estimator used is

$$\min \, r_i' M^{-1} r_i$$

where
$$
\begin{aligned}
r_i' &= (r_1 \dots r_6) \\
r_1 &= \hat{W}^* - W \\
r_2 &= \hat{W}^{*2} - W^2 \\
r_3 &= \hat{I}^* - I \\
r_4 &= \hat{I}^{*2} - I^2 \\
r_5 &= \hat{W}^* \hat{I}^* - WI \\
r_6 &= \hat{H}^* - H
\end{aligned}
$$

and these residuals are obtained by a similar procedure to that described in Section III for the earlier full information approach. The only change needed to the procedure described before is to use the new metric for choosing between multiple solutions.

To distinguish between the full information estimators I shall call the present estimator the 'minimum distance' (MD) estimator and the earlier one using only the hours residual the 'vertical distance' (VD) estimator.

VI   RESULTS II

The three sets of results for the different assumptions about the wage which would equal the marginal rate of substitution of those on a kink are given in columns 5-7 of Table 8.1. For both samples the variation between the three is large. There are two arguments which favour taking the middle estimates ($W = \overline{w}_k$) as the best: first, unless the distribution of the true marginal rates of substitution of those on kinks is very skewed towards the upper or lower end of the range of possible rates on the kink, the average must be closer to the average of the values $\overline{w}$ than to either the average of the wage rates w_{k-1} on the preceding segments or the average of the wage rates w_k on the following segments. Secondly the results favour the middle estimates in that using $\overline{w}$ yields the lowest value of the minimand, and using w_k yields elasticities inconsistent with theory.

Comparing the middle MD estimates in column 6 with the VD estimates in column 4, all the elasticities for married women are higher, while for married men there is virtually no difference.

The results of including preferences were as inconclusive as before and are again not reported.

VII CAUSES OF VARIATION IN THE AMOUNT OF ENDOGENEITY BIAS

Two reasons for endogeneity bias being larger in one sample than another can be distinguished.

First, the bias depends on the proportion of the sample for whom the wage at the hours predicted by the linear approximation procedure is different from their actual wage. This in turn depends on the shape of the budget constraint, the distribution of actual hours and the distribution of the disturbance in supply. If, for example the budget constraint is piecewise linear (and assuming for simplicity that everyone faces the same constraint) and most observations are of hours of work distant from a kink, taking the standard deviation of the disturbance as the unit of distance, there will be very few cases of the marginal wage at predicted hours being different from the marginal wage at actual hours. The possible bias will be small. If, at the other extreme, the budget constraint has short segments or is strictly concave, observations are clustered round the kinks and the variance of the disturbance is high, the possible bias is large.

Whether the actual bias is large in the circumstances identified as giving rise to a large possible bias depends on the second factor: the direction of changes in the slope of the budget constraint. If (assuming again for simplicity everyone faces the same constraint) the constraint has at least one point of inflexion, or at least two kinks alternating in direction, and observations are well spread out either side of each one, a linear or quadratic function will be a poor fit to the budget relationships between hours and the marginal wage rate and between hours and the intercept: there will be relatively little bias if a linear or quadratic supply function is estimated even if the marginal wage rate at predicted hours is different from that at actual hours for a high proportion of the sample. If, on the other hand, the budget constraint is convex along its entire length (or concave over its entire length) a linear or quadratic function is likely to be a very good fit to the budget relationship. There will therefore be serious bias if many of the sample have predicted hours inconsistent with their actual wage.

The operation of these two factors is clearly seen in the difference between the results for married men and women in this chapter. Among the married men there were only 5 per cent whose predicted hours by the linear approximation procedure were inconsistent with their actual wage.

There was some variety among the budget constraints but typically they had two kinks alternating in direction. This and the distribution of actual hours meant that the correlation between the regression (hours) residual and the difference between their actual wage and the wage at predicted hours was small (r = +0.3). Hence the full information and linear approximation results hardly differ. On the other hand 25 per cent of the married women had predicted hours inconsistent with their actual wage. More of these had a convex budget constraint with one kink at the tax threshold so that the correlation between the residual and the wage difference was slightly stronger – and negative: r = –0.4. Hence the large difference between the full information and linear approximation results.

This reasoning suggests what the results would be for other data sets. For the sample of single people used in Chapter 7 10 per cent had inconsistent predicted hours and actual wage and the correlation for these people between the residual and the wage difference was only +0.1, suggesting that the bias would be small.

For a sample who faced a large number of increasing tax rates with fairly close thresholds and for whom extra overtime payments were ignored or zero (as in American studies) the proportion with inconsistent predicted hours and actual wages is likely to be relatively high and the residual-wage difference correlation quite strong suggesting relatively strong bias in the linear approximation procedure.

VIII   SPECIFICATION ERRORS

While the full information approach eliminates one source of bias, there remain other deficiencies in the basic model. There is little evidence from other studies as yet to indicate which are likely to cause serious bias. *A priori* the most important appear likely to be the following:

Interdependence within the household

One assumption of the basic model (see Chapter 7, Section II for a list of assumptions) is that the respondent is an independent decision-maker who takes all other household income as predetermined when deciding on his or her hours of work. As a substantial proportion (see Tables 7.3 and 7.6) of the respondents in both our samples had a working spouse, this assumption is much less likely to be realistic than if a sample were drawn exclusively from single-worker households. Comparing the model used with the neo-classical and Leuthold models of household decision-making (the subject of Chapter 9) exposes two sources of bias: omission of a second relationship – the spouse's supply function – between the husband's and wife's hours, which implies a correlation between the intercept and the disturbance; secondly, the omission of variables – in the neo-classical model of the spouse's wage rate and in the Leuthold model the spouse's leisure time appear in the respondent's supply function in place of the spouse's income.

Non-market work

Another assumption listed in Chapter 7 was that the individual takes a decision between just two homogeneous alternatives, income and leisure. Although the implied supply function was modified in our analysis of preferences to take account of time spent on chores, it remained implicit in our treatment of chores that the quantity to be done was predetermined. The model should recognise that the quantities of market and non-market work may well be determined simultaneously.

Truncation of the sample

As those who worked less than eight hours were excluded from the samples, a person with the same preferences and budget constraint as one of the respondents but a large enough negative disturbance could have been excluded. This biases coefficients towards zero (see, for example, Layard *et al*; 1977). One clue to the extent of such exclusions is the number in the actual sample working little more than eight hours. Using the estimated standard error of the disturbance (from column 4 of Table 8.1) as the unit of distance, 12 per cent of the sample of married women were within one unit of the limit and 48 per cent within two units. Of the married men, none was within two units. This suggests that this source of bias is not important at least for married men. The reason for a gap in the distribution of hours may, however, be fixed costs of working or constraints not identified by the survey, both of which may be important causes of bias since neither are taken account of in the model.

Disequilibrium behaviour

The function used specified the equilibrium hours of work corresponding to given values of the arguments and adds an error term partly to allow for random, short-run disturbances from this equilibrium. As the data are for one week these disturbances may have a high variance. The high residual variance might be taken as evidence of this. If in fact disequilibrium behaviour depends systematically on variables included as equilibrium determinants or variables correlated with them then estimators will be biased.

IX   CONCLUSIONS

This chapter has been concerned mainly with methodological issues in the econometrics of labour supply. Others have demonstrated the presence of endogeneity bias in the linear approximation procedure when budget constraints are piecewise linear using a variety of alternative estimation procedures. In this chapter a supply function of a quadratic form in the wage and intercept has been directly estimated for two British samples, of married women and married men. The results indicate a large bias in the linear approximation procedure for the sample of married women but very little bias for the sample of married men. The reasons for variation in bias between samples have been set out in Section VII: differences in the shape of budget constraints, the distribution of actual hours of work across a sample and the distribution of supply disturbances.

It was argued in Section V that minimum distance estimation is preferable to using only the residual in hours, as the kinks in the budget constraint mean that the latter may be the same for different disturbances in supply. While the onerous data requirements of this method could not be met it has been shown, using a rough estimate of the required error covariance matrices, that the procedure does give different answers. This is particularly so when, as in the case of the married women sample, predicted hours are likely to be on a kink for many individuals. While it is possible that these estimates could be improved on by an iterative technique of the sort suggested in Section V (at the expense of a large increase in the already considerable computing time required), more data is needed before reliable estimates can be obtained: if the data on individuals on a kink of their budget constraint is to provide as much information for estimation as the data on others, an estimate of their marginal rate of substitution is needed. It has been shown that alternative assumptions about this missing data give quite different answers.

Chapter 9

Household Models

ON THE STRUCTURE OF FAMILY LABOUR SUPPLY DECISIONS

In the literature on family labour supply, there are a variety of models employing very different assumptions about the structure of the decision-making process within the household. Two such models are the neo-classical model, and the model originally proposed by Leuthold (1968).

The neo-classical model assumes the household acts as if it were maximizing a single utility function embracing all the various objectives of the household subject to a common budget constraint. The Leuthold model assumes that each member of the household has an independent utility function defined over total household income and the leisure of that household member. Given the hours of work of others each person then decides how much work he is prepared to do in order to increase total household income. Household members adjust their hours of work until their independently derived decisions are mutually consistent.

In this chapter we propose a procedure for specifying these two models so that they can not only be estimated in a consistent fashion on a given body of data, but one can also test one model against the other. This is of interest not only for the light it enables us to throw on the structure of family decision-making but also because, as we shall show, the predicted labour supply elasticities arising from the two models can be very different. It is therefore important for policy purposes to be able to decide which of the two models best fits the data.

We begin by setting out the basic neo-classical model for a two-worker household. We then examine in some detail a fairly natural extension of the Leuthold model in which each household member cares about not only their own leisure but also that of their spouse. We show how this leads to a very obvious procedure for specifying the two models in such a way that one model can be tested against the other.

After a discussion of data problems we present the results of such a test for a sample of UK households. We show that in fact the Leuthold model provides a significantly better fit than the neo-classical model, and compare the supply elasticities arising from the two models.

117

Our procedure enables us to completely explore the structure of interaction between husband and wife in the Leuthold model and this we then do. We show that we cannot reject the hypothesis that each member's preferences between income and their own leisure is independent of the leisure of their spouse.

Our concluding section considers some theoretical and econometric limitations of our estimates.

I   THE MODELS

(a) Neo-classical

There are three goods; consumption denoted c, leisure of the husband ℓ^h, leisure of the wife, ℓ^w. The household has endowments of 1 unit of each type of leisure, and V units of consumption – non-employment income. Time not spent in leisure is spent on market work rewarded at wage rates w^h, w^w for the husband and wife, respectively. The price of consumption is taken to be 1. The household therefore faces a budget constraint

$$c + w^h \ell^h + w^w \ell^w \leqq w^h + w^w + V \tag{1}$$

The consumption possibility set is

$$D = \left\{ (c, \ell^h, \ell^w) \geqq 0 \mid \ell^h \leqq 1, \ell^w \leqq 1 \right\} \tag{2}$$

On D the household has a strictly quasi-concave utility function[1] $u(c, \ell^h, \ell^w)$, and household choice on consumption and the allocation of time is made by maximizing $u(.)$ subject to (1) and (2). This generates, in particular, the labour supply functions

$$H^h \equiv 1-\ell^h = f^h(w^h, w^w, V) \tag{3}$$
$$H^w \equiv 1-\ell^w = f^w(w^h, w^w, V) \tag{4}$$

whose properties are well established.

(b) Leuthold

The assumptions about the budget constraint and consumption-possibility set are those given above in (1) and (2). On D there are now assumed to be two utility functions $u^h(c, \ell^h, \ell^w)$, $u^w(c, \ell^h, \ell^w)$. Before proceeding, it will be helpful to define what we might call the *short-run independent* supply functions

$$H^h = \phi^h(w^h, \ell^w, x) \tag{5}$$
$$H^w = \phi^w(w^w, \ell^h, y) \tag{6}$$

which arise as solutions to the problems

$$\max_{c \geq 0, \, 0 \leq \ell^h \leq 1} u^h(c, \ell^h, \ell^w) \text{ s.t.} c + w^h \ell^h \leq w^h + x \tag{7}$$

and

$$\max_{c \geq 0, \, 0 \leq \ell^w \leq 1} u^w(c, \ell^h, \ell^w) \text{ s.t.} c + w^w \ell^w \leq w^w + y \tag{8}$$

respectively. That is, these are just the supply functions that would arise if each person took the other's hours of work as given and made their hours of work decision, operating, somehow, under independent budget constraints. However, as pointed out above the Leuthold model does not assume independent budget constraints, but, rather, that the husband takes the wife's hours of work as given and then chooses his hours so as to

$$\max_{c \geq 0, \, 0 \leq \ell^h \leq 1} u^h(c, \ell^h, \ell^w) \text{ s.t.} c + w^h \ell^h \leq w^h + V + w^w(1 - \ell^w) \tag{9}$$

while the wife takes the husband's hours of work as constant and then seeks to

$$\max_{c \geq 0, \, 0 \leq \ell^w \leq 1} u^w(c, \ell^h, \ell^w) \text{ s.t.} c + w^w \ell^w \leq w^w + V + w^h(1 - \ell^h) \tag{10}$$

Equations (9) and (10) generate what we will call *short-run interdependent supply functions*

$$H^h = \psi^h(w^h, w^w, V, \ell^w) \equiv \phi^h[w^h, \ell^w, V + w^w(1 - \ell^w)] \tag{11}$$

$$H^w = \psi^w(w^h, w^w, V, \ell^h) \equiv \phi^w[w^w, \ell^h, V + w^h(1 - \ell^h)] \tag{12}$$

Notice that

$$\frac{\partial \psi^h}{\partial \ell^w} = \frac{\partial \phi^h}{\partial \ell^w} - \frac{\partial \phi^h}{\partial x} w^w \tag{13}$$

$$\frac{\partial \psi^w}{\partial \ell^h} = \frac{\partial \phi^w}{\partial \phi^h} - \frac{\partial \phi^w}{\partial y} w^h \tag{14}$$

Equation (13) says that an increase in the wife's leisure will have two effects on the husband's hours of work. There is, first, what we will call the *preference effect*, $\partial\phi^h/\partial\ell^w$, arising from the effect of the change on the husband's preference between income and leisure; secondly there is the *income effect*, $-\partial\phi^h/\partial x, w^w$, which arises from the reduction in (non-employment) income the husband receives because of the wife's reduction in hours of work. If the husband's leisure is a normal good in his preference function then this latter effect is positive. The preference effect can be positive, negative or zero. A similar interpretation applies to (14).

In Leuthold's original model the individual utility functions were assumed to be independent of the leisure of the spouse and so she considered only income effects. More generally, of course, the preference effects will be zero if the individual utility functions are separable in the leisure of the spouse.

As they stand, there need be no consistency between the hours of work entering as independent variables in (11), (12) and the dependent hours of work. To make sense of the model, therefore, we have to introduce a concept of equilibrium. Accordingly, we define the equilibrium of the household to be the values $\bar{H}^h, \bar{H}^w$ satisfying

$$\bar{H}^h = \psi^h\ (w^h, w^w, V, 1-\bar{H}^w) \tag{15}$$

$$\bar{H}^w = \psi^w\ (w^h, w^w, V, 1-\bar{H}^h) \tag{16}$$

Under standard conditions, we can solve (15), (16) to obtain the *long-run supply functions*

$$H^h = g^h\ (w^h, w^w, V) \tag{17}$$

$$H^w = g^w\ (w^h, w^w, V) \tag{18}$$

All the comparative static results on g^h, g^w can be derived from those on ψ^h, ψ^w by the formulae

$$\left.\begin{array}{l} \dfrac{\partial g^h}{\partial\alpha} = \dfrac{1}{D}\ \dfrac{\partial\psi^h}{\partial\alpha} - \dfrac{\partial\psi^h}{\partial\ell^w}\cdot\dfrac{\partial\psi^w}{\partial\alpha} \\[3ex] \dfrac{\partial g^w}{\partial\alpha} = \dfrac{1}{D}\ \dfrac{\partial\psi^w}{\partial\alpha} - \dfrac{\partial\psi^w}{\partial\ell^h}\cdot\dfrac{\partial\psi^h}{\partial\alpha} \end{array}\right\}\quad \alpha = w^w, w^h, V \tag{19}$$

where

$$D = 1 - \frac{\partial \psi^h}{\partial \ell^w} \cdot \frac{\partial \psi^w}{\partial \ell^h}$$

If we wish the equilibrium in (15), (16) to be stable under the usual quantity adjustment process[2] then we require $D > 0$, but there are no further restrictions on the signs of $\partial \psi^h / \partial l^w$, $\partial \psi^w / \partial \ell^h$ so that there is nothing one can say in general about the signs of the long-run effects in (19).

Having outlined the models and their properties, we now consider how to specify them in order to test which best fits a body of data.

II THE SPECIFICATION OF THE MODELS

We begin with a simple remark. If the two utility functions u^h, u^w in the Leuthold model are identical, then the long-run Leuthold equilibrium is identical to the neo-classical equilibrium corresponding to that single utility function.[3] This suggests the following procedure for testing which of the two models best fits a given body of data. If we can specify explicit functional forms for u^h and u^w and estimate the parameters of these functions (using the long-run or reduced form equations (17), (18)), we can then re-estimate the parameters under the restriction that they be identical for the two functions, and test whether the resulting estimates are significantly different from the former.

The functional form we have adopted is the transcendental logarithmic function. While this is, of course, a special form of the utility function, it has some claim to generality in that it will serve as a local second-order approximation to any utility function.[4] Thus in the case of the neo-classical model, the utility function is of the form

$$u(c, \ell^h, \ell^w) = \alpha_9 \log c + \alpha_1 \log \ell^h + \alpha_2 \log \ell^w + \tfrac{1}{2}\alpha_3 (\log c)^2 \\ + \tfrac{1}{2}\alpha_4 (\log \ell^h)^2 + \tfrac{1}{2}\alpha_5 (\log \ell^w)^2 + \alpha_6 (\log c \, \log \ell^h) \\ + \alpha_7 (\log c \, \log \ell^w) + \alpha_8 (\log \ell^h \, \log \ell^w) \qquad (20)$$

On solving the first-order conditions for utility maximization we have the share equations[5]

$$\frac{w^h \ell^h}{w^h + w^w + V} = \frac{\alpha_1 + \alpha_4 \log \ell + \alpha_6 \log c + \alpha_8 \log \ell^w}{E} \qquad (21)$$

$$\frac{w^w \ell^w}{w^h + w^w + V} = \frac{\alpha_2 + \alpha_5 \log \ell^w + \alpha_7 \log c + \alpha_8 \log \ell^h}{E} \qquad (22)$$

where

$$E = \alpha_9 + \alpha_1 + \alpha_2 + \alpha_3 \log c + \alpha_4 \log \ell h + \alpha_5 \log \ell w + \alpha_6 (\log c + \log \ell h)$$
$$+ \alpha_7 (\log c + \log \ell w) + \alpha_8 (\log \ell h + \log \ell w)$$

(21) and (22) are homogeneous of degree zero in $\alpha_1 - \alpha_9$, and so we can employ some normalisation on the parameters.

We have chosen to set

$$\alpha_1 + \alpha_2 + \alpha_9 = 1$$

so (21) and (22) now contain eight parameters with $\alpha_1 + \alpha_2 + \alpha_9$ replaced by 1 in E.

Turning to the Leuthold model, we use the utility functions

$$u^h = \beta_7 \log c + \beta_1 \log \ell h + \delta_1 \log \ell w + \tfrac{1}{2}\beta_2 (\log c)^2 + \tfrac{1}{2}\beta_3 (\log \ell h)^2 \quad (23)$$
$$+ \tfrac{1}{2}\delta_3 (\log \ell w)^2 + \beta_4 (\log c \, \log \ell h) + \beta_5 (\log c \, \log \ell w) + \beta_6 (\log \ell h \, \log \ell w)$$

$$u^w = \delta_7 \log c + \beta_1 \log \ell h + \delta_1 \log \ell w + \tfrac{1}{2}\delta_2 (\log c)^2 + \tfrac{1}{2}\beta_3 (\log \ell h)^2 \quad (24)$$
$$+ \tfrac{1}{2}\delta_3 (\log \ell w)^2 + \delta_4 (\log c \, \log \ell h) + \delta_5 (\log c \, \log \ell w) + \delta_6 (\log \ell h \, \log \ell w)$$

Notice that we have imposed the condition that the coefficients on the terms which are additively separable in the leisure of the spouse should be the same in both functions. Since demand behaviour will be independent of such additively separable terms, this is a restriction which cannot be refuted from empirical observation.

As before, utility maximization leads to the following (short-run) share conditions

$$\frac{w^h \ell h}{w^h + V + w^w (1 - \ell w)} =$$
$$\frac{\beta_1 + \beta_3 \log \ell h + \beta_4 \log c + \beta_6 \log \ell w}{\beta_7 + \beta_1 + \beta_2 \log c + \beta_3 \log \ell h + \beta_4 (\log c + \log \ell h) + (\beta_5 + \beta_6) \log \ell w} \quad (25)$$

$$\frac{w^w \ell w}{w^w + V + w^h (1 - \ell h)} =$$
$$\frac{\delta_1 + \delta_3 \log \ell w + \delta_5 \log c + \delta_6 \log \ell h}{\delta_7 + \delta_1 + \delta_2 \log c + \delta_3 \log \ell w + \delta_5 (\log c + \log \ell w) + (\delta_4 + \delta_6) \log \ell h} \quad (26)$$

Now (25) is homogeneous of degree zero in the β's, and (26) in the δ's.

Hence we can impose two independent normalisations. To be consistent with normalisation employed for the neo-classical model when the β's and δ's are equalised, we set

$$\beta_1 + \beta_7 + \delta_1 = 1$$
$$\delta_1 + \delta_7 + \beta_1 = 1$$

Incorporating these normalisations, and solving (25) and (26) for the long-run functions, we obtain

$$\frac{w^h \ell^h}{w^h + w^w + V} = \frac{n_1(d_2 - n_2)}{d_1 d_2 - n_1 n_2} \qquad (27)$$

$$\frac{w^w \ell^w}{w^h + w^w + V} = \frac{n_2(d_1 - n_1)}{d_1 d_2 - n_1 n_2} \qquad (28)$$

where

$$n_1 = \beta_1 + \beta_3 \log \ell^h + \beta_4 \log c + \beta_6 \log \ell^w$$
$$d_1 = 1 - \delta_1 + \beta_2 \log c + \beta_3 \log \ell^h + \beta_4 (\log c + \log \ell^h) + (\beta_5 + \beta_6) \log \ell^w$$
$$n_2 = \delta_1 + \delta_3 \log \ell^w + \delta_5 \log c + \delta_6 \log \ell^h$$
$$d_2 = 1 - \beta_1 + \delta_2 \log c + \delta_3 \log \ell^w + \delta_5 (\log c + \log \ell^w) + (\delta_4 + \delta_6) \log \ell^h$$

(27) and (28) are the analogues of (21) and (22). They contain the twelve parameters $\beta_1 - \beta_6, \delta_1 - \delta_6$, and it is easy to verify that when we eliminate four parameters by setting $\delta_2 = \beta_2$, $\delta_4 = \beta_4$, $\delta_5 = \beta_5$, $\delta_6 = \beta_6$, then $u^h = u^w$, and (27) and (28) reduce to the neo-classical equations (21) and (22) containing eight parameters.

For the actual estimation of these models we must consider (21), (22), (27) and (28) each with an error term. The error terms employed have a basic assumption of asymptotic normality. This assumption is dictated by our estimating procedure and test. We can see from the above discussion that we are left with a very simple test of the two models. If we can obtain maximum likelihood estimates of $\alpha_1 - \alpha_8$ in (21) and (22) and of $\beta_1 - \beta_6, \delta_1 - \delta_6$ in (27) and (28), we can then use the fact that minus twice the logarithm of the ratio of the two likelihoods is asymptotically distributed as χ^2 with four degrees of freedom to tell us whether the likelihoods are significantly different.[6]

The manner in which we use the logarithms of the likelihood ratio should be considered. Our actual procedure is to first of all minimize the sum of squares for our functions using the conjugate gradient method of

Powell (1964). We then use the condensed logarithmic likelihood function given by

$$\log L = -\frac{n}{2}(1 + \log \frac{2\pi}{n}) - \frac{n}{2}\log S(\hat{\theta}) \qquad (29)$$

where n is the sample size and $S(\hat{\theta})$ is the least squares estimate of θ. It can easily be seen that the same values of θ which maximise the sum of squares will maximise the likelihood function. This result depends on the normality of the error structure but as the chi-square distribution result depends on suitable regularity conditions – basically those that assure the asymptotic normality and efficiency[7] of the maximum likelihood estimator – it would seem reasonable to use it here.

We have performed such a test for a sample of households in the UK, but before giving our results, we will describe the sample and the data.

III   THE SAMPLE AND THE DATA

The estimation we report here is an extension of the work reported in Chapter 5. In that chapter the results of a single-equation model estimated for a sample of male workers[8] are reported. We have obtained our sample by restricting attention to the subset of the Brown–Levin–Ulph sample of married men whose wives worked for more than eight hours in the week and who had no children under eleven years of age. This gave a sample of eighty-eight households. The first restriction is similar to one imposed on husbands in the earlier study. The second constraint was imposed in the light of the findings in the earlier study that the presence of a child under eleven gave rise to a significantly different labour supply equation from that obtained when there was no child under eleven. Since the main objective of this paper was to report on our test procedure we decided to confine our attention to a sample which might best fit the underlying model and postpone a more careful treatment of the wider sample to a later date.

A major problem in measuring the wage and non-employment income variables in empirical studies of this kind is that households do not in fact face simple linear budget constraints of the form assumed in (1), but, rather, piecewise linear constraints arising from switches in the (net) marginal wage due to the presence of overtime, second jobs, progressive income tax schedules, etc. Our procedure for handling this difficulty is that of linearising the budget constraint by using the net marginal wage that individuals faced, given the hours they actually worked, and adjusting the non-employment income term to compensate.[9,10] A detailed discussion of the calculation of the husband's net marginal wage and of making the appropriate adjustments to the non-employment income term has been given in Chapter 5 so we will concentrate our discussion on our procedure for calculating the wife's net marginal wage.

The difficulty we faced in constructing the wife's wage was that we did not have any direct information on it. But we did have data on the total number of hours worked by the wife and the total amount of income coming into the family other than the husband's earnings (the variable called 'other income' in Chapter 5). This will include the wife's total earnings and other sources of income such as state benefits.[11] We had information on what benefits the household was receiving though not the absolute amount of each. However most benefits were paid on clearly defined scales so we were able to subtract these to leave a figure measuring wife's total earnings. We assumed that the wife did no overtime, had no second job, and that if she paid tax she did so at the standard rate. We could therefore construct her gross wage by dividing earnings by hours. If her gross earnings exceeded the tax threshold for married women (in 1971, the year in which our data was collected) we used as wage rate in her marginal wage (= $w(1-t)$ where w is the gross wage and t is the standard rate of tax) and added to non-employment income tT_w where T_w is the wife's tax threshold.

IV   RESULTS

The estimates we obtained for the neo-classical model are given in Table 9.1. For the Leuthold model the estimates were as given in Table 9.2.

Table 9.1   *Estimates of Neo-classical Model*[a]

α_1	0.454	α_5	0.379
α_2	0.345	α_6	−0.0616
α_3	−0.0396	α_7	−0.0403
α_4	0.207	α_8	0.0298

[a] Sum of squares = 1.608.

From (29), minus twice the logarithm of the likelihood ratios is 10.947. As the critical value for $\chi^2(4)$ at the 5 per cent significance level is 9.487 this implies that at a reasonable level of significance the data supports the Leuthold model as against the neo-classical model.

Table 9.2   *Estimates of Leuthold Model*[a]

β_1	1.166	δ_1	−0.0813
β_2	0.275	δ_2	0.0233
β_3	3.628	δ_3	0.136
β_4	0.441	δ_4	−0.127
β_5	−3.311	δ_5	0.0312
β_6	−4.756	δ_6	−0.116

[a] Sum of squares = 1.511

It is worthwhile looking at the labour supply elasticities implied by both models to see how different are the predicted effects when one assumes one model rather than the other. It is of course only meaningful to compare the long-run elasticities in the Leuthold model with those of the neo-classical model.

Before presenting the results, however, let us briefly mention the method of calculation. For the Leuthold model we took the mean values of consumption, husband's leisure and wife's leisure, from our sample and used equations (25) and (26) to solve for $\hat{w}^h$, $\hat{w}^w$ and $\hat{V}$, the predicted wage rates and non-employment income. Equations (25) and (26), along with analogous equations for consumption shares, were differentiated to give all the short-run price, income and cross-quantity effects ($\partial \ell^h / \partial \ell^w$, $\partial \ell^w / \partial \ell^h$). We then used (19) to compute the long-run effects. The neo-classical model was written as a Leuthold model with the four additional equalities, and all the elasticities were then computed in exactly the same way. Let us turn then to the results.

Table 9.3   *Long-Run Labour Supply Elasticities*

	Leuthold	*Neo-classical*
η_{hh}	−1.0047	−0.0259
η_{hw}	0.872	−0.158
η_{hV}	−0.0261	−0.0325
η_{hM}	−8.163	−12.129
η_{hh}^c	0.471	2.1666
η_{hw}^c	1.475	0.753
η_{ww}	−4.461	−1.175
η_{wh}	5.047	1.734
η_{wV}	0.0241	−0.00117
η_{wM}	7.530	−0.434
η_{ww}^c	−5.017	−1.142
η_{wh}^c	6.408	1.812

In Table 9.3 η_{ij} ($\eta^c{}_{ij}$) (i,j = h,w) are the various own and cross-price elasticities (compensated elasticities) of a change in j's wage on i's hours of work. η_{iv} (i = h,w) is the elasticity of a change in non-employment income v on i's hours of work while η_{iM} is the elasticity of a change in full income ($w_w + w_h + V$). This latter elasticity is presented both because it is always well defined (which η_{iv} is not when $V = 0$) and because it features in several areas in which these elasticities might be used.[12] The substitution elasticities have been presented for both models though no particular significance attaches to their sign or magnitude for the Leuthold model.

Notice that in two cases (the cross elasticity of the wife's wage on the husband's labour supply and the income elasticity of wife's labour supply) the elasticities differ in sign and that (apart from the husband's income and his own substitution effect) in all other cases the Leuthold model predicts elasticities which are much larger in absolute magnitude. While we have no way of knowing whether these results are significantly different statistically, the policy implications of using one set of elasticities rather than the other are likely to be very different.

Two further points are worth making about these results. First, the own-substitution effect for the wife is negative, which contradicts a basic property of neo-classical models. Secondly, results obtained by Brown, Levin and Ulph for a sample of married men whose wives did not work and who had no children under eleven[13] gave elasticities η_{hh} = -0.253, η_{hv} = -0.029, η^c_{hh} = 0.472. The income and substitution elasticities are fairly close to those obtained here for the Leuthold model, though the price elasticity is very much smaller in absolute magnitude. For the neo-classical model, only the income elasticity is quite close to the single-equation model.

All these elasticities for the Leuthold model are derived from the underlying short-run supply equations so we now examine these. The results are given in Table 9.4. The definitions of the elasticities are as before with the addition that η^Q_{ij} (i,j = h,w) is the cross-quantity elasticity of an increase in j's working hours on the hours of work of the spouse. Also, it should be remembered that for this case the cross-price effects are pure income effects.

Notice that for the husband the short-run supply function is upward sloping and the substitution elasticity is greater than 1. This means that the standard finding of a long-run supply function which is downward sloping with a long-run substitution elasticity much less than 1 (which is confirmed by our results) seems to arise from the interaction of the husband and wife rather than being intrinsic to the husband's behaviour.

The results for the wife show a backward bending supply curve, but with leisure apparently being inferior and a substitution elasticity which violates the theoretical prediction of the model – we will return to this point in our concluding remarks. All the wife's elasticities are much larger in absolute terms than those for the husband.

The cross-quantity elasticities show that a 1 per cent increase in the work of the wife will (*ceteris paribus*) lead the husband to reduce his hours of work, though by less than 1 per cent, while a 1 per cent increase in the husband's hours of work will lead the wife to increase her hours, though by much more than 1 per cent. If we recall equations (13) and (14) we see that these cross-quantity effects are themselves composed of two other effects – what we have called the 'preference effect' and the 'income effect.'

Table 9.4   *Short-Run Elasticities for Leuthold Model*

Husband		Wife	
η_{hh}	0.479	η_{ww}	−11.279
η_{hv}	−0.0191	η_{wv}	0.2285
$\eta_{\hat{h}h}$	1.555	$\eta_{\hat{w}w}$	−12.327
η_{hw}	−0.4388	η_{wh}	12.898
$\eta_{\hat{h}w}$	−0.294	$\eta_{\hat{w}h}$	7.815

Since we know the income effect it is straightforward to compute the magnitude of the preference effect. We find that for the husband we have

$$-0.294 = \eta_{\hat{h}w}^{Q} = \eta_{\hat{h}w}^{QP} + \eta_{\hat{h}w}^{QI} = 0.146 - 0.44$$

while for the wife

$$7.815 = \eta_{\hat{w}h}^{Q} = \eta_{\hat{w}h}^{QP} + \eta_{\hat{w}h}^{QI} = -5.2312 + 13.046$$

where the η^{QP} are the preference effects expressed as elasticities, while the η^{QI} are the income effects expressed as elasticities.

In both cases the preference effect is of the opposite sign to the total effect and is dominated by the income effect. Moreover the interactions between husband and wife are such that an increase in the wife's hours of work will so alter the husband's preferences for income and leisure as to make him want to work hard (*ceteris paribus*), while the reverse is true for the wife. We decided to test whether or not these preference effects were zero – both for its own interest, and also because this would indicate whether the data supported the simple Leuthold model or the more general one proposed at the beginning of this chapter.

Now, from (23) and (24) the effect on the husband's preferences of of a change in the wife's hours of work comes through the terms β_5 to β_6 while the effects of a change in the husband's hours on the wife's preferences come through the terms δ_4 and δ_6. A sufficient condition for the preference effects to be zero is that these coefficients should be zero, and accordingly we re-estimated the Leuthold model, once under the restriction $\beta_5 = \beta_6 = 0$, and a second time under the restriction $\delta_4 = \delta_6 = 0$.

In the case of the restriction on the β's we found a minimizing sum of squares of 1.519. Upon comparison with our previous Leuthold model we found that the value of minus twice the logarithm of the likelihood ratio was 0.872. As the 5 per cent significance level of $\chi^2(2)$ is 5.991 we could not reject the null hypothesis that $\beta_5 = \beta_6 = 0$ at this level. Using the same procedure for the restriction on the δ's we found that there was a minimizing sum of squares of 1.550 which when compared with the original Leuthold model gave a value of 4.453 in the test. Again, we could not reject the null hypothesis, in this case $\delta_4 = \delta_6 = 0$, at the 5 per cent level of significance.

As we had no basis for rejecting the models with restrictions

Table 9.5   *Long-Run Elasticities*

	$\beta_5 = \beta_6 = 0$	$\delta_4 = \delta_6 = 0$
η_{hh}	−1.413	−0.728
η_{hw}	1.261	0.541
$\eta_{h\nu}$	−0.0288	−0.0001
η_{ww}	−4.175	−3.373
η_{wh}	4.73	3.910
$\eta_{w\nu}$	0.0222	0.00004

Table 9.6   *Short-Run Elasticities*

	$\beta_5 = \beta_6 = 0$	$\delta_4 = \delta_6 = 0$
η_{hh}	0.465	0.328
$\eta_{h\nu}$	−0.02	−0.0001
η_{hh}^c	1.436	1.212
η_{hw}^Q	−0.397	−0.27
η_{ww}	323.62	−11.142
$\eta_{w\nu}$	−7.478	0.0017
η_{ww}^c	467.34	−17.167
η_{ww}^Q	−259.96	14.374

applied we computed the short-run and long-run elasticities under the two restrictions. Comparing Tables 9.5 and 9.6 with Tables 9.3 and 9.4, we see that when $\beta_5 = \beta_6 = 0$, that is, the husband's preferences are independent of the wife's hours of work, we see that while the long-run elasticities and the short-run elasticities of the husband are very similar to those obtained without the restriction imposed, there has been a dramatic change in the short-run elasticities of the wife which now have completely different signs. Thus while the likelihood is fairly insensitive to the values of β_5 and β_6, the short-run elasticities of the wife are not, which means we can place little significance on the results in Table 9.4 for the wife. When we set $\delta_4 = \delta_6 = 0$, all the signs remain the same as in Tables 9.3 and and 9.4, with no dramatic shifts in the magnitudes.

V   CONCLUSIONS

In this chapter we have developed a generalisation of the Leuthold model of family labour supply which allows us to test the Leuthold specification of labour supply against the neo-classical model.

On performing the test on a sample of UK families we have found that the data supports the Leuthold rather than the neo-classical model, and that the predicted labour supply elasticities arising from the two models are markedly different. This suggests that policy prediction is affected by the specification one employs, which makes it important to have a test of one model against the other.

Our model specification also has the advantage of enabling one to explore the underlying structure of the Leuthold model completely. Thus one can compare the short- and long-run elasticities and analyse the structure of interaction between husband and wife. We found that the short-run labour supply behaviour of the husband was very different from the long-run behaviour; that an increase in work by the wife induced the husband to work less hard, but an increase in work by the husband led the wife to work substantially harder. On breaking these latter effects into effects operating through shifts in preferences and effects operating through induced changes in increased income, we found the two effects to be of opposite sign, with the income effect dominant. This suggested that the preference effects might not be significant – a hypothesis we could not refute at the 5 per cent level. This implies that we cannot reject the simple Leuthold model as against the more general proposed at the outset of this chapter.

There are a number of qualifications we would like to make about the work presented here. First, the model is by no means the most general one can construct for analysing household decisions where the members hold different views. Essentially the model limits the area of disagreement to how income should be earned and not to how it should be spent. One possible generalisation would be to allow three types of consumption: general household consumption, consumption specifically for the husband and consumption specifically for the wife. Each member of the household could then make decisions not only about how hard to work but also how he/she would allocate his/her income over the different consumption categories. It is easy to see how the techniques proposed here would generalise to such a situation. Such a model would have the interesting feature that it would now matter to whom non-employment incomes such as state benefits were paid. We have not discussed such a model simply because our data did not distinguish expenditure in a satisfactory fashion to enable us to test it.

The second qualification concerns the empirical results. Apart from some obvious caveats concerning the construction of the data, especially the wife's wage rate, a serious problem which remains is that of endogeneity bias, particularly for the wife. What we are doing in making adjustments to non-employment income to allow for non-linearities in the budget constraint is to add nothing on for wives below the tax threshold and a positive amount for wives above the tax threshold. This will mean that for wives with approximately the same wage rate we will be attributing higher unearned income to those working longer hours. This could well explain the positive income effect we found for the wife in the Leuthold model, and could mean that the income effect found for the wife in the neo-classical model is underestimated. This in turn could account for the wrong signs we have found for the substitution effects of the wife in both models. As we have seen, a great deal of the long-run behaviour of the Leuthold model depends on the interaction effects which depend, in their turn, on the income effects.

While it would be fairly straightforward to eliminate endogeneity bias from the neo-classical model using an estimation procedure recently developed by Wales and Woodland (1979) and ourselves (Chapter 6) this procedure is harder to apply to the Leuthold model. The procedure involves constructing the entire budget constraint for each individual and explicitly solving the utility maximization problem. In the Wales and Woodland version of the procedure, a form for the direct utility function is assumed, and since they need to solve the first-order conditions explicitly, they are limited to using the CES forms. In our version of the procedure a form for the indirect utility function is assumed, and since hours of work can be determined from this by simple differentiation, we can employ a very general functional form.

Our procedure would not be applicable to the Leuthold model since the short-run indirect utility functions will contain not only prices but the leisure of the spouse. Even if the direct utility function is identical for both members, the two short-run indirect utility functions need not be the same. Unless one works with very simple functional forms it is impossible to see what restrictions one puts on the indirect utility functions.

On the other hand, using the Wales and Woodland procedure would strictly limit us to testing the hypothesis that husband and wife operate with the same CES utility function, as against two different CES utility functions. It is not too clear what conclusions one could draw from whatever result such a test produced.

NOTES: CHAPTER 9

1 Throughout this chapter, all utility functions will be taken to be twice continuously differentiable.

2 $\dot{H}_h = \psi^h(w^h, w^w, V, 1-H^w) - H^h$
   $\dot{H}_w = \psi^w(w^h, w^w, V, 1-H^h) - H^w$

3 The first-order conditions for the long-run Leuthold equilibrium are given by

$$\frac{\partial}{\partial c} u^h(c, \ell^h, \ell^w) = \lambda^h \qquad \frac{\partial}{\partial c} u^w(c, \ell^h, \ell^w) = \lambda^w$$

$$\frac{\partial}{\partial \ell^h} u^h(c, \ell^h, \ell^w) = \lambda^h w^h \qquad \frac{\partial}{\partial \ell^w} u^w(c, \ell^h, \ell^w) = \lambda^w w^w$$

$$c + w^w \ell^w + w^h \ell^h = v + w^h + w^w$$

If $u^h = u^w$, $\lambda^h = \lambda^w$ and we have the first-order conditions for the neo-classical model. Given strict quasi-concavity there is a unique solution to these conditions.

4 For proof of this, see Christenson, Jorgenson and Lau (1973) where the other properties of the functional form are established.

5 We give only the two share equations which we employed in estimating the parameters of the neo-classical model. There is, of course, a third equation for the share of consumption, but since this is linearly dependent on the above two, it need not be used when performing the estimation.

6 See Theil (1971, pp. 396–7).

7 Further discussion of this is given in Goldfield and Quandt (1972). There is also consideration of the exact use of the logarithmic likelihood ratio test.

8 For details of the construction of that sample see Chapter 2.

9 For details of this procedure see Chapter 5 for the single-worker case and Wales and Woodland (1976) for the family case.

10 That this procedure may give rise to endogeneity bias in the estimates has been forcefully argued by Greenhalgh (1976) and Wales and Woodland (1979). Wales and Woodland (1979) and ourselves (Chapter 6) have independently devised a procedure for avoiding this bias in neo-classical models. However, we have not, as yet, been able to find a way of applying this procedure to the estimation of our Leuthold equations. We will discuss this matter further in our conclusions.

11 Since the original sample in Chapter 5 was confined to these families where only the husband or only the husband and wife worked, there will be no other earned income in this total.

12 See, for example, Ulph (1978), Hare and Ulph (1980).
13 The sample also eliminated those men who were paid on bonus or who were constrained in their choice of hours – considerations we have ignored here.

Chapter 10

Summary of Results

This chapter brings together and compares our results for individual models.[1,2]

THE BROWN/LEVIN RESULTS (see Chapter 4)

The Brown/Levin results are the only results that cannot be presented in elasticity terms. They found a small effect of tax on men's overtime amounting to perhaps an increase in hours worked of 1 per cent. The impossibility of calculating elasticities is one of the objections to the interview approach. Nevertheless one of the original objectives of the project was to see if there was broad consistency between the interview approach and the econometric approach. No very precise comparison is possible. It may be that the finding of the interview approach that income tax increases overtime hours slightly is not inconsistent with the econometric finding of a low negative price elasticity.

THE BROWN/LEVIN/ULPH RESULTS (see Chapter 5)

The Brown/Levin/Ulph results are based on an endogenous model and are summarized in Table 10.1. It can be seen that the estimated price elasticity is negative (-0.1 to -0.2), that income and substitution elasticities

Table 10.1 *Summary of Brown/Levin/Ulph Results*

| | All | | Not on Bonus | |
Married Men	*Without Preferences* (1)	*With Preferences* (2)	*Without Preferences* (3)	*With Preferences* (4)
Number	434	434	210	210
Elasticities				
Price	−0.11	−0.14	−0.23	−0.26
Income	−0.02	−0.02	−0.01	−0.01
Substitution	0.20	0.16	0.22	0.17
of substitution	0.27	0.22	0.32	0.24

have the expected signs and that the elasticity of substitution is 0.2 to 0.3. The inclusion of preferences as control variables increases somewhat the absolute value of the price elasticity and reduces the other elasticities.

THE ASHWORTH/ULPH RESULTS (see Chapter 6)

Ashworth and Ulph explored the implications of alternative functional forms and of endogeneity bias employing indirect utility functions. Their results are summarized in Table 10.2.

The results for men are given in the top of the table. Column (1) repeats the Brown/Levin/Ulph results. Column (2) is identical in principle except for the reduction in numbers. Numbers are lower because of the higher information requirements of the Ashworth/Ulph technique. It can be seen that the elasticities rise somewhat. It is perhaps to be expected that people who know more about the budget constraints should be more responsive to changes in these constraints. This tends to confirm the incomplete response bias referred to in Chapter 3.

A comparison of columns (2) and (3) shows the effects of including 'other income' in the intercept. The effect is to increase price elasticity and to decrease the substitution elasticity and the elasticity of substitution. The treatment of other income was discussed at length in Chapter 5 where it was pointed out that our measure of other income has substantial amounts of measurement error. It was also pointed out in that chapter that there is no way of handling 'other income' properly within the confines of our individual model. It is thus not possible to be categorical about which treatment is to be preferred within the confines of a single model and indeed there is not unanimity amongst us as to which is second best. (My own view on this issue has not changed since Brown/Levin/ Ulph – see quotation p. 46.) Column (4) shows the effect of a change in functional form from a quadratic labour supply function to a generalized CES utility function. A comparison of columns (3) and (4) suggests that the quadratic approximation reduced elasticities in the Brown/Levin/Ulph results.

Column (5) contains the non-endogenous budget constraint and a comparison of columns (4) and (5) suggests that endogeneity bias is important particularly for the substitution elasticity and the elasticity of substitution. It may be noted that the estimates in columns (1) and (4) are remarkably similar (i.e. the effects of partial response and the inclusion of 'other' income in the intercept roughly cancel out). This implies that Brown/Levin/Ulph were too optimistic in suggesting that endogeneity bias might be unimportant for men.

Table 10.2 *Summary of Ashworth and Ulph Results*

	Endogenous Budget Constraints				Non Endogenous Budget Constraints
	Quadratic labour supply function			Indirect utility function GCES	
	'Other Income' included as separate term	'Other income' in intercept			
	(1)	(2)	(3)	(4)	(5)
Married men					
Number	434	335	335	335	335
Elasticities					
Price	−0.11	−0.00	0.06	−0.13	−0.07
Income	−0.02	−0.02	−0.02	−0.05	−0.10
Substitution	0.20	0.31	0.15	0.23	0.50
Of substitution	0.27	0.41	0.20	0.30	0.58
Married women					
Number		74	74	74	74
Elasticities					
Price		−0.21	−0.09	0.19	0.63
Income		0.00	−0.10	−0.14	−0.35
Substitution		−0.23	−0.04	0.29	0.84
Of substitution				0.22	0.55

The results for married women are given in the lower half of the table. Brown/Levin/Ulph results are not available for women so column (1) is blank. It should be noted that the results are for only seventy-four women so small cell bias and incomplete response bias are both likely to be particularly acute. It may be noted from columns (2) and (3) that the substitution elasticity has the 'wrong' sign – something we found frequently when we estimated endogenous quadratic labour supply functions for women. Columns (4) and (5) suggest that this was due in part to the restricted functional form and in part to the particularly severe endogeneity problem that is revealed by a comparison of columns (4) and (5).

THE RUFFELL RESULTS (see Chapter 8)

The Ruffell results report an exploration of the definition of the marginal wage rate at kinks of different minimands and of endogeneity bias using quadratic labour supply functions. His results are summarized in Table 10.3.

Ruffell's analysis is confined to people who are not paid by bonus (a sample selection is discussed further below). The table gives the Brown/ Levin/Ulph results for no bonus in column (1). It may be noted that there are three fewer people (net) in column (1) than in the subsequent columns. This is because Ruffell found a programming error in the selection criteria used in Brown/Levin/Ulph. There are also detailed differences of definition between Brown/Levin/Ulph and Ruffell. The most important of these – aside from the treatment of 'other' income – is in the marginal wage rate where Ruffell has carefully explored alternative definitions of the wage for people at kinks. Column (2) shows the definition closest to the Brown/Levin/Ulph definition. There are thus several respects in which columns (1) and (2) differ and hence one cannot say categorically why the results differ. Nevertheless it seems likely that the most important reason is the treatment of 'other income'. If this interpretation is accepted it confirms the Ashworth/Ulph finding that putting 'other income' in the intercept reduces elasticities markedly.

Using the mean wage for people at kinks has little effect for men – except, perhaps, in increasing the absolute value of negative price elasticity. Given the higher proportion of women at kinks it is not surprising that the difference is more pronounced for women with elasticities falling.

Ruffell finds little evidence for endogeneity bias for men (in contrast to Ashworth/Ulph and as expected by Brown/Levin/Ulph) but does find,

Table 10.3 Summary of Ruffell Results

	Endogenous Budget Constraints		'Other income' in intercept	Non-endogenous Budget Constraints
	'Other income' included as separate term	Wage rate used for hours of work above kink for those at kink	Mean wage rate used at kink	
	(1)	(2)	(3)	(4)
Married men				
Number	210	213	213	213
Elasticities				
Price	−0.23	−0.04	−0.07	−0.05
Income	−0.01	−0.04	−0.05	−0.02
Substitution	0.22	0.10	0.09	0.03
Of substitution	0.32	0.12	0.11	0.03
Married women				
Number		129	129	129
Elasticities				
Price		0.08	−0.00	0.72
Income		−0.11	−0.11	−0.16
Substitution		0.12	0.04	0.77
Of substitution		0.05	0.02	0.35

as expected, and in broad conformity with the Ashworth/Ulph results, that endogeneity is important for women.

Ruffell finds a low price elasticity for women with the endogenous model but his non-endogenous model confirms the large positive elasticity found by most other researchers.

COMPARISON OF ASHWORTH/ULPH AND RUFFELL RESULTS

For men there is a consistent finding (see Table 10.4) that the price elasticity for men is a low negative number. (This finding appears very stable.) The income elasticity is also consistently found to be a low negative number. Estimates of the substitution elasticity and the elasticity of substitution are much less stable. Table 10.4 reports estimates of the elasticity of substitution between 0.0 and 0.6. In terms of their policy implications this is a wide range. As the substitution effect depends on hours, the price effect and the income effect, it, as well as the derived elasticities, is very sensitive to variations in any of the estimates. In addition elasticity estimates are made at a point and, except with CES functions, the elasticity can, and does, vary from point to point. These elasticities are all subject to confidence intervals so that even some of the larger differences may not be significantly different. It is thus conceivable that the underlying results are not as different as they appear to be.

Taking the results at their face value there are several possible reasons for the' divergence. From the Ashworth/Ulph results it appears that functional form is important and the quadratic labour supply function used by Ruffell is likely to lead to an underestimate of the elasticity. Ruffell as well as Ashworth/Ulph include 'other' income in the intercept and this also reduces the elasticity – in this case of both estimates. There is also the possibility that the results are dependent on the selection criteria adopted. Ruffell's results apply only to people not on bonus, whereas Ashworth/Ulph include people on bonus. Ruffell made considerable efforts to overcome incomplete response bias by using alternative definitions of variables whenever possible.[3]

As we have seen Ashworth/Ulph did not do this and so their results are more likely to suffer from incomplete response bias and it was suggested above that this may have increased their estimated elasticity. It should be stressed that the estimates are based on a low number of cases. The programmes for the non-endogenous routines are complex and large numbers would be a clear advantage.

The small numbers problem is especially acute for women. The

Table 10.4 *Comparison of Ashworth/Ulph and Ruffell Results*

	Endogenous Budget Constraints		Non-endogenous Budget Constraints	
	Ashworth/Ulph	Ruffell	Ashworth/Ulph	Ruffell
Source (Table/column)	10.2/4	10.3/3	10.2/5	10.3/4
Married men				
Number	335	213	335	213
Elasticities				
Price	−0.13	−0.07	−0.07	−0.05
Income	−0.05	−0.05	−0.10	−0.02
Substitution	0.23	0.09	0.50	0.03
Of substitution	0.30	0.11	0.58	0.03
Married women				
Number	74	129	74	129
Elasticities				
Price	0.19	−0.00	0.63	0.72
Income	−0.14	−0.11	−0.35	−0.16
Substitution	0.29	0.04	0.84	0.77
Of substitution	0.22	0.02	0.55	0.35

women's results are also likely to suffer particularly from truncation bias arising from the exclusion of non-workers and from employing an individual model which is probably especially inappropriate in the case of married women due to the larger non-employment income/other income term. The results for women must clearly therefore be regarded as even more provisional than those for men. That being said, both the Ashworth/ Ulph and the Ruffell results have confirmed our expectations that the endogeneity problem is serious for married women. The non-endogenous results are in close agreement with a fairly high positive price elasticity of 0.6 or 0.7 and an elasticity of substitution of 0.4 or 0.5.

PREFERENCES

The evidence from this study suggests that sophistication in the treatment of budget constraints is important but the evidence in favour of sophistication in the treatment of preferences from this study is not strong. The relatively unsophisticated treatment of preferences in Brown Levin/Ulph (see Table 10.1) suggested that the inclusion of preferences increased the absolute value of the price elasticity and reduced the other elasticities but the differences were not great. The Glaister/McGlone/ Ruffell findings (see Table 10.5) which allow for interactions between preference variables and budget constraint variables has also reduced the

Table 10.5   *Glaister/McGlone/Ruffell on Preferences*
Endogenous Model

	Without Preferences	*With Preferences*
Married men		
Number	213	213
Elasticities		
Price	−0.07	−0.02
Income	−0.05	−0.01
Substitution	0.09	−0.06
Of substitution	0.11	−0.07
Married women		
Number	129	129
Elasticities		
Price	−0.00	0.09
Income	−0.11	0.01
Substitution	0.04	0.09
Of substitution	0.02	0.04

elasticity of substitution for men, which have actually become negative contrary to theoretical predictions. The negative elasticity of substitution for men may stem from the inclusion of 'other income' in the intercept. For women the inclusion of preferences increased elasticity slightly. The interactive treatment of preferences did not work with the non-endogenous budget constraint probably because of small numbers. With better data and/or larger numbers the inclusion of interactive preferences might have been more important, but we have no evidence for this view.

CONCLUSION

We have made a great effort to point out throughout the first two parts of this book that there are a large number of potential problems in making labour supply estimates. We believe that we can reasonably claim to have made progress in tackling a number of these. Nevertheless all of our econometric work (and especially the work on households and married women) is based on small numbers. All of the econometric work suffers from small cell bias and/or incomplete response bias. All of the work in principle suffers from truncation bias, and this may be important especially in the case of married women. These deficiencies, coupled with our findings that some of the estimates, in particular, the estimate of the elasticity of substitution, are highly sensitive to details of model specification, mean that all of our estimates must be regarded as provisional.

If more work had been done *some* of the uncertainties concerning the present estimates could have been removed. We could have taken steps to keep numbers up by using alternative definitions of variables to overcome missing data problems. We could have ensured that the two approaches to the endogeneity problem (Chapters 6 and 8) were run on the same definition of variables. Elasticities could have been calculated at the same points and confidence intervals put on all the estimates. We could not however eliminate all of the problems caused by relatively small numbers, nor could the problem of truncation bias have been eliminated. Lack of household data and the resulting problem with other income could not be removed. In the event we have not pursued those improvements which could have been made because we have turned our attention to a new study in which we hope to overcome these and other problems.

There is thus a clear need for new work[4] building on the lessons that we, and others, have learned. Given the problems that have been stressed and the time that has elapsed since our data was collected it would hardly be surprising if new estimates differed substantially from the present estimates.

Until new estimates are available there are two possible courses of action. One, the more easily defensible academically, is to argue that the key lesson that has been learned is that estimates are very sensitive to model specification and that it is unlikely to be fruitful to speculate on either the direction or the magnitude of any change in elasticities that may emerge when these problems are solved. The other, riskier, approach is to point out that while further work should eliminate many problems it is likely that there will always be reasons for criticizing estimates. My personal view, which is not shared by all of my colleagues, is to follow the riskier strategy for men, and to say what is the best available estimate I believe that the best available information is as follows. For men the price elasticity is low and negative (perhaps −0.1), the income elasticity is also low and negative (perhaps of the same order of magnitude) with the elasticity of substitution being somewhat higher than Ruffell found and slightly lower than Ashworth/Ulph found (perhaps 0.5). These figures are broadly in line with other, recent, predominantly US studies.[5] For all of the reasons stressed above my confidence in our findings for women leads me to take the more academically respectable position and simply to point out that our findings are not inconsistent with those of others – that the price elasticity for married women is a fairly large positive number.

NOTES: CHAPTER 10

1 The results from Chapter 9 on household models have not been included in this summary because as the authors of that chapter have pointed out the chapter is best interpreted as an exploration of a method of comparing the neo-classical and Leuthold models rather than as a basis for providing firm estimates of elasticities. The empirical work inevitably must be regarded as even more tentative than our other work as it is based on only eighty-eight cases, we were unable to observe a wage rate for the wife, non-working wives have been excluded and it is based on an endogenous model which we have found to be a particularly serious problem for married women.

2 Because confidence intervals are not available for some of our results it is not possible to say which, if any, of the differences in elasticities are significantly different.

3 And actually gained three people – see above.

4 New work that hopefully will overcome many of the problems we have encountered has now started and is being funded by a grant from HM Treasury.

5 These are surveyed in Brown (1980).

PART THREE IMPLICATIONS

Chapter 11

Labour Supply, Taxation and the Measurement of Inequality

INTRODUCTION

Given the great amount of theoretical and empirical investigation of the effects of income taxation on labour supply that has been undertaken in recent years, it is natural that the empirical results should be embodied in simulation studies of the effects of changes in the tax system on various features of the economy, and in particular on inequality. Yet, as Layard and Zabalza (1979) have pointed out in trying to undertake just such an exercise for the UK, all the standard measures of inequality ignore leisure considerations, while, as shown recently (Ulph, 1978), those that do try to take account of labour supply are not completely satisfactory.

The essence of the problem is easily identified. As argued in Ulph, (1978), it seems natural when considering questions of income taxation to operate within a context in which the individual endowments of labour skills are fixed, and this is certainly the assumption behind much of the work on optimal income taxation. Ignoring the uninteresting case in which everyone has the same skill endowment, this means that in equilibrium different individuals will face different wage rates. This has two implications.

Firstly, one is not going to be able to construct a measure of inequality by including a valuation of leisure into income (i.e. by using full income) and then applying a standard measure of income inequality. For that to be a valid procedure it is necessary that everyone be confronted with the same prices for all commodities, and that is precisely the assumption that does not hold.

144

Secondly, any simple attempt to use Atkinson's 'equally distributed equivalent income' method will run into difficulties. For our purposes the best method of explaining this is to give the following interpretation to the standard Atkinson measure. Start with a given distribution of income, and redistribute this income through a series of lump-sum taxes and transfers until everyone is equally well off. Retaining the strong assumption made by Atkinson that social welfare is the sum of identical individual utility functions each of which is strictly concave in income, this move will increase social welfare. Now impose lump-sum taxes on everyone so that they all remain equally well off but social welfare returns to its original level. The Atkinson measure expresses the total tax so raised as a proportion of initial income. The difficulty that arises when one tries to carry through exactly the same exercise for the case in which individuals face different prices is that there is no guarantee that redistributing income until everyone is just as well off will increase social welfare. Indeed, since in general the optimum (under the additive social welfare function) will be characterised by having some inequality, there must be some starting positions from which the move to equality will entail a reduction in social welfare. In this case the Atkinson measure, as calculated above, will be negative, for people will need to be given a subsidy (negative tax) to restore the original level of social welfare.

Now one response to such a negative measure is that it poses no problems: for the Atkinson measure reflects what society is prepared to give up to achieve equality, and if it is too expensive (in terms of total welfare foregone) to make everyone equal when some people's consumption is very much more expensive than others' then society may not be prepared to give up anything to attain equality, and indeed may need to receive compensation for doing so. But this is to confuse two issues: whether or not there is inequality (and if there is inequality just how great it is) with that of whether or not it is desirable to take steps to remove the inequality. In the standard case in which all individuals face the same prices the two issues are identical and the one measure will serve to answer both questions. When prices differ, however, the simple extension of the Atkinson measure sketched above may serve to illuminate the second issue but is inadequate for dealing with the first.

The major purpose of this chapter is to propose an extension of the Atkinson measure to the case in which individuals face different prices. This will then be applied in the particular context of labour supply in which the different prices are different wage rates, and the problems of analysing the effects of income taxation on inequality will be considered.

The next section begins with the artificial case of a one-commodity model. It is artificial in that we can forget about income and prices and translate everything directly into real consumption and obtain a measure of inequality in real terms. However this is precisely what we want, for since we know what we are trying to do in this case, we can motivate the more complex formula involving prices and incomes and check that it is equivalent to the simple formula. It will then be possible to show how the more complex formula allowing for price differences across individuals will generalise to the *n*-commodity case. It will be argued that while there is also a generalisation of the simpler Atkinson formula in real terms, this is not a satisfactory measure, and is no longer equivalent to the complex measure. General properties of the new measure will then be established.

The subsequent section will consider briefly the problems involved in applying the new measure to a world of labour supply but no taxation. It turns out that some of the general results established in the previous section have to be modified. An income tax is introduced followed by a discussion of what can be said about the effects of tax changes on inequality allowing for labour supply responses.

I   DEFINITION OF THE MEASURE

As mentioned in the Introduction, we begin with the simple case of a one-good model.

(a) The One-Good Case

There are N individuals, indexed $i = 1, \ldots, N$. Individual i has an endowment y_i of income and faces a price p_i for the single consumption good. His consumption is therefore $c_i = y_i/p_i$. All individuals have the same utility function $u(c)$, where $u(.)$ is defined for all $c \geqq 0$, is strictly increasing and strictly concave. Social welfare is

$$W = \sum_{i=1}^{N} u(c_i) \tag{1}$$

Letters without subscripts will denote the N-vector of elements with the i subscript; thus $y = (y_1 \ldots y_N)$ etc. Letters with a bar will denote mean values, thus

$$\bar{y} = \frac{1}{N} \sum_{i=1}^{N} y_i \text{ etc.}$$

Given the price vector p, how unequal is the income distribution y? A natural way of trying to answer this question is to translate income into terms of real consumption and employ a measure of inequality on the consumption vector c. The particular measure we wish to concentrate on is the Atkinson measure, α, defined by

$$u\left\{(1-\alpha)\bar{c}\right\} = \bar{u} \equiv \frac{1}{N} \sum_{i=1}^{N} u(c_i) \qquad (2)$$

But what exactly is the interpretation of α in this case? To see the answer to this, let us assume for the moment that $N = 2$, and give a diagrammatic representation of α for the standard case in which $p_1 = p_2 = 1$. Thus in Figure 11.1 FF is the efficiency frontier giving all combinations of (c_1, c_2) that can be generated by redistributing income by means of lump-sum taxes and subsidies, that is,

$$FF = \left\{ (c_1, c_2) \geqq 0 \,|\, p_1 c_1 + p_2 c_2 = y_1 + y_2 \right\}. \qquad (3)$$

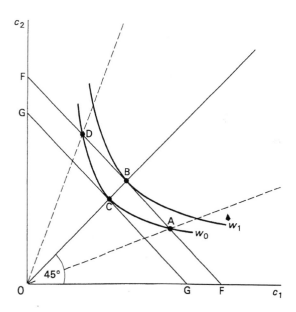

Figure 11.1

The initial allocation is the point A on FF and this gives a level of social welfare represented by the curve w_0 passing through A. Were all income to be equally distributed we could attain the point B and a level of social welfare represented by the curve w_1. GG represents the efficiency frontier after imposing taxes so that when the reduced level of income is equally redistributed, the original level of social welfare w_0 is achieved (this occurs at point C).

Now let us interpret Figure 11.1 in a different way. Let D denote the point which is symmetric around the 45° line to A, that is, at D utility is simply permuted between the two individuals. Given the symmetry of the social welfare function D lies on w_0. The point B can now be thought of as the point which gives each individual exactly half of the total income he receives at the points A and D, while the point C represents the position in which everyone is given just enough income to achieve the average level of welfare in the original position. The Atkinson measure expresses the difference between the total income at B and at C as a proportion of the total income at B.

Put in a more geometric way, the Atkinson measure measures the distance between the line AD which spans the points on w_0 symmetric to A and the 'bottom' of the curve w_0 at C. The measure depends only how far the ray OA (or equivalently OD) is from the 45° line OCB, and on the curvature of the curve w_0 (which reflects the degree of inequality aversion).

The key point to notice is that this second way of interpreting Figure 11.1 no longer relies on any notion of AD lying on the efficiency frontier through A, and so exactly the same construction can be carried out even when the efficiency frontier is not symmetric. To see this, let us consider Figure 11.2 in which the efficiency frontier is no longer symmetric ($p_1 = p_2$). The efficiency frontier through A is once again FF. D is once again symmetric to A, but now it would require more income to support D - as represented by the efficiency frontier F'F'. HH is the efficiency frontier passing through B and so represents an economy with half the total income at A and D, that is, HH lies exactly halfway between FF and F'F'. GG is the efficiency frontier passing through C, the point of perfect equality on w_0. The analogue of the Atkinson measure under the second interpretation of Figure 11.1 is therefore to express the difference in income between B and C as a proportion of income at B.

Notice now what would have happened had we tried to measure inequality in a fashion analogous to that in the first interpretation of Figure 11.1. We would have started at A and moved along the efficiency frontier to the point of perfect equality, in this case E, not B. At E the

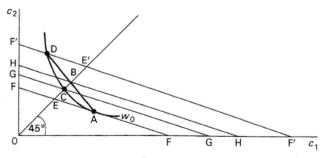

Figure 11.2

economy is worse off than at A and so requires a subsidy measured by the distance EC to restore the original level of welfare. This is precisely the type of negative measure mentioned in the Introduction. Conversely, starting at D we would have moved to E′ and so would have had to impose a tax represented by the distance E′C to restore welfare, and thus have obtained a large positive measure of inequality.

The measure proposed above is independent of whether one starts at A or D and is, in a sense, an average of the measures at A and D under the 'standard' procedure.

Let us now return to the general case of N individuals, and formalise the measure. Let $u_i = u(c_i) = u(y_i/p_i)$ and let $u = (u_1 \ldots u_N)$. Let $J(u)$ be the set of $N!$ permutations of u. We will index permutations by a superscript j running from $j=1, \ldots, N!$ Thus, for all $i, j, u_i^j = u_k$ for some $k = 1, \ldots, N$.

Let $e(p, x)$ be the minimum expenditure required by an individual facing a price p to achieve the utility level x. For the simple one-good model

$$e(p, x) = p.u^{-1}(x)$$

Following the diagrammatical analysis outlined above, the measure of inequality that will be used, denoted by μ, is defined by

$$(1-\mu).\frac{1}{N}\frac{1}{N!} \sum_{i=1}^{N} \sum_{j=1}^{N!} e(p_i, u_i^j) = \frac{1}{N} \sum_{i=1}^{N} e(p_i, \bar{u}) \qquad (4)$$

The expression

$$\frac{1}{N} \sum_{i=1}^{N} e(p_i, u_i^j)$$

is just the average expenditure required to sustain the *j*th permutation of utilities, while

$$\frac{1}{N!}\frac{1}{N} \sum_{i=1}^{N} \sum_{j=1}^{N} e(p_i, u_i^j)$$

is just this expenditure averaged over all permutations. In other words it is just the average expenditure required to support the array of utility $(u_1 \ldots u_N)$ *however these are distributed.* The expression

$$\frac{1}{N} \sum_{i=1}^{N} e(p_i, \bar{u})$$

is just the average expenditure required to support the average utility levels. The measure simply calculates the percentage reduction in average expenditure that could be achieved by moving from a spread of utilities to the mean level of utility.

Equation (4) can be immediately simplified by noting that for each i, k individual i is allocated the utility level u_k in $(N-1)!$ of the permutations. Hence (4) becomes

$$(1-\mu)\frac{1}{N^2} \sum_{i=1}^{N} \sum_{k=1}^{N} e(p_i, u_k) = \frac{1}{N} \sum_{i=1}^{N} e(p_i, \bar{u}) \qquad (5)$$

The claim that, for the one good case, this measure is just the same as the Atkinson measure defined by (2) is justified by:

Theorem 1 when there is only one commodity, $\mu = \alpha$ for all $p \gg 0$.

Proof $e(p_i, u_k) = p_i u^{-1}(u_k) = p_i c_k$. Hence

$$\frac{1}{N^2} \sum_i \sum_k e(p_i, u_k) = \bar{p}.\bar{c}$$

Let $\bar{c}$ be defined by $u(\hat{c}) = \bar{u}$. Then $(1/N)\,\Sigma e(p_i,\bar{u}) = \bar{p}.\hat{c}$. Hence (5) becomes

$$(1-\mu)\bar{p}.\bar{c} = \bar{p}.\hat{c}$$

or

$$(1-\mu)\bar{c} = \hat{c} \tag{6}$$

From (6) it follows that

$$u\left\{(1-\mu)\,\bar{c}\,\right\} = u(\hat{c}) = \bar{u}$$

which is just the definition of α.

Having used the one-good case to motivate the construction of μ let us now look at the problem of generalising the argument to n commodities.

(b) The n-good case

Assume as before that we start with an initial distribution of income y_i, but now assume that each individual faces a price *vector* $p_i \gg 0$ for the n commodities. Assume each individual has, as consumption possibility set, the non-negative orthant of n-dimensional space and that on this he has a well-defined strictly concave utility function $u(.)$ the same for all individuals. Individual i now has an initial utility level u_i given by

$$u_i = v(p_i, y_i) \tag{7}$$

where $v(.)$ is the indirect utility function defined by

$$v(p, y) = \underset{c \geq 0}{\text{Max}}\, u(c) \qquad \text{s.t.}\, pc \leq y \tag{8}$$

As before $e(p, x)$ will be the expenditure function defined by

$$e(p, x) = \underset{c \geq 0}{\text{Min}}\, pc \qquad \text{s.t.}\, u(c) \geq x \tag{9}$$

Further, let $c = d(p,y)$ be the demand function arising from the maximisation in (8). Now there is clearly no problem involved in extending the definition of the measure μ given in (4) and (5) to the case in hand. It is also possible to extend the definition of α given in (2) by simply letting $c_i = d(p_i,\ y_i)$. However, Theorem 1 will no longer apply, for two reasons.

In the first place

$$e(p_i, u_k) \gtreqqless p_i c_k$$

with equality if and only if

$$d^c(p_i, u_k) = d^c(p_k, u_k)$$

where $d^c(p, x)$ is the compensated demand function arising from the minimization in (9). Similarly in the bench-mark position of equality individuals facing different relative prices will, in general, be making different consumption choices. Hence it will not be possible to cancel through the price vectors as was done in Theorem 1, leaving the measure expressed essentially in real terms.

This discussion also suggests why the extension of α to the n-good case may be an inappropriate measure to use, since it presupposes that in pursuing equality it is desirable to give everyone the same consumption vector. However, if price differences are essential to the economy, then this is not the case and efficiency losses will result from the imposition of such a constraint. It has been shown elsewhere that this is precisely what goes wrong with some proposed measures of inequality in the labour-supply context which take a similarly constricted view of the options open to society for achieving equality. For these reasons it will be assumed that while α is perfectly well defined for the n-good case, μ is the more appropriate measure to employ.

Before establishing the general properties of μ, note that if everyone does face the same price vector, p, say, then the Atkinson measure of income inequality, β_p, defined by

$$v\{p, (1-\beta_p)\bar{y}\} = \bar{v} = \frac{1}{N} \sum_{i=1}^{N} v(p_j, y_i) \tag{10}$$

is well defined and is then equivalent to μ.

Theorem 2 For all $p \gg 0, p_i = p$ for all i implies $\mu = \beta_p$.
Proof If $p_i = p$ all i

$$\frac{1}{N^2} \sum_i \sum_k e(p_i, u_k) = \frac{1}{N} \sum_{k=1}^{N} e(p, u_k) = \frac{1}{N} \sum_{k=1}^{N} e\{p, v(p, y_k)\} = \bar{y}$$

while

$$\frac{1}{N} \sum_{i=1}^{N} e(p_i, \bar{u}) = e(p, \bar{u})$$

Hence (5) becomes

$$(1-\mu)\bar{y} = e(p, \bar{u}) \tag{11}$$

Inverting, the expenditure function (11) becomes

$$v\{p, (1-\mu)\bar{y}\} = \bar{u}$$

which is just the definition of β_p.

Theorem 2 shows that μ is a genuine extension of the Atkinson measure of income inequality, since it is equivalent to the Atkinson measure where that is valid, and is well defined in cases where the Atkinson measure is not well defined.

Let us now establish some general properties of μ.

Theorem 3 $\mu \geqq 0$ with equality if and only if $u_i = \bar{u}$ all i.

Proof If $u(.)$ is strictly concave then $e(.)$ is strictly convex, and so

$$\frac{1}{N^2} \sum_{i=1}^{N} \sum_{k=1}^{N} e(p_i, u_k) \geqq \frac{1}{N} \sum_i e(p_i, \bar{u}) \tag{12}$$

with equality if and only if $u_k = \bar{u}$ all k.

Notice that μ depends on the vector of prices $\mathbf{p} = (p_1 \ldots p_N)$ (where each p_i is itself an n-dimensional vector) and on the vector of utilities, $u = (u_1 \ldots u_N)$. It is clear from the construction that μ does not depend on who has the particular utility levels, that is,

$$\mu(\mathbf{p}, u) = \mu(\mathbf{p}, u') \text{ for any } u' \in \mathrm{J}(u)$$

In this sense μ is symmetric or anonymous in utilities.

One final property that it is worth establishing is

Theorem 4 If $\mu(.)$ is homothetic, μ is independent of $\mathbf{p}$ and so depends only on u.

Proof If $u(.)$ is homothetic we can write $e(p, x) = \phi(p) \psi(x)$

Hence

$$\frac{1}{N^2} \sum_{i=1}^{N} \sum_{k=1}^{N} e(p_i, u_k) = \left(\frac{1}{N^2} \sum_{i=1}^{N} \phi(p_i) \right) \left(\frac{1}{N} \sum_{k=1}^{N} \psi(u_k) \right)$$

while

$$\frac{1}{N} \sum_{i=1}^{N} e(p_i, \bar{u}) = \left(\frac{1}{N} \sum_{i=1}^{N} \phi(p_i) \right) . \psi(\bar{u})$$

Hence (5) becomes

$$(1-\mu) \frac{1}{N} \sum_{k=1}^{N} \psi(u_k) = \psi(\bar{u}) \tag{13}$$

which proves the theorem.

Effectively, then, when $u(.)$ is homothetic one uses $\phi(.)$ to convert money income into real income:

$$Z_k = \psi(u_k) = e(p, u_k)/\phi(p_k) = y_k/\phi(p_k) \tag{14}$$

and uses ψ^{-1} as the utility function for real income. Expression (13) can then be rewritten as

$$\psi^{-1} \left\{ (1-\mu)\bar{z} \right\} = \bar{u} \tag{15}$$

which is just the Atkinson measure of inequality of real income, where real income is defined through (14), and where ψ^{-1} is employed as the utility function. Once again the measure μ is equivalent to a natural definition of income inequality where that definition is valid.

Theorem 4 will not, however, translate to the context of labour supply, to which we now turn.

II LABOUR SUPPLY

There are two commodities, income and leisure. Individual i is endowed with s_i units of income and one unit of leisure which he can sell on the market at a real wage n_i. His consumption possibility set is the set of all non-negative combinations of income and leisure with the amount of leisure not exceeding one unit.

Defining the indirect utility function by

$$v(w,y) = \text{Max } u(c,\ell) \quad \text{s.t.} \quad c + w\ell \leq y \tag{16}$$
$$\begin{array}{c} 0 \leq c \\ 0 \leq \ell \leq 1 \end{array}$$

and the expenditure function by

$$e(w, x) = \text{Min } c + w\ell \quad \text{s.t.} \quad u(c,\ell) \geq x$$
$$\begin{array}{c} 0 \leq c \\ 0 \leq \ell \leq 1 \end{array}$$

μ can be defined by

$$(1-\mu)\frac{1}{N^2} \sum_i \sum_k e(w_i, u_k) = \sum_i e(w_i, \bar{u}) \tag{17}$$

where

$$u_k = v(w_k, w_k + s_k) \tag{18}$$

Theorem 2 applies as before, ensuring that when everyone has the same wage rate, the measure just reduces to the Atkinson measure of full income. Similarly, Theorem 3 translates immediately to this context. Theorem 4 will not, however, generally apply. As long as $\ell^c(w, x) < 1$ (where ℓ^c is the compensated demand function for leisure) then, given homotheticity, it is still possible to write $e(w, x) = \phi(w)\psi(x)$; but when $\ell^c(w, x) = 1$ then $e(w, x) = w + g(x)$ where $u\{g(x), 1\} = x$. The expenditure function is therefore of a completely different nature over the two parts of the space and the cancellation argument used in the proof of Theorem 4 will not, in general, be possible. However, it is clear that the proof of Theorem 4 will establish:

Theorem 4' If $u(.)$ is homothetic and if $\ell^c(w_i, u_k) < 1$ for all i, k then μ is locally independent of wage rates.

The additional condition of Theorem 4' is immediately violated if there is any voluntary unemployment in the initial equilibrium. Even if there is no initial unemployment the condition can impose quite severe limits on the variation of wage rates, as the following example will show.

Example Suppose $u(.)$ is of the CES form

$$u(c,\ell) = \frac{\alpha}{1-b} c^{1-b} + \frac{(1-\alpha)}{1-b} \ell^{1-b}$$

where $\epsilon = 1/b$ is the elasticity of substitution, that everyone has zero unearned income and that initially everyone is employed. It is then easily checked that for two individuals facing wages w_1 w_2, $\ell = \ell^c\{w_1, u(w_2)\}$ satisfies

$$\ell^{1-b}\left[(\frac{\alpha}{1-\alpha})^{1/b} w_2^{(1-b)/b} + 1\right] = \left[(\frac{\alpha}{1-\alpha})^{1/b} w_1^{(1-b)/b} + 1\right]^b$$

(provided $\ell < 1$). If we now take w to be the wage of the lowest paid individual and normalise it to be 1, then the maximum value that w_2 can take and still have $\ell < 1$ is given in the following table, 11.1. Thus, for this

Table 11.1

ϵ \ α	0.1	0.5	0.9
0.1	17.6	18.7	19.9
0.5	4.6	5.8	9.0
0.9	3.1	4.2	11.4

range of values (which encompasses many of the empirical estimates of labour supply that have been obtained) if we are to justify using (15) rather than (5) to compute the inequality measure, then the highest wage rate must be no more than 20 times the lowest wage rate, and in some cases the ratio may have to be as low as 5 or 6 to 1.

It is certainly possible to find income distributions in which the ratio of highest to lowest earned income exceeds 20:1, though it is difficult to convert this into a corresponding spread of wage rates, since, for example, the higher prices tend to be salaried. Nevertheless it is clear that in discussing inequality in gross earnings one cannot, in a cavalier fashion, employ the simpler formula given in (15).

It may be argued, however, that if one is discussing inequality in net income then under progressive taxation the spread of net wage rates could be narrow enough to justify the use of (15). Let us consider then the problem of measuring inequality under income taxation.

The introduction of an income tax affects individuals by altering both their utility levels and the net wage they face for their labour. Consequently there are a number of different comparisons of inequality that can be made. For example, one could argue that the important question is how unequally utility is distributed before and after the introduction of the tax. In this case it is appropriate to make the comparison of inequality holding the vector of individual wage rates constant, and the natural ones to choose would be either the original vector or the new one. Even here there are difficulties for the post-tax vector of utilities will not lie on the original efficiency frontier, and one may want to eliminate the effects of scale changes by shrinking the original frontier until it passes through the new set of utility levels.

However, the whole rationale of the measure being proposed in this paper is that, at least in principle, the degree of inequality in society depends not only on the distribution of utility levels, but also on how those utility levels are achieved, that is, on the individual wage rates and levels of unearned income.[1]

Accordingly it will be assumed that in general the impact on inequality of the introduction of an income tax will be measured by comparing the pre-tax inequality measure given by (5) with a post-tax measure given by (5), but in which both the individual utility levels and the net wage rates are changed.[2] This is the method adopted in Chapter 12.

Of course if (15) holds, then the effect of changes in taxation on inequality derives solely from the consequent changes in utility levels. The resulting simplification in the formula allows one to obtain some rather natural comparative statics results about the impact of tax changes on inequality.

The results are concerned solely with the effects of changes in *linear* income tax schedules which may be characterised through the equation

$$c = (1-t)(\theta+Y)$$

where c is net income (consumption), Y is gross income, t is the constant marginal tax rate and θ is a gross income handout from the government. If $\theta > 0$ then the tax is progressive in the sense that the average tax rate rises with income.

Notice now that if we have two linear tax schedules (θ_1, t_1), (θ_2, t_2) then the absolute difference in net income under these schedules for an individual with gross income Y is

$$\Delta c = (1-t_2)(\theta_2+Y) - (1-t_1)(\theta_1+Y)$$
$$= (1-t_2)\theta_2 - (1-t_1)\theta_1 - (t_2-t_1)Y$$

and so is a decreasing function of Y if and only if $t_2 > t_1$ while the percentage difference in net income is

$$\frac{\Delta c}{c} = \frac{(1-t_2)\theta_2 - (1-t_1)\theta_1 - (t_2-t_1)Y}{(1-t_1)(\theta_1+Y)}$$

which is easily shown to be decreasing in Y if and only if $\theta_2 > \theta_1$. That is, one linear tax schedule is 'more progressive' than another in the sense that the rich lose more (gain less) in absolute terms than the poor if and only if it has a higher marginal tax rate, while it is more progressive in the sense that the rich lose more (gain less) in percentage terms than the poor if and only if it has a higher gross lump-sum handout.

Are these changes also more progressive in the sense of being inequality reducing? An answer is given in the following:

Theorem 5 If (1) $u(.)$ is a CES utility function

$$
u = \begin{cases} \dfrac{\alpha}{1-b}c^{1-b} + \dfrac{(1-\alpha)}{1-b}\,\ell^{1-b} & b > 0 \qquad b \neq 1 \\[2mm] \alpha\log c + (1-\alpha)\log\ell & b = 1 \end{cases}
$$

(2) Individuals have no unearned income other than the gross handout they receive from the government.

(3) The tax schedule $(\theta_1\ t)$ and the initial distribution of wage rates are such that hours of work are strictly positive for all individuals under all utility permutations.

Then

$$
\frac{\partial\mu}{\partial\theta} < 0
$$

and

$$
\frac{\partial\mu}{\partial t} \lessgtr 1 \text{ as } \epsilon = \gtrless
$$

where ϵ is the elasticity of substitution.

Proof Under conditions (1), (2) and (3) it is easily shown that we can write the definition of μ as given by (13) in the form

$$
(1-\mu)\frac{1}{N}\sum_i\left((1-b)v_i\right)^{1/1-b} = \left((1-b)\frac{1}{N}\sum v_i\right)^{1/1-b} \tag{19}
$$

where

$$
v_i = \frac{[(1-t)\,(\theta+w_i)]^{\,1-b}}{1-b}\left[\alpha(\alpha^{(1-b)/b}) + (1-\alpha)\ \frac{1-\alpha}{w_i(1-t)}\ ^{(1-b)/b}\right]^b \tag{20}
$$

Let $\nu = 1 - \mu$, $\gamma(x) = \left[\alpha(\alpha^{(1-b)/b}) + (1-\alpha)\left(\dfrac{1-\alpha}{x}\right)^{(1-b)/b}\right]^{b/1-b}$ then (19) becomes

$$\nu \frac{1}{N}\sum_i (\theta + w_i)\,\gamma\,(w_i\,(1-t)) = \left(\frac{1}{N}\sum_i [(\theta + w_i)\,\gamma\,(w_i\,(1-t))]^{1-b}\right)^{1/1-b}$$

(21)

Differentiate (21) logarithmically with respect to θ and we have

$$\frac{\partial \nu/\partial \theta}{\nu} = \sum \pi_i'\cdot\frac{1}{(\theta + w_i)} - \sum \pi_i\left(\frac{1}{\theta + w_i}\right)$$

(22)

where

$$\pi_i' = \frac{(1/1-b)z(w_i)^{1-b}}{\sum_i (1/1-b)\,z(w_i)^{1-b}}\,, \qquad \pi_i = \frac{z(w_i)}{\sum_i z(w_i)}\,,$$

$$z(w_i) = (\theta + w_i)\gamma(w_i(1-t))$$

Differentiating (21) logarithmically with respect to t gives

$$\frac{\partial \nu/\partial t}{\nu} = \sum_i \pi_i'\beta(\dot{w}_i\,(1-t)) - \sum_i \pi_i\beta(w_i(1-t))$$

(23)

where

$$\beta(x) = \frac{-x\gamma'(x)}{\gamma(x)} = \frac{1}{1 + [\alpha\epsilon/(1-\alpha)\epsilon]\,x^{\epsilon-1}}$$

(24)

Now notice the following:

(1) $z(.)$ is just a monotonic increasing transformation of the indirect utility function, and since the latter is strictly increasing in w_i, so too is $z(.)$.
(2) $(1/1-b)z(w_i)^{1-b}$ is a strictly concave function of $z(w_i)$, and consequently the weight π_i' will be greater than the weight π_i for low values of w_i (and here $z(w_i)$) and less than π_i for high values of w_i.
(3) $1/(\theta + w_i)$ is decreasing in w_i.
(4) $\beta(.)$ is increasing in w_i if $\epsilon < 1$ and decreasing if $\epsilon > 1$.

It follows then from (22) and (23) that

$$\frac{\partial v}{\partial \theta} > 0 \text{ while } \frac{\partial v}{\partial t} \gtreqless 0 \text{ as } \epsilon \gtreqless 1$$

That is,

$$\frac{\partial \mu}{\partial \theta} < 0, \text{ and } \frac{\partial \mu}{\partial t} \lesseqgtr 0 \text{ as } \epsilon \gtreqless 1$$

The heuristic proof in the second part of the theorem can be substantiated by a formal proof which is left to the more technically minded reader.

While Theorem 5 is very far from being a general theorem on the effects of tax changes on inequality, it is nevertheless of some interest in two respects. Firstly, it presents a group of cases, those with $\epsilon < 1$, which is certainly empirically interesting, for which what appears *a priori* to be a change to a more progressive tax system turns out to be inequality increasing rather than decreasing. Now of course it is largely a semantic question as to how one classifies tax systems into more and less progressive categories, but there is certainly a general notion that 'more progressive' is to be identified with 'more equality generating'. If we wish to preserve such an identity then a second consequence of the theorem is that one cannot classify one tax system as more progressive than another independently of the nature of individual work/leisure preferences.

Secondly, the results of the theorem contrast with those one would obtain using the standard Atkinson measure of inequality with an iso-elastic indirect utility function for income. Under such a measure, while a rise in θ is once again inequality reducing, changes in t have absolutely no effect on inequality. If the measure proposed in this chapter is accepted, then this implies that under some circumstances the Atkinson measure will give a misleading impression of the *qualitative* changes in inequality that are taking place.

CONCLUSIONS

This chapter has been concerned with developing an inequality measure that will be appropriate for examining the redistributive effects of tax changes allowing for the full effects of these changes on individual labour supply and utility. The key problem in developing such a measure is that, unlike the standard context in which inequality measures are discussed, the interesting case when considering labour supply and taxation is one in which different individuals face different prices. It has been shown how one can obtain a measure that is a genuine extension of the Atkinson measure in that it is equivalent to the Atkinson measure ·where that is appropriate (e.g. when individuals do happen to face the same prices) but is well defined in other circumstances. The measure is computationally more demanding than the standard Atkinson measure in that it involves double summation rather than single summation, and while under some circumstances some considerable simplification can be made, it has been shown that in the labour supply context the conditions for employing the simpler formula are quite restrictive. Finally, some simple comparative statics results have been obtained concerning the effects of tax changes on inequality. In particular it has been possible to show that for linear tax schedules raising the tax rate will not always reduce inequality, and indeed for what are probably the most empirically interesting cases considered, raising the tax rate will increase inequality. If the measure proposed is accepted as being reasonable, this latter finding could have important implications for the view taken about the redistributive efforts of the government.

As pointed out earlier in this chapter, there are some unresolved questions about how exactly one makes comparisons of inequality when taxes are being changed. For since changing taxes will, in many cases, involve a change in the prices that consumers face, and since the measure

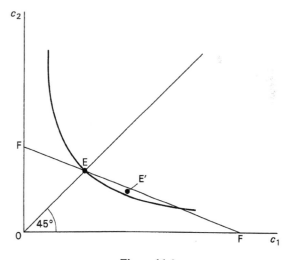

Figure 11.3

proposed here explicity includes prices, it is not clear whether one should try to remove the effects of price changes when making the comparison. As already mentioned it may be possible to resolve this question by appeal to a theory of how to decompose welfare changes into efficiency changes and distributional changes. However, when individuals face different prices, this decomposition is not as straightforward as it might at first appear, as Figure 11.3 will show. Figure 11.3 is a simplified version of Figure 11.2 with just the one efficiency frontier FF. E is the point of perfect equality on FF. Consider now the point E'. This is neither efficient nor equitable and yet is socially preferred to E. In other words, the move from E to E' would entail both an 'efficiency loss' and a 'distributional loss' and yet would constitute a social gain.

NOTES: CHAPTER 11

1 A measure which has the property of depending solely on the distribution of utilities is that proposed by Kolm (1969). However, for reasons discussed by Allingham (1972) and by Ulph (1978) this measure is unsatisfactory.
2 The justification for this is admittedly *ad hoc*. Ideally, the correct procedure for measuring the change in inequality should come from a theory of how to decompose welfare changes into efficiency gains and losses and equity gains and losses. However, as I point out later in the text, this decomposition is not as simple as it might seem when the efficiency frontier is non-symmetric.

Chapter 12

Labour Supply Responses to Tax Changes
A Simulation Exercise for the UK

It is well known that the estimation of labour supply elasticities is complicated by the fact that the budget constraint that many individuals face is non-linear. This non-linearity arises for a variety of reasons – the structure of the tax/benefit scheme, overtime rates, second jobs, etc.

However, these non-linearities also cause problems when it comes to interpreting the policy implications of the estimates. Consider, for example, assessing the effects of an increase in the basic rate of income tax when we take account of the non-linearity introduced by the presence of an exemption level of income. As we shall show in the next section, the effect of this change on someone who is paying tax at the standard rate is not necessarily best understood by looking at an estimate of the price, elasticity of labour supply. For one has to take account of the income effect arising from the increased value of the tax exemptions, and how important this is depends on how close the individual is to his tax threshold. Indeed, for someone paying very little tax, the effect of the change on his hours of work is better represented by the substitution elasticity. Since most estimates of labour supply show that for men the price elasticity is negative while the substitution elasticity is positive, then for some sections of the population one could mistake not just the magnitude but also the direction of the effects of the tax change by looking at the price elasticity. How serious this is will clearly depend on the distribution of the population around their tax thresholds, which in turn depends on the underlying distribution of gross wages and tax thresholds in the population.

As we shall show, this is by no means the only complication to which non-linearities give rise, and in principle one has to know the distribution of a large number of characteristics of individuals (their basic wage rates, standard working weeks, overtime premium, tax threshold, etc.) in order to make an accurate assessment of the effects of tax changes.

It is natural to ask just how important these complications are, and it

163

is to this question that this paper is addressed. There are a number of ways of answering this question, and we have chosen to answer it by undertaking a simulation exercise for a sample of weekly paid married male workers in the UK. For this sample we have calculated the effects of various types of tax changes, taking account of as many non-linearities in the budget constraint as we had information on, and have tried to assess how our predictions differ from those we would have reached had we ignored the non-linearities. Our conclusion is that the presence of the non-linearities matters a great deal in assessing both the aggregate impact of the tax changes on GNP and in examining the distribution consequences of the changes.

The plan of this chapter is as follows: in Section I we outline a number of complications which can arise because of the presence of non-linearities. Section II outlines the basic structure of the simulation model, while Section III reports our findings. The final section offers some concluding remarks.

I   RATIONALE FOR SIMULATION

In this section we will explain why, for a variety of reasons, knowledge of the labour supply function is insufficient to enable one to predict the effects of various changes in the tax system.

The first set of reasons can be illustrated by consideration of the following simple model of individual labour supply. Consider an individual who has unearned income N, and who faces a gross wage of w. In the absence of any tax system his hours of work, H, would be determined by the supply function

$$H = f(w, N) \tag{1}$$

derived in the usual way from his utility function and budget constraint. Now suppose an income tax is introduced under which the individual pays tax at the rate t on all income in excess of his tax threshold, E. His budget constraint is now non-linear, but, as is well known, if the individual is paying a positive amount of tax his hours of work can be determined by the equation

$$H = f(w(1 - t), N + te) \tag{2}$$

That is, we treat the individual as if he paid tax at the rate t on all his income and is reimbursed with a lump sum handout of the amount tE for the tax he should not have paid on the first E units of income. If we now change the tax rate, the effect of this on the individual's hours of work will be given by[1]

$$\frac{\partial H}{\partial t} = -f_1 w + f_2 E \tag{3}$$

Substituting the Slutsky-Hicks equation $f_1 = f_1{}^c + f_2 H$ we have

$$\frac{\partial H}{\partial t} = -\left[f_1{}^c w + f_2 (wH - E) \right] \tag{4}$$

where f^c is the compensated supply function. This gives,

$$\frac{\partial H}{\partial t} = -w \left[f_1{}^c + f_2 (H - \frac{E}{w}) \right] \tag{5}$$

Equation (5) shows that the effect of the tax on the individual cannot be predicted from knowledge of the price, income or substitution effects alone but depends on how close the individual's hours are to those that he would have to work to just reach the tax threshold. In particular, for individuals very close to the tax threshold, the effect of raising the tax rate will be almost a pure substitution effect and so there will be a reduction in the hours of work even if the price effect is negative. Since people who do not pay tax will be unaffected by the increase in the tax rate, we can see that the aggregate effect of the tax change will depend on the distribution of people around the tax threshold as well as on the nature of the supply function.

Another instance in which the distribution of people around the tax threshold can be important occurs when we consider the effects of a change in the exemption level. For people who are paying tax the effect of this is given by

$$\frac{\partial H}{\partial E} = tf_2 \tag{6}$$

and so, if leisure is a normal good, their hours of work will decline. For people who previously worked less than E/w hours there will be no effect on their hours of work, but for people who chose to work right up to the tax threshold, but chose not to start paying tax, hours of work are given by

$$H = \frac{E}{w},$$

and so, for small changes in E

$$\frac{\partial H}{\partial E} = \frac{1}{w} \tag{7}$$

Expressed in percentage terms (6) becomes

$$\frac{E}{H} \frac{\partial H}{\partial E} = \left(\frac{tE}{N + tE} \right)^{\epsilon_N} \tag{8}$$

where ϵ_N is the income elasticity of labour supply, while (7) becomes

$$\frac{E}{H} \frac{\partial H}{\partial E} = 1 \tag{9}$$

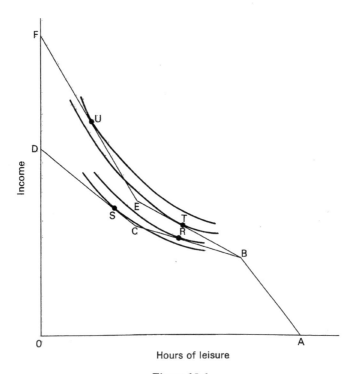

Figure 12.1

Since ϵ_N is typically very small in absolute magnitude, then, if N is close to zero, we can see that the overall effect in (8) is likely to be small in percentage terms, while the effect in (9) is large. It does not therefore require a very large percentage of the population to be on the tax threshold for the positive effect in (9) to offset the negative effect in (8) on aggregate. Whichever way the balance goes, however, it is still true that the overall effect of the change in the tax allowance is going to depend on the distribution of individuals around the tax threshold as well as on the nature of the labour supply function.

Further complications arise when we recognise the possibility that changes in the tax system can lead the individual to change from one segment of his budget constraint to another. Such a possibility is illustrated in Figure 12.1.

The individual initially faces the budget constraint ABCD; thus he has no unearned income and has a gross wage given by the slope of AB. At the income level prevailing at B he starts to pay tax and his net wage is now given by the slope of BC. Beyond the hours of work prevailing at C the individual is paid overtime and his net wage is now given by the slope of CD. Given his preferences he would wish to work at the point S if he were forced to work overtime, but finds that point R is preferable to this (assuming he is not forced to work the standard working week). His initial equilibrium is therefore at R. If the tax rate is cut his budget line now becomes ABEF, and it is important to note that while the net wage rate changes by the same percentage amount whether or not he works overtime, his net overtime wage rate increases by a greater absolute amount than his basic net wage rate. It is now possible that he would prefer to work overtime, and this is illustrated by having point U lie on a higher indifference curve than point T. Two points should be noted about this.

First, had we tried to predict the effect of the tax change on his hours of work, on the assumption that he stayed on the same segment, we would have predicted that his hours would have changed from those at R to those at T. Consequently we would have mispredicted not just the magnitude but also the direction of change.

Secondly, whether or not the individual will switch segments will depend on his basic wage rate, standard working week, overtime premium and tax threshold, for all of these will influence the precise position of the various segments of his budget constraint.

Once again, then, knowledge of the labour supply function $f(.)$ is just not sufficient to predict the effect of tax changes. Indeed to predict the overall effect of tax changes allowing for the possibility illustrated above, it is necessary to know not just the distribution of individuals around their tax thresholds, but also the distribution of a large number of other personal characteristics.

All these arguments imply that one is just not going to be able to say much about the effects of tax changes using a 'representative individual' approach, and that to understand even the direction of change in the aggregate one will need information on the distribution of individuals in different categories. This suggests that the best approach to understanding the effects of tax changes is to simulate them on a representative sample of the population.

Unfortunately, given the amount of information required of each individual, it is very difficult to obtain such a sample. What we have done in this chapter is to undertake a simulation exercise for a sample of weekly-paid married male workers in the UK. This sample is described in some detail in Brown, Levin and Ulph (1976) and Ashworth and Ulph (1977a) but for our present purposes it is sufficient to notice that the sample is unrepresentative of (1) the entire working population in that it includes only married male weekly-paid workers who worked for more than eight hours in the week previous to their interview, (2) even this limited sub-sample in that we had to exclude various workers who did not know some of the information relevant to undertaking the simulation exercise.

The limitations imposed by the restrictions under (1) are obvious, but as people in this category form a large percentage of the labour force information obtained from such a sub-sample can still be of some importance. Unfortunately we do not know what sorts of biases are being introduced by the restrictions under (2).

II   THE SIMULATION MODEL

We begin with the sample of 335 married male workers which Ashworth and Ulph (1977a) used in obtaining labour supply estimates. For each individual we have information on his basic wage rate, standard working week, overtime premium, tax threshold, tax rate (in 1971, the year in which the sample was collected), second job wage rate (if any), and this enables us to construct his entire piecewise linear budget constraint.

We assumed everyone had the same CES utility function in which, initially, the elasticity of substitution was set to 0.5. The CES function was chosen solely for its tractability, while the value of 0.5 was chosen in the light of the estimates of the elasticity of substitution obtained by Ashworth and Ulph (1977a). Once a particular weight to consumption is chosen it is then possible to calculate the hours of work everyone would choose to work given their budget constraint. Again details of the algorithm used in this computation are given in Ashworth and Ulph (1977a). As in other simulation work (e.g. Whalley, 1975) it is important to leave degrees of freedom so that the initial equilibrium is in some sense close to the actual position in which people found themselves and we used the weight to consumption as our degree of freedom. This was therefore adjusted until the sum of squares of deviations of predicted hours from actual hours of work was minimized. Given this information we could compute for each individual their gross income, net income, tax payments and utility in the initial position.

We then considered the effects of changing (1) the tax rate by some fixed percentage, (2) the tax threshold by some fixed percentage, (3) both simultaneously.

For any such change we re-computed each individual's entire budget constraint and resolved the utility maximization problem. We were thus able to predict the change in individual hours of work, gross and net incomes and tax revenue which these tax changes entailed. It is important to note that in this exercise we assumed that there were no changes in gross wage rates, overtime premia or standard working week thus ignoring any general equilibrium effects of the tax changes. Moreover, if individuals faced constraints in their hours of work (e.g. an upper limit on the amount of overtime they could do) we assumed these constraints remained the same, thus ignoring any macroeconomic expansion or contraction effects of the tax changes. We could have avoided making these restrictive assumptions only by making alternative and equally *ad hoc* assumptions or by undertaking a much more complex simulation exercise.

Knowing the changes in individual tax revenue we could compute the aggregate change, and were thus able to explore the effects of equal revenue changes in the tax system. This we did by making a given change in the tax rate and then adjusting allowances until the percentage change in aggregate tax revenue was sufficiently small.[2]

As we saw in the previous section, the effects of tax changes can differ in direction as well as magnitude across different sections of the population. To completely isolate all the possible cases would have required a fine subdivision of the sample by a number of different criteria (tax paid, overtime rate, basic wage rate for example). However, computing restrictions required that we employ a fairly coarse subdivision by a single criterion, and we chose to subdivide the sample into deciles according to utility. Utility was chosen as the criterion because we wanted to examine some of the distributional impact of tax policy, and since we had a direct measure of welfare it seemed best to employ this as our criterion. As we shall see this subdivision is sufficient to enable us to pick up a number of differential effects.

An alternative means of picking up the distributional incidence of tax changes adapted was the use of a variety of summary measures of inequality. Thus we computed the Gini coefficient of gross and net income before and after the tax changes, as well as the Atkinson measure of inequality of net income. However, since utility is being affected by both income and leisure, it seemed important to employ a measure of inequality which incorporated leisure as well as income. There are a number of conceptual problems in developing such a measure which have been discussed by one of the authors elsewhere (Ulph 1978a, b) and the measure we have adopted is that proposed by Ulph (1978a). The spirit of this measure is that one employs an Atkinson measure of inequality of real income, where real income is defined as Becker full income deflated by a price index to take account of the fact that different individuals face different prices (different net wage rates). Since real income is not always well defined (even with a CES utility function) the measure actually employed a generalisation of the above procedure, which turns out to be well defined in all situations. For details the reader is referred to the cited paper.

In summary, the simulation programme operates by constructing each individual's entire budget constraint before and after the tax change, and then, given a specification of the individual utility function, computes each individual's equilibrium on the two constraints. This information is used to compute aggregated and disaggregated effects of the tax changes. We turn now to the results of these exercises.

Before presenting the results there is a point of terminology that is worth clarifying. We will want to distinguish between the situation in which we change the tax rate by, say, one percentage point from 30 per cent to 31 per cent, from the case in which we make a 1 per cent change in the tax rate by which we will mean a change from 30 per cent to 30.3 per cent, that is, a change by 0.3 percentage points.

III   THE RESULTS

Before examining the effects of tax changes it will be helpful to examine some features of the sample in the initial equilibrium.

(a) *The Initial Equilibrium*
Although, as pointed out in the previous section, the number of people included in the sample can vary from exercise to exercise, the effects of

this on the broad features of the model are negligible. Accordingly, the results to be presented correspond to a sample of 333 individuals.

Recalling that, initially, the elasticity of substitution was set to 0.5, it was found that for this sample the weight to consumption in the utility function, which gave the closest fit between the initial equilibrium hours of work and those actually being worked by individuals, was 0.825. With these values of the utility parameters it was found that while the average weekly hours of work for the sample was 47.9, the average hours predicted in the initial equilibrium was 45.5. Average predicted gross income was £35.95 (in 1971 prices); the average tax paid was £4.4, giving an average tax rate of 12.2 per cent and an average level of net income of £31.55.

For later purposes it will be useful to note that for this utility function the price and substitution elasticities computed at the mean values for the net wage rate and unearned income for the entire sample were -0.16 and 0.48, respectively. These compare with figures of -0.07 and 0.50 for the more general functional form employed by Ashworth and Ulph. Thus the price effect is negative, though tiny.

Using a social welfare function of the form

$$W = \sum_i \frac{1}{1-\alpha} c_i^{1-\alpha}$$

it was found that when $\alpha = 1.0$ the Atkinson measure of inequality of net income was 0.021 while when $\alpha = 2.0$ the measure of inequality was 0.041. Thus society would be prepared to give up about 2 per cent (resp. 4 per cent) of net income to eliminate inequality. These somewhat low figures presumably reflect the rather uniform nature of the sample.

The Gini coefficient of net income was 0.105 while that for gross income was 0.108. Using the same weights as in the Atkinson measure, the Ulph measure of inequality was 0.008 (resp. 0.015). However, it should be borne in mind that the Ulph measure expresses what society is prepared to give up to achieve equality as a percentage of real full income, not of GNP, and since people work about one quarter of the week it is clear that the Ulph measure is giving a measure of inequality very much in line with that of the Atkinson measure. However, as we shall see, the two measures can give different views of what happens to inequality as taxes are changed.

In what follows, it will be important to know about the characteristics of the various deciles of the population, and these are given in Table 12.1. Deciles are numbered 1 to 10 from worst off decile to best off.

Notice that there is a more or less monotonic rise in gross and net income and in leisure as we move to successively better off deciles, but

172 Taxation and Labour Supply

Table 12.1

Decile No.	Gross Income	Hours	Net Income	Tax
1	29.1	65.1	22.3	6.8
2	31.8	56.2	26.3	5.5
3	32.3	50.5	28.0	4.3
4	34.2	49.9	30.3	3.9
5	37.4	49.4	32.2	5.2
6	37.3	46.5	32.7	4.6
7	38.0	42.4	33.0	5.0
8	38.8	39.0	34.6	4.2
9	37.1	32.9	35.2	2.2
10	42.8	25.0	40.5	2.3

that there is a general tendency for the better off to pay less tax than the worse off, though this is a much less monotonic relation. This is a point to which we shall return. Notice also that we have not treated the standard working week as a minimum constraint on hours, and this has produced a wider spread in hours than was found in the sample. This presumably also accounts for the under prediction of mean hours.

(b) *The effects of a Change in the Standard Rate of Tax*

The first set of tax changes which we wish to analyse are the effects of changing the standard rate of tax leaving other rates and the level of tax allowances constant. We took the standard rate to be 30 per cent and considered changing this to 25 per cent, 28 per cent, 32 per cent and 35 per cent. The aggregate effects of these changes are shown in Table 12.2.

A number of points should be noted about these results. In the first place they neatly illustrate the point made in the first section about the effect of a tax threshold on the predictions that can be made about the effects of changes in the tax rate. For notice that while we found the price effect to be negative the effect of raising the tax rate is to reduce hours of work, which is not what the price effect would predict. Moreover,

Table 12.2

Percentage change in	Tax Rate			
	25%	*28%*	*32%*	*35%*
Mean hour	0.83	0.37	−0.55	−1.35
Mean gross income	0.60	0.27	−0.40	−0.99
Mean tax revenue	−15.32	−6.04	5.76	13.94

the order of magnitude of the effects of tax changes are much closer to those that would be predicted by the substitution elasticity. This can be seen by noting that a change in the tax rate by 5 per cent (resp. 2 per cent) is equivalent to a change in the net wage rate by 7.1 per cent (resp. 2.9 per cent). Consequently we can express the first line of Table 12.2 as a 'price' elasticity, π, by dividing the percentage change in hours by the percentage change in the net wage rate. Figures for π are given in Table 12.2a. They range from 25% to 40% of the substitution elasticity

Table 12.2a

Tax Rate	25%	28%	32%	35%
π	0.117	0.128	0.190	0.190

(assuming an average figure for π of 0.16 this is 33 per cent of the substitution elasticity), which bears out our point that with low levels of tax being paid by people in our sample the effects of changes in the tax rate can be approximated to a pure substitution effect.

The effects of tax changes on GNP are of the same sign as those on hours though of a lower percentage magnitude (almost exactly 73 per cent in all cases). To see why this might be so, note that we can write gross income Y as

$$Y = \sum_i y_i = \sum f_i (H_i)$$

so, assuming for the moment that everything is differentiable, we can write

$$\frac{dY}{dt} = \sum_i f_i' \cdot \frac{dH_i}{dt}$$

and consequently

$$\frac{dY/dt}{Y} = \sum_i \frac{y_i}{Y} \cdot \left(\frac{f_i'}{y_i/H_i} \right) \left(\frac{dH_i/dt}{H_i} \right)$$

This shows that even if everybody's hours of work change by the same percentage, the percentage change in GNP will be greater or less than that in hours depending on whether or not the ratio of the marginal to the average gross wage rate is, on average, greater than or less than 1. While for those who work overtime and have no second job we would expect the marginal gross wage rate to exceed the average – for those working in a second job, we may well expect the marginal wage to be lower than the average. (In fact this was so for everybody in our sample.) Of course the percentage change in hours is unlikely to be the same for everybody (and we shall see shortly just how it varies across different deciles) so the full explanation of why the percentage change in GNP is less than that in hours is going to turn on a variety of distributional considerations. Since this is not the main concern of this chapter we shall not pursue this further.

Turning to the effects on tax revenue, Table 12.2 shows that while a reduction in the tax rate will increase GNP, this increase is not sufficient to offset the effect on revenue of the tax cut. Indeed the reductions in tax revenue are quite large in percentage terms. A better way of understanding these figures is to notice that a reduction in the marginal tax rate from 30 per cent to 28 per cent (25 per cent) represents a 6.7 per cent (16.7 per cent) reduction in the tax rate, so that expressing the last line of Table 12.2 in elasticity form (that is the percentage change in tax revenue divided by the percentage change in tax rate) we obtain the figures set out in Table 12.2b.

Table 12.2b

Tax Rate	25%	28%	32%	35%
Elasticity of tax revenue (ϵ)	0.917	0.902	0.860	0.835

This table indicates that the rise in GNP only offsets about 10 per cent of the effects of a fall in the tax rate, while the fall in GNP is sufficient to offset about 15 per cent of the gain in revenue from increasing the tax rate. To understand why the elasticity is higher for tax cuts than for tax increases, notice that if we assume that everyone pays tax at the standard rate both before and after the change in the tax rate, then the change in tax revenue, ΔR, that results from changing the marginal tax rate from t_0 to t_1 can be written

$$\Delta R = t_1 \sum_i (y_i^1 - s_i) - t_0 \sum_i (y_i^0 - s_i)$$

where $y_i^0 (y_i^1)$ is individual i's gross income before (after) the tax change and s_i is his tax threshold. After some straightforward manipulation, this yields the formula

$$\epsilon = 1 + \frac{t_1}{\text{ATR}_0} \cdot \eta$$

where ϵ is the elasticity of tax revenue, ATR_0 is the average tax rate in the initial position and η is the elasticity of GNP with respect to the tax rate (the percentage change in GNP divided by the percentage change in the tax rate). The values of η corresponding to the four tax rates in Table 12.2 are given in Table 12.2c.

Table 12.2c

Tax Rate	25%	28%	32%	35%
η	−0.036	−0.040	0.060	0.060

Recalling that ATR_0 is 12 per cent, we see that when the tax rate is raised, t_1/ATR_0 becomes approximately 3 while when it is lowered it becomes approximately 2. Since η is more or less constant, we can conclude that the apparent asymmetry in the elasticity is a consequence of the rather large changes in tax rates that have been made. Had the change been small we could have replaced t_1 by t_0 in the above formula, which would give a value of t_0/ATR_0 of 2.5 and consequently a value of ϵ of about 0.7.

One final point to note about Table 12.2 is that when expressed in the form of the elasticities π, η and ϵ the figures are fairly uniform across the table, apart from the asymmetry in ϵ which we have just discussed. We will exploit this uniformity when reporting the results of our sensitivity studies, by presenting a single figure for each of these elasticities rather than the four figures for the four tax rates considered.

Having considered the aggregate effects of changes in the tax rate, let us now examine the effects in a more disaggregated form. The figures we present relate to changes in hours of work and to net income rather than gross income, since it is these magnitudes which will be relevant in assessing the impact of the tax changes on the welfare of different groups.[3] Table 12.3 presents figures for the percentage change in hours of work and in net income for each of the deciles and for each of the four tax rates discussed above. For each tax rate and for each decile the left-hand column gives the figure for the percentage change in hours ($\Delta H/H$) and the right-hand for the percentage change in net income ($\Delta C/C$).

It should be noted that the direction of change in hours of work is not the same in all deciles and there is considerable variation in the magnitude of the percentage change. The general pattern that emerges is that the absolute magnitude of the percentage change increases over

Table 12.3

				Tax Rate				
	25%		*28%*		*32%*		*35%*	
Decile	$\Delta H/H$	$\Delta C/C$	$\Delta H/H$	$\Delta C/C$	$\Delta H/H$	$\Delta C/C$	$\Delta H/H$	$\Delta C/C$
1	−0.578	3.86	−0.232	1.55	0.234	−1.57	0.586	−3.95
2	−0.006	3.35	0.005	1.35	−0.017	−1.36	−0.069	−3.42
3	0.500	2.89	0.216	1.12	−0.234	−1.42	−0.596	−3.14
4	0.847	2.82	0.361	1.14	−0.797	−1.41	−1.47	−3.13
5	0.572	3.01	0.247	1.21	−0.819	−1.59	−1.30	−3.43
6	0.944	2.97	0.402	1.19	−1.09	−1.55	−3.24	−4.06
7	2.21	3.66	1.14	1.59	−0.524	−1.24	−2.60	−3.73
8	1.67	2.90	0.678	1.15	−1.25	−1.43	−2.49	−3.18
9	2.07	1.84	0.856	0.733	−0.863	−0.807	−2.25	−1.89
10	1.98	1.57	0.834	0.673	−0.834	−0.592	−2.03	−1.52

the first four deciles, oscillates, then becomes very large for the seventh decile, and then falls steadily, though remaining substantially higher than in the worst off deciles. Given the variety of factors that can determine how individuals respond to tax changes, it is not easy to give a complete explanation of this pattern, but if we look back at Table 12.1 we will see that the worst off deciles pay more tax than the top deciles and so are probably further from their tax threshold. This should give greater strength to the income effect in the bottom deciles, thus dampening down the overall size of the change.

There is very little systematic behaviour in the changes in net income. The percentage changes are higher in absolute magnitude for the bottom two deciles than for the top two deciles, and is dropping over the last four deciles.

Given this rather unclear pattern in the behaviour of net income it is not too surprising to find that the summary measures of inequality do not show any clear pattern. Thus in Table 12.4 we have presented figures showing the changes in inequality as measured by the Gini coefficient of net income, the Atkinson measure of inequality of net income using

Table 12.4

	Tax Rate	
Measure	*25%*	*35%*
Gini (net)	−0.0013	0.0024
Atkinson (net)	−0.0005	0.0010
Gini (gross)	−0.0021	0.0042
Ulph	−0.0009	0.0012

the higher of the two values of a, the Gini coefficient of gross income and the Ulph measure of inequality (again using the higher value of a). We have presented the figures for only two tax changes since the results for other tax rates are very much in line with those shown.

(c) *The effects of a change in allowances*
In this section we will consider the effects of a 10 per cent increase and decrease in the level of tax allowances. The results for the 10 per cent

Table 12.5

Group	Percentage change in	Hours	Gross Income	Tax Revenue	Consumption
Overall sample		−0.937	−0.832	−11.91	
Decile	1	−0.82	−1.03	−6.63	0.67
	2	−0.97	−1.03	−9.31	0.74
	3	−0.99	−0.95	−11.60	0.79
	4	−1.54	−1.45	−15.12	0.32
	5	−1.59	−1.53	−12.50	0.18
	6	−1.34	−1.24	−12.53	0.36
	7	−1.25	−0.93	−11.48	−0.63
	8	−1.38	−1.16	−15.20	0.51
	9	0.52	−0.014	−15.79	1.13
	10	1.41	0.55	−16.56	1.54

Table 12.6

Group	Percentage change in	Hours	Gross Income	Tax Revenue	Consumption
Overall sample		0.78	0.75	12.12	
Decile	1	0.82	1.03	6.63	−0.67
	2	1.01	1.05	9.31	−0.26
	3	0.998	0.95	11.6	−0.79
	4	0.98	0.97	14.45	−0.78
	5	0.81	0.90	11.47	−0.75
	6	0.74	0.84	11.55	−0.68
	7	1.67	1.33	12.40	−0.31
	8	1.19	0.99	14.85	−0.66
	9	−0.50	0.07	19.07	−1.30
	10	−0.92	−0.27	20.75	−1.50

increase are presented in Table 12.5 and those for the decrease in Table 12.6. In both tables the effects on the overall sample are given in the first line; those for the various deciles then follow.

A number of points of interest arise from these results. First, the overall direction of change in hours of work is what one would have predicted by assuming that the change in allowances would act as an income effect. However, the magnitude of the effect is quite small, with a 10 per cent change in allowances leading to a change in hours of less than 1 per cent, giving an elasticity of about 0.08–0.09. This low elasticity is partly a reflection of the low income elasticities of labour supply, but also reflects the fact that some of the offsetting effects discussed in Section II of this chapter are operative.

In particular, we see that for deciles 9 and 10, which we had earlier seen to have the lowest per capita tax payments (and, presumably, the largest percentage of individuals on the tax threshold), the effects of the change are in the direction we would predict for those on the tax threshold. Moreover, as we discussed in Section II, the order of magnitude of the change is relatively large compared to those for the other deciles.

The deciles for which this 'threshold effect' of the tax change operates are also those for which the change in consumption is greatest, which is again just the result we would expect.

As to the effects on inequality, it was found that when the allowances were cut by 10 per cent, the Gini coefficient on gross income rose from 0.1080 to 0.1084, reflecting a slight increase in inequality. A decrease in the inequality of net income was recorded by both the Gini coefficient (which fell from 0.1054 to 0.1050) and the Atkinson measure (which fell from 0.0410 to 0.0408 when the larger figure for the degree of inequality aversion was employed) while the Ulph measure of inequality showed virtually no change (0.0154 to 0.0155 for the same value for inequality aversion), which could reflect the fact that while those in deciles 5 to 8 were enjoying much smaller percentage reductions in their consumption (in some cases even an increase) than those in the lower deciles, they were suffering much larger percentage increases in their hours of work.

(d) *Equal revenue changes*

Having dealt with the effects of individual changes in tax rates and allowances in the previous two subsections we now consider the effects of changing these parameters simultaneously. This is a particularly important case for policy purposes as it may be necessary to compensate for a given change in the tax rate by changing the level of allowances in order to leave total tax revenue unchanged. For example, it is interesting to know by how much the government would have to change the level of allowances to obtain equal revenue when a 1 percent change in the tax rate is made. In what follows we define an 'allowance elasticity', τ, as the percentage change in allowances necessary to bring tax revenue back to its original level following a change in the tax rate of one percentage point.

Starting from the initial equilibrium (as described in Section III(a)) for a given change in the tax rate the level of allowances was permitted to vary in order to leave the level of tax revenue unchanged. It was not possible to force the change in tax revenue to zero for all cases because of rounding errors and cases of non-convergence; however it was allowed to approach as close to zero as possible given the computational time involved.

Table 12.7

Tax Rate	25%	28%	32%	35%
τ	2.36	2.05	1.90	1.80

The allowance elasticity defined above is shown in Table 12.7. To understand the significance of τ consider a tax rate change from 30 per cent to 32 per cent, that is, a change in the tax rate of two percentage points; allowances must then rise by approximately 4% in order to leave tax revenue unchanged.

The aggregate effects of a simultaneous change in the tax rate and level of allowances to leave the tax revenue unchanged are shown in Table 12.8, along with π the 'price elasticity' defined in Section III(b).

Table 12.8

% change in	Tax rate 25%	28%	32%	35%
Mean hours	1.65	0.621	−0.837	−2.04
Mean gross income	1.39	0.502	−0.692	−1.72
π	0.23	0.21	0.29	0.28

Comparing the results of Table 12.8 with those presented in Tables 12.2 and 12.2a it may be seen that the respective figures are all of slightly greater magnitude for the present case. This shows that the change in allowances is reinforcing the effect of the change in the tax rate. A fall in the tax rate increases the net wage and, given the strong substitution effect shown above, this leads to an increase in hours worked. Allowances are reduced in order to keep tax revenue the same which, with a negative income effect, reinforces the increase in hours worked. The converse applies for an increase in the tax rate. For example, changing the tax rate by two percentage points from 30 per cent to 28 per cent gives a percentage change in mean hours of 0.621 compared to a percentage change of 0.37 when allowances remain unchanged. This is reflected in the higher values of π.

The values of η (the elasticity of GNP with respect to the tax rate) corresponding to the four tax rates when allowances are varied to leave

Table 12.9

Tax Rate	25%	28%	32%	35%
π	−0.08	−0.07	−0.10	−0.12

tax revenue unchanged are shown in Table 12.9. Once more η is more or less constant but of greater magnitude than the corresponding elasticities shown in Table 12.2c. This again is a reflection of the reinforcing effects of changing allowances at the same time as the tax rate.

At a more disaggregated level the effects of changing tax rates and allowances simultaneously are shown in Table 12.10, for each decile of the sample. The general pattern of change in hours of work which emerges

Table 12.10

				Tax Rate				
	25%		28%		32%		35%	
Decile	$\Delta H/H$	$\Delta C/C$	$\Delta H/H$	$\Delta C/C$	$\Delta H/H$	$\Delta C/C$	$\Delta H/H$	$\Delta C/C$
1	0.185	3.21	0.078	1.29	−0.022	−1.43	0.071	−3.37
2	0.837	2.65	0.350	1.07	−0.393	−1.07	−1.08	−2.65
3	1.02	1.98	0.584	0.861	−0.443	−1.12	−0.985	−2.07
4	1.90	2.23	0.791	0.911	−1.27	−1.17	−2.53	−2.47
5	1.33	2.42	0.470	0.855	−0.986	−0.233	−2.55	−1.91
6	1.76	2.34	0.780	0.923	−1.42	−1.27	−4.07	−3.33
7	3.18	3.06	1.47	1.33	−1.43	−1.25	−3.35	−2.88
8	4.13	3.03	1.07	0.890	−1.60	−1.11	−3.34	−2.31
9	2.33	1.05	0.644	0.260	−0.632	−0.308	−2.81	−1.27
10	1.12	0.059	0.402	−0.303	−0.596	−0.193	−0.970	−0.298

for this case is broadly the same as that for the case where only the tax rate is changed, as shown in Table 12.3. The direction of change in hours of work is the same in all deciles except for the first decile when tax rate is changed to 35 per cent. There is considerable variation in the magnitude of the percentage changes. Again the absolute magnitude of the percentage change rises until the fourth decile and then falls.

Changing the level of allowances at the same time as the tax rate highlights the stronger income effects for those in the lower deciles, as may be seen by comparing Tables 12.3 and 12.10. The percentage change in hours becomes greater for all deciles except the top two, where (as mentioned above) the individuals are close to their tax threshold. As in Table 12.3 there is no discernible change in net income for the case considered here.

The changes in the inequality measures for a simultaneous change in tax rates and allowances are shown in Table 12.11 for two typical changes.

Table 12.11

Measure	Tax rate 25%	35%
Gini (net)	−0.0007	0.0028
Atkinson (net)	−0.0002	0.0012
Gini (gross)	−0.0018	0.0013
Ulph	−0.0008	0.0011

(e) *Sensitivity Analysis*
Given the wide range of estimates of the elasticity of substitution that have been obtained in the literature, we felt it was important to see how sensitive our conclusions were to this parameter. Thus we undertook our simulation exercise for values of the elasticity of substitution running from 0.2 to 0.9. In each case the weight to consumption in the utility function was also varied to make the predicted values for hours of work before the tax changes as close as possible to the observed hours. For each case we examined the consequences of the four changes in tax rates discussed in Section III(b), but, as we saw there, when expressed in the form of the elasticities π, η, ϵ there is not a great deal of variation in the results across these different tax rates so the values of the elasticities were averaged, and it is this average value which is reported here.

We consider first the consequences of changes in the tax rate with no corresponding changes in tax allowances. The results are reported in Table 12.12. The first line of this table gives the assumed value of the

Table 12.12

Elasticity of Substitution	0.2	0.3	0.4	0.5	0.6	0.7	0.8	0.9
Substitution elasticity	0.15	0.225	0.3	0.375	0.45	0.525	0.6	0.675
Price elasticity	-0.62	-0.545	-0.47	-0.395	-0.32	-0.245	-0.17	-0.095
π	-0.11	-0.05	0.05	0.15	0.24	0.37	0.45	0.55
η	0.05	0.02	-0.01	-0.05	-0.08	-0.12	-0.15	-0.19
ϵ	1.125	1.05	0.975	0.875	0.8	0.7	0.625	0.525
π – Price Elasticity	0.51	0.495	0.52	0.545	0.56	0.615	0.62	0.56

elasticity of substitution. The next two lines present the values of the standard neo-classical substitution elasticity and price elasticity computed at the mean net-wage rate and mean unearned income of the sample. The following line of the table shows the value of π, the 'price elasticity' of the tax change allowing for all the complications introduced by the presence of the exemption level. There then follows figures for the GNP elasticity η and the tax revenue elasticity ϵ. The final row of the table shows the difference between rows 3 and 4 and hence gives an idea of how the error from using the neo-classical price elasticity rather than the 'price elasticity' π varies with elasticity of substitution.

Most of the effects here are exactly as one would expect. Thus as the elasticity of substitution increases, so does the substitution elasticity, which causes the price elasticity to rise (become a smaller absolute negative number). This in turn is reflected in the behaviour of π, the 'price elasticity', corrected for the presence of allowances which goes from being negative for small values of the elasticity of substitution to being virtually zero for values of the elasticity of substitution around 0.3–0.4. The figures for η show that the effects on GNP of increasing the tax rate by 1 per cent are virtually zero for small values of the elasticity of substitution (so resulting in a virtually equivalent increase in tax revenue as the figures for ϵ show), while for higher values of the elasticity of substitution the reduction in GNP from increasing the tax rate becomes more significant and goes much further towards offsetting the effects on tax revenue of making the tax change.

While the directions of these movements are very much what one would expect to happen from a strengthening of the substitution elasticity, the magnitudes of the differences are appreciable, giving quite different predictions about the direction and magnitude of the aggregate effects of tax changes depending on where within the range of estimates of the elasticity of substitution that have been obtained one thinks the 'true' figure lies.

Probably the most interesting finding from the sensitivity study comes from comparing π with the neo-classical price elasticity, for as the last line of the table shows the difference between these is more or less constant. This implies that it is precisely when the neo-classical price elasticity suggests that increasing the tax rate may have a relatively strong positive effect on aggregate hours of work that it in fact has very little aggregate effect; and that when the neo-classical elasticity suggests there would be a very small effect arising from a tax change that the actual change would be quite large and negative.

Table 12.13

Elasticity of Substitution	0.2	0.3	0.4	0.5	0.6	0.7	0.8	0.9
π	0.06	0.13	0.19	0.25	0.36	0.42	0.52	0.62
η	-0.02	-0.05	-0.07	-0.09	-0.13	-0.16	-0.19	-0.23
τ	2.8	2.6	2.3	2.03	1.85	1.84	1.57	1.46

Turning to the effects of equal revenue changes, Table 12.13 presents values for π, η and τ for the same range of values of the elasticity of substitution. As noted in the previous section, the effect of changing the allowances to restore revenue produces an income effect acting to depress GNP. Thus the values for η are now uniformly negative, and where they were previously negative are now larger in absolute magnitude. Once again the figures move appreciably with the elasticity of substitution, producing, for example, a value for τ (the percentage change in allowances required to restore revenue when the tax rate is raised by one percentage point) that is almost twice as great for the lowest values of the elasticity of substitution as for the highest.

Table 12.14

Tax Rate	Elasticity of Substitution Measure of Inequality	0.2	0.3	0.4	0.5	0.6	0.7	0.8	0.9
0.25		0.019	0.017	0.015	0.014	0.014	0.014	0.014	0.014
0.3	Ulph measure	0.02	0.018	0.016	0.015	0.015	0.015	0.015	0.015
0.35		0.021	0.019	0.017	0.016	0.016	0.016		
0.25	Atkinson measure	0.031	0.034	0.036	0.04	0.046	0.053	0.059	0.067
0.3	of	0.032	0.035	0.037	0.041	0.045	0.052	0.058	0.066
0.35	net income	0.034	0.036	0.038	0.042	0.046	0.052	0.058	0.065

Table 12.15

Tax Rate	Elasticity of Substitution / Measure of Inequality	0.2	0.3	0.4	0.5	0.6	0.7	0.8	0.9
0.25		0.019	0.017	0.015	0.015	0.014	0.014	0.014	0.014
0.3	Ulph measure	0.02	0.018	0.016	0.016	0.015	0.015	0.015	0.015
0.35		0.021	0.019	0.017	0.016	0.016	0.016	0.016	0.016
0.15	Atkinson measure	0.032	0.034	0.037	0.041	0.046	0.054	0.060	0.069
0.3	of	0.032	0.035	0.037	0.041	0.045	0.052	0.058	0.066
0.35	net income	0.033	0.036	0.038	0.042	0.046	0.052	0.057	0.065

The sensitivity of our conclusions about the effects of tax changes on inequality can be gauged by considering Tables 12.14 and 12.15. These show the values of the Ulph measure of inequality and the Atkinson measure of inequality of net income (corresponding to the higher value of the inequality aversion) for all the values of the elasticity and for standard rates of tax of 25 per cent, 30 per cent and 35 per cent. Table 12.14 shows the figures for the case in which there is no change in allowances and Table 12.15 for the case of an equal revenue change in allowances. Table 12.14 shows that for all values of the tax rate the Ulph measure falls initially as the elasticity of substitution is increased and then stays virtually constant, while the Atkinson measure rises steadily with the elasticity of substitution for all tax rates.

The conclusion that inequality as measured by the Ulph measure falls as the tax rate is cut and rises when it is raised remains valid for all values of the elasticity of substitution. The reverse conclusion about the effects on inequality as measured by the Atkinson measure of net income remain valid only for high levels of the elasticity of substitution, while for values of the elasticity of 0.5 and below the effects of the tax changes are as predicted by the Ulph measure of inequality. Table 12.15 shows that equal revenue tax adjustments change the inequality measures in the same direction as no equal revenue changes, with inequality (as measured by the Ulph method) decreasing as tax rates are cut and increasing when they are increased.

(f) Alternative treatment of unearned income
We pointed out in Section III(a), from an inspection of the decile ranges, that there is a tendency for the amount of tax paid to decline as the individuals become better off. This is largely explained by the way we have treated household income other than the respondent's earned

income. The better off members of the sample have working wives whose net income we have treated as a constant component of the husband's unearned income. This produces the tendency shown in the deciles for individuals to become better off and yet to pay less tax. We have attempted to correct for this tendency by making some *ad hoc* adjustments to the basic model.

First, we count into the tax bill of the household both the tax paid by the wife and the tax paid by the husband. Secondly, the tax paid by the wife is allowed to vary as the tax rate is changed. It should be noted, however, that the hours of work of the wife remain constant so we are ignoring any labour supply effects on the wife. In this respect the model is not a household model of labour supply but a crude attempt to take into account variations in tax paid by working wives.

An important reason for wives seeking employment may be due to the need to support children when the husband's wage rate is low. So the second adjustment we make is to introduce a 'need' variable. This variable is a simple measure of need based on the amount of supplementary benefit that would be received by a family depending on the number and ages of the children. The need variable is subtracted from unearned income to give a measure of consumption unrelated to need. It is this consumption figure which enters the utility function when computing utility for the purposes of ranking.

Table 12.16

Decile No.	Consumption	Hours	Need	Tax
1	9.207	60.88	12.98	6.109
2	13.36	52.95	11.79	3.859
3	18.64	57.92	12.07	5.77
4	18.73	51.48	11.87	4.948
5	21.42	53.63	12.08	6.072
6	22.34	50.37	11.95	5.542
7	23.93	48.40	10.95	6.366
8	26.45	47.68	11.79	6.925
9	25.73	38.60	10.76	4.918
10	31.62	29.92	11.38	5.978

In Table 12.16 we show the adjusted measures of consumption, hours, need and tax paid by the household after these changes to the initial position have been made. The value of the elasticity of substitution assumed is the value of 0.8.[4] It can be seen that need is more or less constant over the deciles, and now tax paid does not show any distinct tendency to fall as welfare rises.

Table 12.17

Tax Rate	25%	35%
π	0.0518	0.0924
η	-0.015	-0.0294
ϵ	0.9678	0.9324

Having made these adjustments to our initial position we changed the tax rate by 5 per cent and the results are shown in Table 12.17. Once more π, η and ϵ represent price elasticity, elasticity of GNP and elasticity of tax revenue, respectively. If we compare these results with those of, say, Table 12.12 we see that the figures for π and η are very much smaller in absolute magnitude. This presumably reflects the fact that when, say, the tax rate is cut this increases the net income of the wife, consequently producing an income effect leading the husband to reduce his hours of work. This is now reflected in the values of ϵ being much closer to unity.

Similar conclusions apply to the case when equal revenue changes in allowances are made. Now, however, these changes can be made in a variety of ways - in the husband's allowances, the wife's allowances or both. Table 12.18 presents the effects of changing the tax rate by 5 per

Table 12.18

		Tax rate	
		25%	35%
Both allowances changed	π	0.2296	0.2506
	η	-0.0834	-0.0888
	τ	3.08	2.4
Only husband's allowance changed	π	0.2184	0.2254
	η	-0.0798	-0.0810
	τ	3.3	2.66

cent when, first, both allowances are changed by the same percentage to restore revenue, and secondly when only the husband's allowances are changed. Comparing these figures with those in Table 12.13 we can see once again that the price elasticity and the elasticity of GNP are much smaller in magnitude due to the income effect on the husband's hours of work of changing the wife's income. The measure of allowance elasticity, τ, is much higher in the present case since the elasticity of tax revenue has risen from 0.625 to around 0.94 and a correspondingly larger rise in allowances is necessary to bring the change in tax revenue back to zero. Also the change is larger for the case where only the husband's allowance is altered. Finally, comparing Tables 12.17 and 12.18 we can see that the effect of changing allowances to obtain equal revenue once more reinforces the tax rate change and so the effect on elasticities is larger for the equal revenue case.

Finally in this section we wish to comment on the changes in the inequality measures. Table 12.19 reports the Ulph and Atkinson measures

Table 12.19

Tax Rate	Ulph Inequality	Atkinson Inequality
25%	0.038	0.242
30%	0.040	0.239
35%	0.043	0.238

of inequality which are analogous to those presented in Table 12.4 above for the case where the tax rate is changed without adjusting allowances. The other two cases of this section are not considered in detail; however, the following comments apply. The first point to note is that the absolute value of each of the measures is greater than the corresponding measures reported in Table 12.4. This is because these figures have been calculated after the need element has been subtracted from the level of income. The need figure was fairly constant across all deciles and it is well known that subtracting a constant from income increases the Atkinson measure of inequality.

It may be observed from Table 12.19 that in the case of the Ulph measure a reduction in the tax rate reduces inequality while raising the tax rate leads to greater inequality. The converse applies to the Atkinson measure of inequality.

IV   CONCLUSION

We have found that recognising the presence of the exemption level seems to be crucial in understanding the aggregate impact of tax changes on our sample of married male workers. Clearly in a wider sample that would include a large proportion of people paying more tax than the people in our sample, the importance of this point would diminish; it would be interesting to run the exercise on such a sample to find out just how much it does diminish.

In assessing the distributional impact, the presence of the exemption level and a variety of other complications arising from non-linearity all seem to be important in forming a complete picture.

It is a major limitation of our work that because we had poor information on the work characteristics of other household members (especially
the wife), we were constrained to treat the man as a single worker, and
this has given rise to some anomalous findings. However, we hope to be
able to undertake an analogous exercise on a household basis in the
future.

To keep the exercise as simple as possible we have also ignored
heterogeneity of tastes both in obtaining the initial estimates of labour
supply and in performing the simulation exercise. Again this is an aspect
of the model we hope to improve in future work.

NOTES: CHAPTER 12

1 Here and throughout the paper, f_i will be the ith partial derivative of f.
2 This led to a problem in practice, for the optimization algorithm would not
   always produce a solution to the individual utility maximization problem. The
   difficulty was that sometimes the algorithm would work for a given individual
   before the tax change but not afterwards, and vice versa. Since in making equal
   revenue comparisons it is important to have the same population before and after
   the tax change we had to drop people for whom there was no solution to their
   optimization problem before or after the change. But this has a bearing on how
   close the initial equilibrium is to the initial position in which people find themselves, and hence on the choice of consumption weight. Conversely, the choice of
   consumption weight affects the utility function and hence whether or not an
   individual's maximization problem would possess a solution. Accordingly we had
   to compute the equal revenue adjustment to the tax threshold and the initial
   weight to consumption *simultaneously* so as to minimize the sum of squares and
   the percentage change in tax revenue on a constant population. This has the
   implication that the effective population on which the simulation exercise is
   run will not always be 335. Moreover, since whether or not there is solution to
   the individual optimisation problem can depend on both the nature and the
   size of the tax changes being contemplated, the population need not be
   constant when looking at different types of change in the tax system. This
   qualification should be borne in mind when considering the results to be presented in the next section. We will report effective sample sizes when considering
   various tax changes. However, it will be seen that the sample never drops below
   331 and is constant for many tax changes, so it is unlikely that there is any
   serious distortion being introduced into our results on account of changing population size.
3 The disaggregated breakdown of figures for changes in gross income and tax
   revenue are available from the authors on request.
4 The elasticity of substitution used in this section is a measure of
   0.8, which was based on an early estimate obtained by Ashworth and Ulph
   (1977a). It was not possible to replicate this section using the lower measure
   of 0.5 so the results presented should be viewed as illustrative of the method.

Chapter 13

Implications for Optimal Income Taxation

I INTRODUCTION

An important motivation for the study of labour supply is the recognition that the nature of individual utility functions (which determines the supply of effort) is an important factor in the design of income tax schedules. It has been long realised that in discussing the merits of alternative income tax schedules it is necessary to balance the resulting distortionary welfare losses against distributional welfare gains. However, only recently, following the seminal work of Mirrlees (1971), have economists attempted to assess how the various factors underlying the gains and losses combine to determine optimal tax schedules. As Stern (1976) notes, the four main ingredients of models of optimal income taxation are a welfare function, individual utility functions, a distribution of labour skills and a production function. The second of these ingredients has been the focus of the research presented in the rest of this book.

As Mirrlees (1971) demonstrated, the derivation of optimal income tax schedules is in general quite complex, and in the second part of his paper he examined a number of special cases for which numerical examples could be readily computed. Stern (1976) extended his work to allow for different utility functions, although he confined himself to linear tax schedules, a restriction for which the more general approach of Mirrlees provides some justification. In the next section of this chapter we will briefly review the models of Mirrlees and Stern, demonstrating what the estimates of labour supply functions derived elsewhere in this book imply for tax rates, within the context of these models.

It needs to be emphasised that work on optimal income taxation is not designed to prescribe tax rates for real world economies, for the models are too simple yet for that purpose. The aim of these models is to assess how sensitive tax schedules might be to the underlying assumptions of the model. The rest of this chapter will pursue this program of research by examining one particular feature of optimal tax models – what happens to the revenue raised by income tax. In much of the work on optimal income taxation, the revenue is simply redistributed. Even where revenue is raised for public expenditure, as in the models of Mirrlees and Stern already referred to, this is seen simply as a drain from consumption. The effects of increasing government expenditure on optimal tax rates in such models will be discussed in Section II.

A natural extension to these models of optimal taxation is to allow individuals to benefit from government expenditure. A simple method of doing this was provided by Feldstein (1973). It was assumed that government expenditure could be treated as equivalent to a transfer in kind. Thus, in the individual utility functions the value of the lump-sum grant is just replaced by the sum of the cash grant and the value to the individual of the public expenditure. Feldstein suggested that this simply acts like raising the cash grant, and so it would reduce labour supply. Including public expenditure in this way, therefore, would act to reduce the optimal tax rate and the size of the cash grant. So Feldstein concluded that 'the more valuable the public expenditure to the individuals, the more regressive would be the optimal method of financing that expenditure'.

One point to make about Feldstein's analysis is that the effect of including public expenditure in individual's utility functions is twofold. In the first place, it can change individual preferences between consumption and leisure, and hence the individual supply function. This is clearly the effect Feldstein has in mind. But it can also alter the relative marginal utilities of income of different individuals in society, and hence the distributional effects of different tax schedules. It is not clear whether Feldstein took the second effect into account in reaching his conclusions, and in Section III of this chapter we will offer a brief analysis of Feldstein's model when both effects are recognised.

A more serious objection to the Feldstein model is the extreme way in which public expenditure is introduced to the utility function. Feldstein assumes an infinite elasticity of substitution between private and public expenditure. To the extent that public expenditure takes the form of free provision of goods and services individuals would otherwise have bought through the market, this assumption is plausible. However it is more questionable when the government expenditure is devoted to the provision of goods like defence, which would not normally be provided by market economies. It would seem sensible, then, to allow government expenditure to enter the utility function in a more general way.

The remaining sections of this chapter will explore the implications for optimal income taxation of including the benefits of government expenditure in individual utility functions in a more general way than that analysed by Feldstein. However, we shall make two restrictions on this analysis. First, we confine ourselves to linear tax schedules. Secondly, we shall assume that government expenditure is *separable* from consumption and leisure in the individual utility function. Government expenditure, therefore, will not affect labour supply, and its impact is solely through the effect on marginal utilities of income. The justification for this rather severe restriction is, first, tractability and, secondly, the introspective view that defence expenditure may not have much to do with one's choice of hours of work. One could approach actual government expenditure as a combination of two kinds – one which is a close substitute for private expenditure and can be treated as equivalent to a lump-sum handout in cash, and one which is quite distinct from private consumption and does not affect consumption/leisure choices, but does affect marginal utility. A judicious interpolation between the results of Feldstein's analysis and our own may suggest the consequences for optimal income taxes of a more general case where there are both labour supply and marginal utility effects.

In Section IV, then, we set out a general model of optimal linear taxation where government expenditure enters utility functions in a separable form. For this section, the level of government expenditure will be assumed exogenous. To derive precise predictions we need to specialise to the particular utility functions, welfare function, production function and skill distribution used in the Stern model.

One difficulty with the model of Section IV is that the optimum tax rate (and subsidy) will depend not only on the assumed exogenous level of government expenditure, but also on the weight attached to government spending in the utility function. There is no empirical evidence, however, to suggest plausible figures for such a weight. One way out of this difficulty is to find, for any given weight attached to government expenditure, the optimal values of tax rate, subsidy and government expenditure. Since we can observe actual levels of government expenditure (more precisely, it is the share of public expenditure in GNP that is relevant), we can find by inverse inference the optimum tax rate corresponding to any level of government expenditure *on the assumption that this is the optimal level of expenditure*. Analysis of this full optimum is of interest in its own right, of course. The discussion of this model is presented in Section V.

II THE SIMPLE MODEL

In this section we outline the model used by Stern (1976), which is based, in turn, on the work of Mirrlees (1971). Individuals have identical preferences represented by a CES utility function for consumption and leisure:

$$U(C,L) = [\alpha L^{-\mu} + (1-\alpha)C^{-\mu}]^{-1/\mu} \tag{1}$$

where $\epsilon = 1/(\mu + 1)$ is the elasticity of substitution between consumption and leisure. To each individual there corresponds a skill level, n, such that if the individual works for H hours ($H + L = 1$), he provides Hn units of labour. With a linear tax system with tax rate t and lump-sum handout s, an n-individual chooses C_n, L_n to maximise (1) subject to the budget constraint

$$C_n = (1-t)\,n\,(1-L_n) + s \tag{2}$$

In (2), the wage rate for an efficiency unit of labour is assumed to be 1. Skills are distributed with density function $f(n)$, assumed known.

The social welfare function is of the iso-elastic form

$$\frac{1}{1-\nu} \int_0^\infty U^{1-\nu}(C_n, L_n)\,f(n)\,d_n, \nu \geq 0 \tag{3}$$

and the government has to choose t and s to maximise (3) subject to the production constraint

$$t . \int_{n_t}^\infty n H_n f(n) dn = s + g \tag{4}$$

where n_t is the skill level below which individuals do no work, and g is the required level of per capita expenditure on public goods. In this simple model, g is treated as an exogenous leakage from consumption. Indeed an alternative interpretation of g is as a fixed cost of production.

Stern followed Mirrlees in assuming a lognormal distribution for $f(n)$, with mean and standard deviation of -1 and 0.39, respectively, for the associated normal distribution. The parameter α in the utility function was set so that an individual with mean skill would work for two-thirds of the time with $\epsilon = \frac{1}{2}$ when there was no taxation. The optimum rate of tax was then calculated for the various values of the remaining parameters, ν, ϵ and g, as shown in Table 13.1. Higher values of ν indicate greater concern for equality, with the welfare function becoming Rawlsian

Table 13.1 *Optimal Linear Tax Rates*

ν	ϵ	g = 0	.05	.10	.15
	.2	.362	.406	.456	.513
	.4	.223	.254	.351	.504
0	.6	.170	.189	.366	.530
	.8	.141	.197	.386	.565
	.99	.127	.206	.409	.613
	.2	.627	.681	.733	.784
	.4	.477	.540	.605	.675
2	.6	.389	.450	.520	.600
	.8	.331	.389	.460	.565
	.99	.291	.347	.417	.613
	.2	.670	.720	.767	.812
	.4	.527	.588	.651	.716
3	.6	.438	.501	.571	.648
	.8	.376	.438	.513	.528
	.99	.334	.395	.470	.613
	.2	.926	.938	⩾.950	⩾.950
	.4	.839	.867	.893	.917
∞	.6	.756	.798	.839	.877
	.8	.682	.736	.792	.848
	.99	.621	.685	.756	.831

Source: Stern (1976), Table 3.

as $\nu \to \infty$. The example studied by Mirrlees corresponds to $\mu = 0$, $\nu = 1$. It should be noted, also, that for most of the examples GNP usually lies between .25 and .30, so that the non-zero values of g represent substantial shares of GNP spent on government expenditure (remembering that transfer income, s, is over and above g).

Some comment on the results are in order. As one might expect, greater concern for equity (higher values of ν) increases the optimal tax rate; high values of g also increase the optimal tax rate. However, while for $g = 0$ tax rates are higher with lower elasticities of substitution (i.e. smaller distortionary effects), this monotonic relation ceases to hold with high values of g and low values of ν. The reason is that the need to raise revenue to pay for government expenditure acts as a constraint on the rate of tax one can set, and with higher elasticities a higher tax rate is needed; this conflicts with the desire to lower taxes as elasticities rise, and so for some values of g and ν there is a U-shaped relationship between the elasticity of substitution and the optimal tax rate.

From the estimates of labour supply derived earlier in this book, we would take a value of $\epsilon = .4$ as the most plausible value to use. Taking $g = .05$ as the closest approximation to the actual UK share of government expenditure in GNP[1], values for the optimal tax rate vary between .254 and .867 depending on the attitude adopted towards equity. If $\nu = 2$ or 3 were thought to represent a reasonable weight for equity, then tax rates around 55 per cent would seem to be called for. However, we stress again that the literature on optimal taxation is not designed to prescribe tax rates for real economies.

III   FELDSTEIN'S MODEL

In the previous section government expenditure was treated simply as a drain on consumption, and its effect on optimal tax rates come mainly through the effect it had in constraining feasible tax rates. In this section we allow government expenditure to affect individual utility functions in the way suggested by Feldstein, that is, as a perfect substitute for the cash subsidy. However, to establish notation for this and subsequent sections we begin by setting up a general model.

Individual utility functions are now written as $U(C,L,g)$, where for this and the next section g is treated as exogenously fixed. The welfare function $W(C,L,g) = h(U)$, where $h(.)$ is the increasing transformation used before adding up utilities in the social welfare function, and will reflect society's preferences for equity.

Let

$$V(n(1-t), s, g) \equiv \underset{C,L}{\text{Max}}\ W(C,L,g) \tag{5}$$
$$\text{s.t. } C = n(1-t)(1-L) + s$$

be the indirect social utility of a person of skill n when the tax rate is t, the lump-sum handout is s, and government expenditure (per head) is g. Let $H(n(1-t), s, g)$ be the corresponding supply of labour function generated by the maximisation performed in (5).

Then the optimal tax rate and subsidy are the solutions of the problem

$$\underset{t,s \geqslant 0}{\text{Max}} \int_0^\infty V(n(1-t), s, g) f(n)\, dn \tag{6}$$
$$\text{s.t } t \int_0^\infty nH(n(1-t), s, g) f(n)\, dn = s + g$$

We now turn to the analysis of the Feldstein model. This consists of the special case of the utility function

$$U(C,L,g) \equiv \tilde{U}(C + \gamma g, L)$$

where γ is the weight the individual attaches to government expenditure. Defining $\tilde{V}$ and $\tilde{H}$ analogously (6) becomes

$$\underset{t,s}{\text{Max}} \int_0^\infty \tilde{V}(n(1-t), s + \gamma g) f(n) dn$$

$$\text{s.t. } t \int_0^\infty n\tilde{H}(n(1-t), s + \gamma g) f(n) dn = s + g \qquad (7)$$

Let $t = T(\gamma,g)$ and $s = S(\gamma,g)$ be the optimal tax rate and subsidy when the parameters are γ and g. We are interested in the effects on the optimal tax rate and subsidy of an increase in the value that individuals attach to government expenditure, that is, we are interested in $T_1(\gamma, g)$ and $S_1(\gamma, g)$. Notice now that $T(0, g)$ and $S(0, g)$ give the solutions to the problem when government expenditure does not enter the individual utility functions, and that if in (7) we make the substitution $\sigma = s + \gamma g$, $G = (1 - \gamma)g$, we can rewrite (7) as:

$$\underset{\sigma,t}{\text{Max}} \int_0^\infty \tilde{V}(n(1-t), \sigma) f(n) dn \text{ s.t. } t \int_0^\infty n\tilde{H}(n(1-t), \sigma) f(n) dn = \sigma + G$$

and so we have

$$T(\gamma,g) \equiv T(0, (1-\gamma)g), S(\gamma,g) \equiv S(0, (1-\gamma)g) - \gamma g$$

We therefore find that

$$T_1(\gamma, g) = -g T_2(0, (1-\gamma)g), S_1(\gamma, g) = -g(1 + S_2(0, (1-\gamma)g))$$

In general, $T_2(0, G)$ and $(1 + S_2(0, G))$ are unsigned, though we show in the appendix that if $T_2 > 0$ then $(1 + S_2) > 0$. However, as illustrated in Table 13.1, Stern found that for the case where $f(.)$ is lognormal and $u(.)$ is CES then $T_2 > 0$. This confirms a similar finding by Feldstein. Hence we can conclude that, for the class of cases considered by Feldstein and Stern, increasing the value attached to government expenditure (treating this expenditure as equivalent to a cash grant) will indeed lead to lower tax rates and lump-sum handouts.

Thus we have shown that for the cases considered by Feldstein, the conjecture that increasing the value attached to government expenditure lowers optimal tax rates is correct, allowing for the effects on both labour supply and the valuation of marginal utility.

IV A MORE GENERAL TREATMENT OF GOVERNMENT EXPENDITURE

The Feldstein analysis assumes that government expenditure (appropriately weighted) is a perfect substitute for a cash handout. In this section we return to the more general model outlined at the beginning of the previous section, where g is a distinct argument of an individual's utility function. However, we make the important restriction that government expenditure is separable from consumption and leisure in the utility function.

For comparability with the previous section we introduce a parameter γ to reflect the strength of people's preferences for government expenditure, so that we can write the indirect utility function as $V(n(1-t), s, g: \gamma)$.

Let us further write

$$\phi(t, s, g: \gamma) \equiv \int_0^\infty V(n(1-t), s, g: \gamma))f(n)\, dn \tag{8}$$

and

$$\psi(t, s, g) \equiv t \int_0^\infty nH(n(1-t), s)f(n)dn - s - g \tag{9}$$

where, given separability, $H(.)$ is independent of g and γ.

Then the objective is to choose t and s to maximise ϕ subject to $\psi = 0$, which yields the following first-order conditions:

$$\phi_t(t, s, g; \gamma) = \lambda \psi_t(t, s, g) \tag{10}$$

$$\phi_s(t, s, g; \gamma) = \lambda \psi_s(t, s, g) \tag{11}$$

$$\psi(t, s, g) = 0 \tag{12}$$

where λ is the marginal social utility of income. Differentiate these first-order conditions with respect to γ and we obtain

$$\begin{pmatrix} \phi_{tt} - \lambda\psi_{tt} & \phi_{ts} - \lambda\psi_{ts} & -\psi_t \\ \phi_{st} - \lambda\psi_{st} & \phi_{ss} - \lambda\psi_{ss} & -\psi_s \\ -\psi_t & -\psi_s & 0 \end{pmatrix} \begin{pmatrix} \partial t/\partial\gamma \\ \partial s/\partial\gamma \\ \partial\lambda/\partial\gamma \end{pmatrix} = \begin{pmatrix} -\phi_{t\gamma} \\ -\phi_{s\gamma} \\ 0 \end{pmatrix} \tag{13}$$

Letting A be the determinant of the matrix in (13), carrying out the inversion and substituting from (10) and (11) yields

$$\frac{\partial t}{\partial\gamma} = \frac{-\phi_t(\phi_s)^2}{\lambda^2 A} \left(\frac{\phi_{s\gamma}}{\phi_s} - \frac{\phi_{t\gamma}}{\phi_t} \right) \tag{14}$$

$$\frac{\partial s}{\partial\gamma} = \frac{\phi_s(\phi_t)^2}{\lambda^2 A} \left(\frac{\phi_{s\gamma}}{\phi_s} - \frac{\phi_{t\gamma}}{\phi_t} \right) \tag{15}$$

Now

$$\phi_s = \int_0^\infty V_s(n(1-t), s, g{:}\gamma)f(n)dn > 0 \tag{16}$$

$$\phi_t = -\int_0^\infty nV_s(n(1-t), s, g{:}\gamma)H(n(1-t), s)f(n)dn < 0 \tag{17}$$

Moreover, second-order conditions of maximisation give $A > 0$, thus

$$\text{sign} \frac{\partial t}{\partial\gamma} = \text{sign} \frac{\partial s}{\partial\gamma} = \text{sign}\left(\frac{\phi_{s\gamma}}{\phi_s} - \frac{\phi_{t\gamma}}{\phi_t} \right) \tag{18}$$

Hence the effect on the optimal tax rate of introducing government expenditure into the utility function depends on the sign of

$$\frac{\int_0^\infty V_{s\gamma}(n)f(n)dn}{\int_0^\infty V_s(n)f(n)\,dn} - \frac{\int_0^\infty nV_{s\gamma}(n)H(n)f(n)dn}{\int_0^\infty nV_s(n)H(n)f(n)dn} \tag{19}$$

which is just the difference between the percentage change in the mean value of the social marginal utility of income and the percentage change in the mean value of the social marginal valuation of income.

The expression in (19) tells us that when a change in γ alters everyone's social marginal utility of income in the same proportion, then optimal tax rates are unaffected. An obvious case in which this would be true is that in which $U(C,L,g) = U^1(C,L).U^2(g)$ and $h(.)$ is iso-elastic. This would include cases in which the welfare function, $W(.)$, was additively separable. At this level of generality, however, it is difficult to say much more about the sign of (19). We therefore examined some special cases to get a feel of the factors that might influence the changes in the tax rate. We considered the class of cases in which $U(.)$ is CES so that

$$U(C,L,g) = \begin{cases} (\alpha C^{-\mu} + \beta L^{-\mu} + \gamma g^{-\mu})^{-1/\mu} & \mu > -1, \mu \neq 0 \\ C^{\alpha}L^{\beta}g^{\gamma} & \mu = 0 \end{cases}$$

and

$$h(U) = \begin{cases} \dfrac{1}{1-\nu} U^{1-\nu} & \nu \geq 0, \nu \neq 1 \\ \log U & \nu = 1 \end{cases}$$

that is, h is iso-elastic.

From our above discussion, we immediately get the result that in the Cobb–Douglas case ($\mu = 0$), the optimal tax rate is independent of γ. When $\mu \neq 0$ we have

$$V_{s\gamma}(n(1-t), s, g) = \frac{-(1/\epsilon-\nu)g^{-\mu}}{(1/\epsilon-1)} \zeta(n(1-t), s, g) V_s(n(1-t), s, g) \quad (20)$$

where $\epsilon = 1/1+\mu$ is the elasticity of substitution and

$$\zeta(n(1-t), s, g) = [\alpha C(n(1-t),s)^{-\mu} + \beta L(n(1-t),s)^{-\mu} + \gamma g^{-\mu}]^{-1}$$

Substituting (20) into (19), we have

$$\text{sign } \frac{\partial t}{\partial \gamma} = \text{sign } \left\{ \frac{(1/\epsilon-\nu)}{(1/\epsilon-1)} \left[\frac{\int_0^{\infty} n\zeta(n)V_s(n)H(n)f(n)dn}{\int_0^{\infty} nV_s(n) H(n) f(n) dn} - \frac{\int_0^{\infty}\zeta(n) V_s(n)f(n)dn}{\int_0^{\infty} V_s(n)f(n)dn} \right] \right\}$$
$$(21)$$

(21) shows that a second case in which the optimal tax rate is independent of γ is that in which $\nu = 1/\dot{\epsilon}$. This again reflects our above discussion, for in this case $W(.)$ is additively separable.

To say anything about the remaining cases we need to evaluate the expression in square brackets in (21). This we have done for a number of cases. We have considered the case $\gamma = 0$, which corresponds to the problem solved by Stern, and for which some results were presented earlier in Table 13.1. The parameter values are the same as for Table 13.1, except that we ignore the case $g = 0, \nu = \infty$, and consider a more detailed range of values of ϵ, from 0.2 to 0.9. The values of the optimal tax rates were derived form Stern, and the optimal lump-sum handouts were computed by

Table 13.2 The Values of x for Different Values of ν and ε: The Case of g = 0.05

ε	ν = 0.0			ν = 2.0			ν = 3.0		
	t	s	x	t	s	x	t	s	x
0.2	0.406	0.0617	−75.6228	0.681	0.1319	−53.6855	0.720	0.1411	−51.6118
0.3	0.309	0.0341	−5.0287	0.6	0.1059	−3.8881	0.646	0.1162	−3.7106
0.4	0.254	0.0185	−1.1956	0.54	0.0869	−0.9751	0.588	0.0971	−0.9287
0.5	0.217	0.008	−0.4656	0.49	0.0716	−0.3947	0.541	0.082	−0.379
0.6	0.189	0.0	0.0	0.45	0.0594	−0.1984	0.501	0.0694	−0.1924
0.7	0.193	0.0	0.0	0.417	0.0493	−0.1082	0.467	0.0588	−0.106
0.8	0.197	0.0	0.0	0.389	0.0409	−0.0573	0.438	0.0498	−0.0568
0.9	0.201	0.0	0.0	0.366	0.0338	−0.0241	0.414	0.0422	−0.0242
1.1	0.211	0.0	0.0	0.334	0.0233	0.019	0.376	0.0301	0.0194
1.2	0.216	0.0	0.0	0.324	0.0194	0.0348	0.363	0.0254	0.0356

Table 13.3 *The Values of x for Different Values of ν and ε: The Case of g = 0.1*

ε	ν = 0.0			ν = 2.0			ν = 3.0		
	t	s	x	t	s	x	t	s	x
0.2	0.456	0.0333	−218.461	0.733	0.1079	−124	0.767	0.1164	−119.0746
0.3	0.344	0.0	0.0	0.661	0.0828	−6.6095	0.703	0.0926	−6.2956
0.4	0.351	0.0	0.0	0.605	0.0632	−1.3831	0.651	0.0739	−1.3183
0.5	0.358	0.0	0.0	0.559	0.0481	−0.5014	0.608	0.0586	−0.4786
0.6	0.366	0.0	0.0	0.520	0.0353	−0.2321	0.571	0.0457	−0.2236
0.7	0.375	0.0	0.0	0.488	0.0247	−0.1191	0.54	0.0349	−0.1160
0.8	0.386	0.0	0.0	0.460	0.0155	−0.0602	0.513	0.0255	−0.0594
0.9	0.398	0.0	0.0	0.436	0.0076	−0.0245	0.488	0.0136	−0.0242
1.1	0.422	0.0	0.0	0.422	0.0	0.0	0.44	0.0022	0.0186
1.2	0.434	0.0	0.0	0.434	0.0	0.0	0.434	0.0	0.0

Table 13.4 The Values of x for Different Values of v and ε: The Case of g = 0.15

ε	v = 0.0			v = 2.0			v = 3.0		
	t	s	x	t	s	x	t	s	x
0.2	0.513	0.0086	-843.366	0.784	0.0854	-333.087	0.812	0.0929	-312.861
0.3	0.494	0.0	0.0	0.723	0.0622	-12.3275	0.759	0.071	-11.6583
0.4	0.504	0.0	0.0	0.675	0.0439	-2.1356	0.716	0.0535	-1.72
0.5	0.516	0.0	0.0	0.634	0.0287	-0.672	0.68	0.039	-0.6385
0.6	0.530	0.0	0.0	0.6	0.0161	-0.2831	0.648	0.0263	-0.2706
0.7	0.546	0.0	0.0	0.571	0.0054	-0.1351	0.621	0.0156	-0.1305
0.8	0.565	0.0	0.0	0.565	0.0	0.0	0.598	0.0063	-0.0631
0.9	0.588	0.0	0.0	0.588	0.0	0.0	0.588	0.0	0.0
1.1	0.636	0.0	0.0	0.636	0.0	0.0	0.636	0.0	0.0
1.2	0.671	0.0	0.0	0.671	0.0	0.0	0.671	0.0	0.0

solving the budget constraint for the government. The expression in square brackets in (21) can then be computed and this is shown as x in Tables 13.2-13.4. Two points about these calculations should be noted.

First, as we have noted, when $\epsilon = 1$, $dt/d\gamma = 0$. It seems important therefore to know what is going to happen to the expression in square brackets for $\epsilon > 1$. To find this out, we have extrapolated the values of the optimal tax rate given by Stern to the cases $\epsilon = 1.1$ and $\epsilon = 1.2$, carried out the calculations of the lump-sum subsidy as indicated above and hence the value of the expression in square brackets. Secondly, as Stern has demonstrated, for high values of the elasticity of substitution or of the level of government expenditure, the optimal lump-sum subsidy is zero. Except for borderline cases, the optimal subsidy will continue to be zero when a marginal change is made in γ. This will therefore leave the optimal tax rate unaffected, and this is indicated in the tables by a value of zero for x.

From the tables it can be seen that, ignoring cases where x is zero, x is negative for $\epsilon < 1$ and positive for $\epsilon > 1$, which in turn implies from (21) that (again ignoring zero values)

$$\text{sign } (dt/d\gamma) = \text{sign } [(\nu-1)/\epsilon] \qquad (22)$$

This result is somewhat striking for its ultimate simplicity, though it has to be remembered that the calculations have been performed for a very special set of cases. Despite this, however, the result does serve to point up the difference between the approach adopted in this section and that adopted by Feldstein. For example, if we accept a value for the elasticity of substitution of 0.5, then we only require values of $\nu > 2$ in order to argue that consideration of the benefits of government expenditure should lead us to raise tax rates beyond what we would consider optimal in the absence of such considerations. This is the reverse of the conclusion reached for Feldstein's model in Section III.

V   THE FULL OPTIMUM

In the analysis so far it has been assumed that the level of government expenditure was given exogenously. We now wish to compute the full optimum in which both the tax rate and the level of spending are selected optimally.

Actually, discussing the *level* of expenditure is not very revealing in our model since output has been scaled to equal input, so we will carry out our discussion in terms of the optimal percentage of GNP that is to be devoted to government expenditure. Moreover, we will continue to analyse the special case in which government expenditure enters the utility function in a separable form.

We begin by examining what can be said about the optimal share of government expenditure in GNP. The problem is to

$$\text{Max} \int_0^\infty V[n(1-t), s, g] f(n)dn \quad \text{s.t.} \quad t \int_0^\infty nH[n(1-t), s] f(n)dn = s+g \quad (23)$$

$$t, s, g \geqq 0$$

The first-order conditions for this maximisation are

$$\int_0^\infty nV_1(n(1-t), s, g)f(n)dn + \lambda t \int_0^\infty n^2 H_1(n(1-t), s)f(n)dn$$

$$= \lambda \int_0^\infty nH(n(1-t), s)f(n)dn \quad (24)$$

$$\int_0^\infty V_2(n(1-t), s, g)f(n)dn + \lambda t \int_0^\infty nH_2(n(1-t), s)f(n)dn = \lambda \quad (25)$$

$$\int_0^\infty V_3(n(1-t), s, g)f(n)dn = \lambda \quad (26)$$

where λ is the marginal social utility of income.

(24) × (1-t) + (25) ×s gives

$$\int_0^\infty V_2(n) [s+n(1-t)H(n)] f(n) dn + \lambda t \int_0^\infty n[sH_2(n)+n(1-t)H_1(n)] f(n)dn$$

$$= \lambda(1-t)y+\lambda s \quad (27)$$

where $y = \int_0^\infty nH(n(1-t), s)f(n)dn$ is per capita GNP.

(27) + (26) × g gives

$$\int_0^\infty V_2(n)c(n)f(n)dn + g\int_0^\infty V_3(n)f(n)dn = \lambda y - \lambda t \int_0^\infty n[H_2(n)s +$$

$$n(1-t)H_1(n)]\,f(n)dn \tag{28}$$

where $c(n) = s + n(1-t)H(n)$ is the private consumption of an n-man.

[(26) $\times$ g] /(27) yields

$$\frac{g}{y} = \frac{\int_0^\infty V_3(n)gf(n)dn}{\int_0^\infty V_3(n)gf(n)dn + \int_0^\infty V_2(n)c(n)f(n)dn}$$

$$\times \left(1 - \frac{t\int_0^\infty n[H_2(n)s + n(1-t)H_1(n)]\,f(n)dn}{y}\right) \tag{29}$$

A little manipulation will show that (29) can also be written in the form

$$\frac{g}{y} = \frac{\int_0^\infty V_3(n)gf(n)dn}{\int_0^\infty V_3(n)gf(n)dn + \int_0^\infty V_2(n)c(n)f(n)dn} \cdot t\,[1 - \eta_s - \eta_T] \tag{30}$$

where η_s is the elasticity of government revenue with respect to a change in the lump-sum handout and η_T is the elasticity of government revenue with respect to a change in the *net* marginal tax rate $\tau = (1-t)$. At the optimum both these elasticities are negative.

Expressions (29) and (30) are still fairly complex, and so to obtain further insight into the way in which various factors influence the optimal tax rate and share of government expenditure, we 'solved explicitly' for these variables for a number of different cases of the CES utility function and iso-elastic social welfare function employed in the previous section.

We began by characterising the CES function in terms of the parameters ϵ (the elasticity of substitution = $1/1+\mu$), γ(the weight given to government expenditure) and $\delta = \alpha/\beta$ (the relative weight given to consumption as against leisure). Using the normalisation $\alpha + \beta + \gamma = 1$ it is always possible to solve for α, β knowing δ and γ. The reason for this slight change is that if one wishes to estimate the (separable) CES supply function one would determine only ϵ and δ, and would have to know γ before obtaining α, β. Thus if individuals had a CES utility function, ϵ and δ could be treated as empirically determined from data on labour supply leaving γ to be inferred from the assumption that a given share of GNP going to government expenditure was optimal.

One result that is easily obtained without explicit solution is that of the Cobb–Douglas case[2] ($\epsilon=1$)

$$\frac{g}{y} = \frac{\gamma}{\alpha + \gamma} = \frac{\gamma(1+\delta)}{\delta + \gamma} \tag{31}$$

which is just the standard result that Cobb–Douglas functions generate constant shares given by the exponents of the particular variables in the Cobb–Douglas function. Beyond this case, however, we have to employ direct calculations.

Our calculations were done as follows: We assumed a population of 250 individuals drawn at random from the lognormal distribution used in the previous section. For each of a set of values for the parameters δ, γ, ϵ and ν we then performed the following calculations. We took a particular tax rate, t, and a particular percentage of government revenue to be allocated to government expenditure, z (the remaining percentage going to the lumpsum handout), and solved the government budget constraint by an iterative procedure to find the value of the lump-sum handout (s) (and hence government expenditure, g). With these values of t, s, g we were then able to compute total social welfare. These calculations were repeated for each of 420 values of (t, z) with t running at 0.05 intervals from 0.0 to 0.95 and z at 0.05 intervals from 0.0 to 1.0, and the values of (t, z) which gave the highest social welfare were identified. For these values the optimum tax rate, lump-sum handout and percentage of GNP devoted to government expenditure (tz) were recorded.

The set of parameter values chosen were those generated by giving ν the values 0.0, 0.99, 11, 101, γ the values 0.0 (the Feldstein/Stern case), 0.1, 0.2, 0.3, 0.4 and 0.5, ϵ the values 0.5, 1.0, 1.5 and δ the values 19 and 3. These latter values were obtained from empirical estimates found by fitting a CES consumption/leisure utility function to UK data. The results of these calculations are reported in tables 13.5 and 13.6. We have also included in these tables the values for $\gamma(1+\delta)/(\delta+\gamma)$ for the Cobb–Douglas case, which it will be recalled are the precise values of g/y for this case. It can be seen that our fairly rough grid of points has thrown up some discrepancies, though never more than 5 per cent.

There are several features of these results that we would like to note. First, as we would expect, higher values of γ lead to higher shares of government expenditure in GNP and, on the whole, to non-decreasing optimal tax rates. However, the variation in the optimal tax rate with γ is less marked the higher the value of ν.

Secondly, the optimal share of government expenditure in GNP seems

Table 13.5 Optimal Tax and Expenditure Parameters: The Case where δ = 19

		ε = 0.5						ε = 1.0						ε = 1.5					
ν	γ	0.0	0.1	0.2	0.3	0.4	0.5	0.0	0.1	0.2	0.3	0.4	0.5	0.0	0.1	0.2	0.3	0.4	0.5
0.0	t	0.25	0.5	0.55	0.60	0.65	0.65	0.10	0.25	0.35	0.45	0.5	0.55	0.1	0.15	0.25	0.35	0.45	0.55
	s	0.037	0.088	0.078	0.075	0.07	0.059	0.039	0.067	0.06	0.06	0.038	0.021	0.031	0.054	0.028	0.056	0.036	0.022
	g/y	0.0	0.25	0.33	0.39	0.45	0.49	0.0	0.075	0.19	0.29	0.4	0.5	0.0	0.02	0.1	0.21	0.36	0.5
0.99	t	0.35	0.55	0.60	0.6	0.65	0.70	0.35	0.40	0.40	0.45	0.5	0.6	0.1	0.35	0.40	0.45	0.50	0.55
	s	0.121	0.106	0.095	0.075	0.07	0.075	0.132	0.121	0.08	0.06	0.038	0.034	0.031	0.138	0.118	0.097	0.059	0.022
	g/y	0.0	0.25	0.33	0.39	0.45	0.49	0.0	0.08	0.18	0.29	0.4	0.51	0.0	0.0	0.1	0.20	0.35	0.5
11	t	0.60	0.65	0.65	0.7	0.7	0.70	0.60	0.60	0.6	0.6	0.65	0.65	0.3	0.6	0.6	0.60	0.65	0.65
	s	0.197	0.145	0.113	0.11	0.087	0.075	0.216	0.186	0.155	0.112	0.097	0.062	0.081	0.227	0.194	0.150	0.112	0.063
	g/y	0.0	0.23	0.33	0.39	0.45	0.49	0.0	0.09	0.18	0.3	0.39	0.49	0.0	0.0	0.09	0.21	0.36	0.49
101	t	0.80	0.8	0.8	0.8	0.8	0.85	0.75	0.75	0.75	0.75	0.75	0.8	0.5	0.75	0.75	0.75	0.75	0.75
	s	0.245	0.182	0.159	0.137	0.124	0.117	0.252	0.230	0.155	0.16	0.135	0.101	0.109	0.263	0.228	0.191	0.153	0.1
	g/y	0.0	0.24	0.32	0.40	0.44	0.51	0.0	0.075	0.19	0.3	0.375	0.52	0.0	0.0	0.11	0.225	0.34	0.49
$\frac{\gamma(1+\delta)}{\delta+\gamma}$								0.0	0.105	0.208	0.311	0.412	0.513						

Table 13.6 Optimal Tax and Expenditure Parameters: The Case where $\delta = 3$

ν		$\epsilon=0.5$						$\epsilon=1.0$						$\epsilon=1.5$					
	γ	0.0	0.1	0.2	0.3	0.4	0.5	0.0	0.1	0.2	0.3	0.4	0.5	0.0	0.1	0.2	0.3	0.4	0.5
0.0	t	0.2	0.4	0.45	0.5	0.55	0.6	0.1	0.2	0.25	0.35	0.45	0.55	0.1	0.1	0.15	0.25	0.4	0.55
	s	0.058	0.042	0.028	0.023	0.017	0.019	0.031	0.03	0.008	0.0	0.0	0.0	0.031	0.025	0.007	0.0	0.0	0.0
	g/y	0.0	0.28	0.36	0.43	0.49	0.54	0.0	0.1	0.23	0.35	0.45	0.55	0.0	0.02	0.13	0.25	0.4	0.55
0.99	t	0.2	0.45	0.5	0.5	0.60	0.6	0.2	0.25	0.25	0.35	0.45	0.55	0.1	0.15	0.15	0.25	0.4	0.55
	s	0.058	0.054	0.045	0.023	0.037	0.019	0.058	0.044	0.008	0.0	0.0	0.0	0.031	0.038	0.07	0.0	0.0	0.0
	g/y	0.0	0.27	0.35	0.43	0.48	0.54	0.0	0.1	0.23	0.35	0.45	0.55	0.0	0.02	0.13	0.25	0.4	0.55
11	t	0.5	0.55	0.6	0.6	0.65	0.65	0.35	0.35	0.40	0.40	0.45	0.55	0.3	0.25	0.3	0.35	0.4	0.55
	s	0.132	0.087	0.071	0.055	0.05	0.04	0.094	0.074	0.052	0.017	0.0	0.0	0.081	0.064	0.051	0.02	0.0	0.0
	g/y	0.0	0.25	0.36	0.42	0.49	0.52	0.0	0.09	0.22	0.34	0.45	0.55	0.0	0.03	0.12	0.28	0.4	0.55
101	t	0.7	0.7	0.75	0.75	0.75	0.75	0.60	0.55	0.6	0.60	0.65	0.65	0.5	0.5	0.5	0.5	0.55	0.6
	s	0.170	0.122	0.112	0.117	0.078	0.07	0.133	0.113	0.09	0.071	0.053	0.028	0.109	0.109	0.084	0.063	0.036	0.008
	g/y	0.0	0.25	0.34	0.41	0.49	0.52	0.0	0.08	0.24	0.33	0.46	0.55	0.0	0.0	0.15	0.25	0.41	0.57
$\dfrac{\gamma(1+\delta)}{\delta+\gamma}$								0.0	0.129	0.25	0.364	0.471	0.571						

to be largely independent of ν, the weight to distribution in the social welfare function. One suspects that such a strong result should be capable of analytic demonstration, but as yet we have no proof.

Thirdly, over the range of values we have considered the optimal tax rate is a non-increasing function of the elasticity of substitution. This result contrasts with the case considered in Section IV in which the level of government expenditure was held fixed, where there is a U-shaped relationship between the optimal tax rate and elasticity, as can be seen by examining values for the optimal tax rate in Tables 13.2–13.4.

The movement of the share of government expenditure with the elasticity of substitution is more complex. For low (but positive) values of the weight to government expenditure, a higher elasticity of substitution goes along with a lower share of government expenditure in GNP. However, as the weight given expenditure is raised the rate at which the share falls with elasticity declines until, in Table 13.5, when the weight is 0.5 the share of government expenditure in GNP is virtually the same for all three values of the elasticity of substitution, while in Table 13.6 it starts to rise with the elasticity of substitution.

A possible explanation of this phenomenon would be as follows. If we go back to the Feldstein case where there is an infinite elasticity of substitution, then if γ (the *relative* weight of government expenditure to consumption, in the Feldstein model) is less than 1, the optimal policy is to have no government expenditure and to devote all tax revenue to the lump-sum handout. If γ is greater than 1 the optimal policy is to have no handout but to spend all revenue on government production.

In the CES model the *relative* weight of consumption to government expenditure is $(\delta/(1 + \delta)) . ((1 - \gamma)\gamma)$ so that when, for example, $\delta = 3$, as γ moves from 0.4 to 0.5 the relative weight of government expenditure to consumption rises through unity, causing a sharp rise in the share of government expenditure when the elasticity of substitution is high.

Finally we note that the optimal tax rate is a non-decreasing function and the share of government expenditure a non-increasing function of δ, the relative weight of consumption to leisure.

Turning to calculations of the inverse optimum, we can see that if we assume that it is optimal to have a share of government expenditure of between 20 and 25 per cent (figures which are quite appropriate for the UK) then if $\nu = 0.99$, $\delta = 19$ and $\epsilon = 0.5$ the optimal tax rate is around 55 per cent while if $\epsilon = 1.0$ the optimal tax rate is between 40 and 45 per cent and if $\epsilon = 1.5$ the optimal tax rate is around 45 per cent. On the other hand if $\nu = 11$, then for $\epsilon = 0.5$ the optimal tax rate is about 65 per cent while if $\epsilon = 1$ the optimal tax rate is 60 per cent, as it is if $\epsilon = 1.5$.

Comparison of these results with those of Stern are complicated by the fact that he uses a much lower value of δ (1.588) and computes his optimal tax rate on a much finer grid, but he found that when g was exogenously fixed at 0.05 this corresponded to about 20 per cent of GNP for values of ϵ around 0.4. In particular, we can see from Table 13.2 that for $\epsilon = 0.5$, $\nu = 2.0$ the optimal tax rate he obtained was 0.49, while with $\nu = 3.0$ it was 0.54. Since the somewhat higher values of the optimal tax rate that we have found could well be explained by the higher value of δ we have used, it remains an open question whether the optimal tax rate one obtains when government expenditure is exogenously given is higher or lower than the inverse optimal tax rate.

Now there is, of course, no reason whatever to assume that the individual function is CES; in particular there is no reason to believe that the elasticity of substitution between consumption and leisure is the same as that between consumption and government expenditure. To conclude this chapter we therefore report briefly on a first attempt to explore the robustness of our conclusion when the CES assumption is dropped. We have employed a two-level CES function

$$U = [\gamma g^{-\lambda} + (1-\gamma)(\delta C^{-\mu} + L^{-\mu})^{\lambda/\mu}]^{-1/\lambda}$$

where, $\epsilon = 1/(1+\mu)$ is the elasticity of substitution between consumption and leisure and $\phi = 1/(1+\lambda)$ is the elasticity of substitution between

Table 13.7 $\delta = 3$

		γ			0.1					
		ϵ	0.5			1.0			1.5	
ν	ϕ		0.5	1.0	1.5	0.5	1.0	1.5	0.5	1.0	1.5
	t		0.4	0.3	0.3	0.3	0.2	0.2	0.25	0.15	0.1
0.0	s		0.042	0.057	0.057	0.014	0.03	0.03	0.0	0.016	0.025
	g/y		0.28	0.1	0.1	0.26	0.1	0.1	0.25	0.1	0.02
	t		0.45	0.35	0.35	0.3	0.25	0.25	0.25	0.2	0.15
0.99	s		0.054	0.071	0.071	0.014	0.044	0.044	0.0	0.03	0.038
	g/y		0.27	0.1	0.1	0.26	0.1	0.1	0.25	0.1	0.02
	t		0.55	0.5	0.5	0.4	0.35	0.35	0.35	0.3	0.25
11	s		0.087	0.11	0.11	0.041	0.074	0.074	0.03	0.059	0.064
	g/y		0.25	0.1	0.1	0.26	0.09	0.09	0.24	0.09	0.03
	t		0.7	0.7	0.7	0.6	0.55	0.55	0.5	0.5	0.5
101	s		0.122	0.151	0.151	0.084	0.113	0.113	0.063	0.092	0.109
	g/y		0.25	0.11	0.11	0.27	0.08	0.08	0.25	0.1	0.0

Table 13.8   δ = 3

γ		0.3								
ε		0.5			1.0			1.5		
ν	φ	0.5	1.0	1.5	0.5	1.0	1.5	0.5	1.0	1.5
0.0	t	0.5	0.4	0.4	0.4	0.35	0.35	0.4	0.35	0.25
	s	0.023	0.012	0.012	0.0	0.0	0.0	0.0	0.0	0.0
	g/y	0.43	0.36	0.36	0.4	0.35	0.35	0.4	0.35	0.25
0.99	t	0.5	0.45	0.45	0.4	0.35	0.35	0.4	0.35	0.25
	s	0.023	0.028	0.028	0.0	0.0	0.0	0.0	0.0	0.0
	g/y	0.43	0.36	0.36	0.4	0.35	0.35	0.4	0.35	0.25
11	t	0.6	0.55	0.55	0.5	0.40	0.4	0.4	0.35	0.35
	s	0.055	0.058	0.050	0.022	0.018	0.018	0.0	0.0	0.02
	g/y	0.42	0.36	0.36	0.43	0.34	0.34	0.4	0.35	0.28
101	t	0.75	0.75	0.75	0.65	0.60	0.6	0.55	0.55	0.5
	s	0.117	0.104	0.104	0.06	0.071	0.071	0.036	0.048	0.063
	g/y	0.41	0.38	0.38	0.42	0.33	0.33	0.41	0.36	0.25

Table 13.9   δ = 3

γ		0.5								
ε		0.5			1.0			1.5		
ν	φ	0.5	1.0	1.5	0.5	1.0	1.5	0.5	1.0	1.5
0.0	t	0.6	0.6	0.6	0.55	0.55	0.55	0.55	0.55	0.55
	s	0.019	0.01	0.01	0.0	0.0	0.0	0.0	0.0	0.0
	g/y	0.54	0.57	0.57	0.55	0.55	0.55	0.55	0.55	0.55
0.99	t	0.6	0.6	0.6	0.55	0.55	0.55	0.55	0.55	0.55
	s	0.019	0.01	0.01	0.0	0.0	0.0	0.0	0.0	0.0
	g/y	0.54	0.57	0.57	0.55	0.55	0.55	0.55	0.55	0.55
11	t	0.65	0.65	0.65	0.55	0.55	0.55	0.55	0.55	0.55
	s	0.04	0.021	0.021	0.0	0.0	0.0	0.0	0.0	0.0
	g/y	0.52	0.58	0.58	0.55	0.55	0.55	0.55	0.55	0.55
101	t	0.75	0.8	0.8	0.65	0.65	0.65	0.55	0.6	0.6
	s	0.07	0.061	0.061	0.036	0.028	0.028	0.015	0.008	0.003
	g/y	0.52	0.6	0.6	0.52	0.55	0.55	0.5	0.57	0.57

consumption and government expenditure. We have allowed ϕ and ϵ to range over the three values 0.5, 1.0 and 1.5 while δ is fixed at the value 3 used in Table 13.6 and we have confined γ to the three values 0.1, 0.3 and 0.5. The results of our calculations are shown in Tables 13.7–13.9.

We can see from these tables that in the case where $\epsilon = 0.5$, for low values of $\gamma(0.1, 0.3)$, moving away from the CES case ($\phi = 0.5$) to the case $\phi = 1.0$ results in a cut in the optimal tax rate and a substantial reduction in the optimal percentage of GNP devoted to public expenditure. However, raising ϕ further to 1.5 does not result in any further change in the optimal tax rate and share of public expenditure. On the other hand, when $\gamma = 0.5$ raising ϕ to 1.0 now increases the optimal share of government expenditure for reasons similar to those given above. Once again, however, raising ϕ to 1.5 makes no further difference to the results.

This suggests that our results are sensitive to the CES assumption, at least over certain ranges of ϕ, and that there is scope for refining the calculations over narrower bands of the parameters, and narrower bands for the optimal tax rate.

SUMMARY

We have seen that when the benefits as well as the costs of government expenditure are introduced into the analysis of optimal income taxation, not only are the optimal tax rates altered but, more important, the particular way in which the results are affected depends crucially on the specification of how government expenditure enters the individual utility function. Thus, while Feldstein's arguments that allowing for the benefits of expenditure will reduce the optimal tax rate is correct for the case in which government expenditure is a perfect substitute for private expenditure, this is not the case when they are imperfect substitutes. In this latter case the effect on the optimal tax rate depends on the degree of substitutability and the degree of inequality aversion.

When the level of government expenditure is optimally chosen rather than exogenously imposed on the model, then some of the conclusions reached by Stern (1976) concerning the relationship between the optimal tax rate and the elasticity of substitution between consumption and leisure are also altered when the benefits of expenditure are recognised.

In the absence of hard evidence on what might be a plausible utility function to use when considering the benefits of government expenditure, we have had to employ purely illustrative functions, so the particular numbers we have generated for the optimal tax rates should be viewed in this light. Nevertheless our results suggest that in any empirical work to discover the nature of individual preferences for public expenditure particular care should be taken in specifying the functional form in as general a way as possible, since the particular specification can have a major bearing on the policy conclusion to be drawn.

APPENDIX

We have to find $\partial t/\partial g$ and $(1 + \partial s/\partial g)$ where t and s are solutions to the problem

$$\text{Max} \int_0^\infty V(n(1-t), s)f(n)dn$$

$$\text{s.t. } t \int_0^\infty nH(n(1-t), s)f(n)dn = s + g$$

This may be written as

$$\text{Max } \phi(t, s) \text{ s.t. } \psi(t, s) = s + g$$

which has first-order conditions

$$\phi_t = \lambda\psi_t$$
$$\phi_s = \lambda(\psi_s - 1)$$

Since $\phi_t < 0$, $\phi_s > 0$, we conclude that at the optimum $\psi_t < 0 \; (\psi_s - 1) > 0$.

Now differentiate the budget constraint totally with respect to g to obtain

$$\psi_t \frac{\partial t}{\partial g} + \psi_s \frac{\partial s}{\partial g} = \frac{\partial s}{\partial g} + 1$$

or, on re-arranging,

$$(1 + \partial s/\partial g)(\psi_s - 1) = \psi_s - \psi_t \, \partial t/\partial g$$

which proves that if $\partial t/\partial g > 0$ then $1 + \partial s/\partial g > 0$, as required.

NOTES: CHAPTER 13

1 When g includes all government expenditure on goods and services. (It may be noted that this is a wider definition of g than that adopted by Mirrlees (1978.)
2 This result is most easily seen from (29) where $V_3g = \gamma v$, $V_2c = \alpha v$ and, since $H = (\delta w - s)/(\delta w + w)$, $H_1 w + H_2 s = 0$.

Chapter 14

Macroeconomic Implications I

Income Taxation and Employment – An Integration of
Neo-classical and Keynesian Approaches

In this chapter and the next some of the macroeconomic implications of
our work are explored. The present chapter shows the implications of
incorporating the results from the microeconomic analysis of labour
supply into a standard macroeconomic model. The amounts of labour
actually employed, the full employment level of income and the levels of
unemployment are all altered relative to the standard model. These
differences in the model follow from the differences between the microeconomic treatment of labour supply and the standard macroeconomic
treatment.

First, in the standard microeconomic neo-classical treatment[1], individuals are assumed to maximise their satisfaction given certain
preferences, as for example between real consumption goods and
leisure, and given their budget constraints which depend among other
things on a *net* real wage rate. In the standard Keynesian macroeconomic treatment equilibrium in the labour market occurs where the
aggregate supply curve of labour intersects the aggregate demand curve
for labour. While it is typically *not* emphasised, this aggregate supply
curve for labour shows the amount of labour that will be supplied at
various *gross* wage rates (which are sometimes assumed to be money
wages and sometimes real wages – see Branson, 1972).

Another inconsistency between the micro- and macroeconomic treatments of taxation and labour supply is in the assumption(s) about the
elasticity of labour supply. Microeconomic treatments consider both the
possibility that the individual's supply curve of labour is positively
sloped (i.e. that elasticity is greater than zero) and the possibility that the
individual supply curve is negatively sloped (elasticity less than zero).
Macroeconomic treatments often assume that the aggregate supply of
labour has a positive elasticity.[2]

A final difference between the micro- and macro-treatments is that textbook macro-treatments are typically confined to very simple assumptions about the nature of the tax systems (e.g. that there is a proportional income tax). Microeconomic treatments, on the other hand, consider the effects of more complex tax systems (e.g. those that are progressive).

In this chapter we show the effects of integrating these three aspects into a static macroeconomic model familiar to readers of standard macroeconomic textbooks. The macroeconomic model that is used is thought to be fairly representative of Keynesian models in standard intermediate textbooks. It is not suggested that such models are especially realistic, but a fully realistic model is not necessary to the argument, which is designed to incorporate some missing elements into a familiar theoretical structure and thereby increase the realism of the models. Section I incorporates the effects of assuming that labour supply depends on the net rather than the gross wage assuming a positive elasticity of supply and a proportional income tax. The possibility of a negative elasticity of labour supply is considered in Section II, where the assumption of proportional taxes is retained. In Section III we look at the macroeconomic implications of non-proportional taxes, and in Section IV the combined results from Sections I, II and III are summarised.

In order to keep the analysis as simple as possible we assume throughout that:

(1) Individuals' utility depends on net income and leisure.
(2) All variables (except the price level) are measured in real terms. In particular it should be noted that it is assumed that the supply of labour depends on the real net wage.[3]
(3) There is a fixed money wage W_0 .[4]
(4) At the initial price level, P_0, the real wage W_0/P_0 is above the full employment level.
(5) The government has decided to eliminate the resulting unemployment by a cut in income taxation.
(6) The government is able to calculate the required reduction in income taxation accurately[5] and is thus able to eliminate unemployment.
(7) When the demand for labour is less than the supply of labour it is assumed that the actual level of employment is determined by the demand for labour. It is also assumed that when there is disequilibrium in the labour market goods markets reach a position of (constrained) equilibrium.
(8) There are no other restrictions on labour supply.
(9) The supply of labour is measured in hours.

(10) All individuals have the same preferences and the same wage rate, which means that aggregate labour supply is the supply of a representative individual times the number of individuals.

(11) Unemployment is any excess of hours supplied over hours demanded at the current net wage rate.

(12) Income and leisure are both normal goods (this is consistent with the empirical evidence presented).

I INCORPORATION OF TAXATION AND LABOUR SUPPLY

The purpose of this section is to show how the incorporation of taxation and labour supply can affect a familiar macroeconomical model. It is assumed throughout this section that the tax under consideration is a proportional income tax.

The model is represented graphically in Figure 14.1, part (a) which has real national income on the vertical axis and the level of prices on the horizontal axis, contains aggregate supply[6] *(AS)* and demand curves[7]

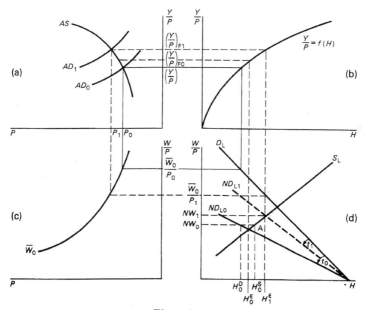

Figure 14.1

(AD) and shows the equilibrium level of output and prices. Part (b), with output on the vertical axis and labour hours on the horizontal axis, shows the short-run production function, which is assumed to exhibit diminishing returns. Part (c), with real wages on the vertical axis and prices on the horizontal axis, shows the relationship between real wages and prices given the fixed money wage.

Part (d) represents the labour market. The horizontal axis shows total hours of labour supplied and *the vertical axis represents both gross and net real-wage rates*. The (derived) demand curve for labour is shown as D_L. This (gross) demand curve for labour shows the amount of labour that employers will wish to hire and the gross wage rate is the cost to the employer of hiring various amounts of labour. When there is tax on income employees do not receive the gross wage, as part of this wage or income is paid in income taxation. With a proportional income tax, the income tax deduction will be a constant proportion of the gross wage irrespective of either the level of the gross wage or the number of hours worked. Thus if the proportional tax rate is t_0, the net of tax demand curve for labour will be ND_{L0}.

We know from standard microeconomics that it is assumed that the supply of labour depends on the net wage rate, which means that the labour market equilibrium would occur where S_L and ND_{L0} intersect at H_0^E hours. Thus, while the demand for labour depends on the gross wage, the supply of labour depends on the net wage. This means that labour market equilibrium occurs where the supply of labour is equal to the net wage rate.

With the current level of wages ($\overline{W}_0$) and of prices (P_0), the real gross wage is $\overline{W}_0/P_0$. At this gross wage the demand for labour is H_0^E and, by assumption, that is the actual level of employment as well. When the gross wage is $\overline{W}_0/P_0$ it can be seen that the net wage is NW_0. With a net wage of NW_0 the supply of labour is H_0^S. This means that with a gross wage of W_0/P_0 and a net wage of NW_0 there will be unemployment amounting to H_0^S less H_0^D. It is assumed that the government decides to eliminate unemployment by reducing the (proportional) income tax. By assumption the reduction in income tax will just eliminate the unemployment. This cut in the tax rate will have both supply and demand effects. The cut will increase the net demand curve from ND_{L0} to ND_{L1}. This will raise the equilibrium level of employment from H_0^E to H_1^E. It will also raise the amount of labour supplied from H_0^S to H_1^E. On the demand side, the cut in tax raises disposable incomes, which increases the demand for goods[8]; and with appropriate multiplier effects this will increase the level of aggregate demand from AD_0 to AD_1.

It can be seen from part (a) that this increase in aggregate demand will raise the full employment level of income from $(Y/P)_{F0}$ to $(Y/P)_{F1}$ and the equilibrium level of prices from P_0 to P_1. From part (b) it can be seen that the demand for labour will increase. That is to say there will be a movement down the gross demand curve for labour. It can be seen that the increase in the amount of labour demanded is from H_0^D to H_1^E. From part (c) it may be seen that with the money wage fixed at $\overline{W}_0$ the increase in the price level reduces the real wage to $\overline{W}_0/P_1$. This cut in the gross real wage is consistent with the increase in the demand for labour to H_1^E. It may be noted that, while the *gross* real wage falls, the *net* real wage *rises*. Thus, from the employer's point of view the expansion in employment is associated with a falling wage, while from the employee's point of view the expansion in employment is brought about by an increase in the real wage. It also seems highly probable that real disposable income will rise (the only possible exception is if the labour supply curve bent backwards very sharply).

II NEGATIVE ELASTICITY OF LABOUR SUPPLY

The situation is rather different when the labour supply curve is negatively sloped. The position may be analyzed with the aid of Figure 14.2 which is identical to Figure 14.1 except for the slope of the labour supply curve. The labour supply curve in Figure 14.2 (d) is constructed so that the initial level of employment is the same as in Figure 14.1 (d). Thus S_L in Figure 14.2 (d) passes through the point A so that in both cases the initial level of unemployment is $H_0^S - H_0^D$. The cut in the tax rate raises the net of tax demand curve from ND_{L0} to ND_{L1} and the (actual) net wage rises from NW_0 to NW_1. This reduces the equilibrium supply of labour from H_0^F to H_1^F. It also reduces the amount of labour supplied at the current net wage rate. When, originally, the net wage was NW_0 the amount of labour supplied was H_0^S. When the net wage rises to NW_1 the amount of labour supplied falls to H_1^E.

On the demand side, however, the effects are as before. The cut in tax raises aggregate demand, which raises the equilibrium levels of income and of price in Figure 14.2 (a). This raises the demand for labour in part (b) and reduces the gross real wage in part (c) so that the demand for labour rises to H_1^E in part (d). Thus, with a negatively sloped supply curve, the supply effects tend to reduce unemployment, and hence the actual increase in employment is due entirely to the demand effect.

It has been assumed that the government is able to calculate the

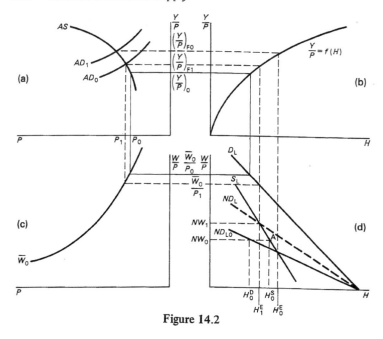

Figure 14.2

required tax cut so that unemployment is eliminated in both cases. However, the effects of the tax cut differ in most other respects. The key to the difference is that, with a positively sloped supply curve, the equilibrium level of employment rises, while with a negatively sloped supply curve the equilibrium level of employment falls. Thus the actual level of employment rises by more with a positively sloped supply curve than it does with a negatively sloped supply curve. A higher level of employment means a higher level of real income when the supply curve is positively sloped. This higher level of real income can be achieved only by a lower gross real wage. With a given money wage a lower gross real wage means higher prices. Thus the achievement of full employment requires a larger rise in prices when the supply curve is positively sloped.

III MACROECONOMIC IMPLICATIONS OF NON-PROPORTIONAL TAXES

In this section we consider the macroeconomic effects of non-proportional taxes by examining the implications of changes in allowances in

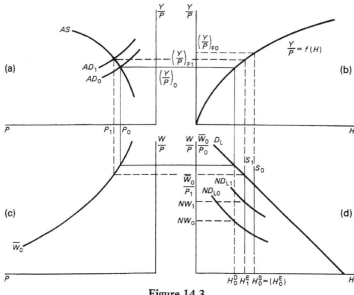

Figure 14.3

basic rates in the UK tax structure. It is shown in Brown (1980) Chapter 2 that an increase in allowances will shift the supply curve of labour in the direction of less work, and a cut in the basic tax rate will shift the supply curve in the direction of more work. Non-proportional taxes will also affect the net of tax demand curve for labour. With the non-proportional taxes the net of tax demand curve will no longer be a straight line (as with a proportional tax) but instead will be a curved line of the sort shown in Figures 14.3 and 14.4 where for convenience we have assumed that the supply curve of labour is vertical.

An increase in allowances will cause the net demand curve to shift up from ND_{L0} to ND_{L1} in Figure 14.3 and will cause the supply curve to shift to the *left* (the direction of less work) to S_{L1} (for the reasons explained in Brown 1980). The important consequence in this case is that the leftward shift in the supply curve *reduces* the equilibrium employment level to H_1^E and *reduces* the full employment level of income from $(Y/P)_{F0}$ to $(Y/P)_{F1}$. A cut in the rate tax, on the other hand, will cause the supply curve to shift to the *right*, to S_{L1} in Figure 14.4. The shift of the net demand curve to ND_{L1} will *increase* the equilibrium level of income from $(Y/P)_{F0}$ to $(Y/P)_{F1}$.

The argument could be easily extended to include supply curves with

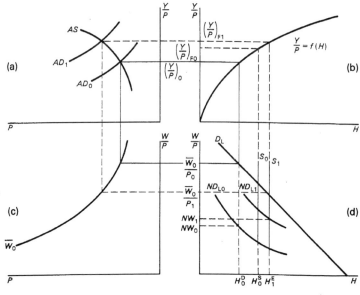

Figure 14.4

positive and negative slopes. The essential point is that an increase in the exemption level shifts the supply curve to the left, reducing the full employment level of income relative to the level determined by the original supply curve, while a reduction in the tax rate shifts the supply curve to the right, increasing the full employment level relative to the original supply curve.

IV SUMMARY

It has been demonstrated that a change in income taxation will change both the actual level of employment and the full employment level. Thus a tax change designed to bring the economy to a particular full employment target may cause that target to shift. The recognition of this interaction between policy instruments and policy goals is perhaps the most important practical implication of the integration of the neoclassical and Keynesian approaches. A cut in taxation may either increase or decrease the full employment level of income depending on the elasticity of labour supply, on the one hand, and the nature of the tax

Table 14.1 *Effect of a tax cut on the full employment level of income*

Nature of effect from tax cut	*Elasticity of labour supply*		
	Positive	*Zero*	*Negative*
Positive income effect (e.g. increase in exemption level	Uncertain	Falls	Falls
Pure price effect (e.g. cut in proportional tax rate)	Rises	No change	Falls
Price effect plus negative income effect (e.g. cut in basic tax rate)	Rises	Rises	Uncertain

cut, on the other. These effects are summarised in Table 14.1. If we knew the elasticity of labour supply we could then predict the direction of the effect of different types of tax changes in the level of national income. If all the underlying relationships in the model were fully known it should also be possible to predict the amount by which the actual and full employment levels of income would change.

NOTES: CHAPTER 14

1   As the microeconomic treatment of taxation and labour supply is in the neo-classical tradition, the terms neo-classical and microeconomic are used more or less interchangeably and similarly the 'macroeconomic' and 'Keynesian' are used as near synonyms for the present purpose.

2   This neglect of negative supply elasticities at the macro-level is perhaps even more surprising given the increasing evidence that individual price elasticities are negative. However, in defence of the standard assumption it should be pointed out both that elasticity estimates for married women are typically positive and that the simple extrapolation from the micro- to the macro-level is complicated when labour supply decisions are made on a household rather than an individual basis.

3   The reader is referred to Branson (1972) for a discussion of the implications of assuming that labour supply depends on the money wage rather than the real wage.

4   For alternative assumptions the reader is again referred to Branson (1972).

5   If it cannot, then of course there may be over-full employment or unemployment after the tax cut.

6   The aggregate supply curve is derived from the production function in part (b), the demand for labour in part (d), and the fixed money wage is part (c).

7   The aggregate demand curve is assumed to be derived from a standard *IS/LM* curve.

8   Changes in tax receipts (and government expenditure) shift the *IS* curve and as a consequence the AD curve.

Chapter 15

Macroeconomic Implications II
Labour Supply and Fiscal Policy in a Disequilibrium Model

INTRODUCTION

An analysis of the macroeconomic effects of changes in income tax parameters through their effect on the labour market will, to a large extent, be concerned with the concept of equilibrium in the labour market and departures from it. In order to identify such equilibrium and disequilibrium situations one must have a frame of reference for the concept of 'full' employment and the nature and significance of unemployment. The particular construction of the macroeconomic model which is analysed will largely define such a phenomenon. In the classical model[1] unemployment is viewed as being 'voluntary' and the labour market equilibrium condition is satisfied where demand for workers is equated with the supply of workers. Keynes' critique of the classical theory showed that involuntary unemployment can exist and that a state of full employment exists only in the absence of involuntary unemployment. The controversy which followed Keynes' diagnosis of the sources of unemployment led to a 'neo-classical synthesis' which challenged the Keynesian model and maintained that involuntary unemployment can only be a long-run phenomenon if money wage rates and prices are downwardly rigid. In all of this analysis unemployment is said to occur only where individuals are entirely without work. Unemployment in terms of workers being employed for fewer hours than they wish is generally neglected. A more promising paradigm for the study of unemployment has developed however from a reappraisal of Keynes' theory, which provides new foundations for macroeconomic analysis. The new analysis is in terms of 'constrained' general equilibrium or general disequilibrium.

Several 'macroeconomic disequilibrium' models have been developed recently (e.g. those by Barro and Grossman, 1976, Malinvaud, 1977, and

223

Muellbauer and Portes, 1978 which emphasise the failure of prices to adjust quickly to produce a Walrasian equilibrium, so that a temporary equilibrium is established via the adjustment of quantities. A discussion of such a model is presented here with the intention of looking more closely at the role of fiscal policy and to give rather more consideration to the assumptions regarding labour supply than hitherto.

The rest of the chapter proceeds as follows: Section I discusses the antecedents of the modern reappraisal of Keynesian theory; Section II sets out the basic model; Section III elaborates on the possible types of equilibria largely in terms of Muellbauer and Portes' 'double wedge' diagram approach. Comparative statics are discussed in Section IV where discrete switching between regimes is assumed through the use of fiscal policy. Section V develops Ehemann's (1974) argument that in general a single policy instrument is usually unable to bring both markets to Walrasian equilibrium simultaneously. Also an attempt is made to show that assumptions made regarding the labour market affect the direction of use of fiscal policy. Section VI briefly introduces a more progressive tax structure, while Section VII concludes the chapter.

I ANTECEDENTS[2]

The antecedents of the modern reappraisal of Keynesian theory stems from the work of Clower (1965) who introduced the distinction between 'notional' and 'effective' equilibrium. Clower was able to make the distinction by pointing out that, in the absence of a Walrasian auctioneer, trade would typically take place at non-Walrasian prices. Moreover, effective excess demand functions would not only depend on the vector of relative prices but also on the vector of actual trades. The implications of this analysis for the theory of employment were not fully developed however, and it was left to Leijonhufvud (1968) to extend and elaborate on the theme suggested by Clower.

As Leijonhufvud (1968, p.81) notes, Clower emphasises that the excess demand relations of the conventional general equilibrium model are based on the assumption that all traders can buy and sell whatever quantities they desire at the market prices at which trading actually takes place. In considering his purchases or sales of a particular good for any announced vector of prices the trader is supposed to face infinitely elastic supply and demand functions in all markets. His trading plans are drawn up so that the total value of his purchases will be financed by the total value of his sales and on the presumption that he will be able to realize any sales he desires at the announced price vector. Excess demand schedules derived in this manner Clower terms 'notional' excess demand functions.

All the notional transactions planned in this way can be carried out *only if* all markets clear at the price vector actually prevailing during trading. If actual demand falls short of notional supply in some markets, some suppliers in those markets find that they cannot finance their notional demands in other markets in the way originally planned. They must therefore curtail their demands in the latter markets. Market excess demand functions which take into account constraints on the transactions quantities that people expect to be able to realize are termed 'effective' excess demand functions.

Clower argues that Walras' Law, although valid as usual with reference to notional market excess demands, is in general irrelevant to any but 'full' employment situations. To show this Clower distinguishes between Walras' Law and Say's Law. 'The familiar household budget constraint ... asserts ... that no transactor consciously plans to purchase units of any commodity without at the same time planning to finance the purchases either from profit receipts or from the sale of units of some other commodity' (Clower, 1965, p. 16). It follows that the individual budget has the property that the value of net demand and supply will sum to zero. This is essentially Say's Law. The quantities entering into this budget are 'planned' by an individual who has not considered the possibility that, at the 'given' prices he may not succeed in selling all he wants to (in a deflationary disequilibrium) or buying all he wants to (in an inflationary disequilibrium). The values of these notional net demands and supplies sum to zero. If everyone falls into this category, Walras' Law, in Clower's sense, is obtained for the system as a whole.

An important departure from the Walrasian analysis is to enquire of the consequences of the Walrasian pricetaker failing to realize some of his notional sales. One problem, as Leijonhufvud (1968, p.84) puts it, is: 'who is ever going to know what his notional demand quantities were?' If, in fact, no one knows then the notional demands do not provide the relevant market signals, as the information which traders acquire is based primarily on the actually realized exchanges. Transactors with un-employed resources will generally reduce their expenditures in other markets so effective demands are reduced also in markets on which the initial disturbance may have had no impact. Unemployed resources emerge in these markets also and the search instituted by unemployed workers and producers with excess capacity will yield information on effective demands and not on notional demands. 'The "multiplier" repercussions thus set in motion make the information acquired "dated" even while it is being gathered' (Leijonhufvud, 1968, p. 85).

The conclusion is that the Walrasian portrayal of the situation is irrelevant to the movement of the Keynesian system because in that system all exchanges involve money on one side of the transaction – workers looking for jobs demand money, not commodities. Their notional demand for commodities is not communicated to producers; being unable to perceive this potential demand for their products, producers will be unwilling to absorb the excess supply of labour at a wage corresponding to the real wage that would 'solve' the Walrasian system. The fact that there exists a potential barter bargain of goods for labour services that would be mutually agreeable to producers as a group and labour as a group is irrelevant to the motion of the system. In summary, in economies relying on a means of payment, the excess demand for wage goods corresponding to an excess supply of labour is merely 'notional'; it is not communicated to employers as effective demand for output. 'The resulting miseries are "involuntary" all around' (Leijonhufvud, 1968, p.98).

The essence of Leijonhufvud's interpretation of Keynes is that 'what Keynes calls equilibrium should be viewed as persistent disequilibrium, and what appears to be comparative statics is really shrewd and incisive if awkward, dynamic, analysis' (Tobin, 1972, p.4). Consequently involuntary unemployment means that labour markets are not in equilibrium.

As indicated at the beginning of this section the conceptual breakthrough made by Clower and amplified by Leijonhufvud form the antecedents of more recent developments in the theory of employment couched in terms of a constrained general equilibrium. A fundamental feature of the general disequilibrium class of models is the assumption of voluntary exchange so that on each market the quantity traded is the minimum of effective demand and effective supply. This means that if prices are assumed sticky and so fail to adjust, the 'short' side of the market is the amount actually transacted and the 'long' side is rationed. This leads to the distinction between notional and effective demands and supplies as discussed above. The notional functions are derived assuming no quantity constraints on the economic agents, that is, given the wage-price vector a Walrasian equilibrium is assumed. Where transactors do face quantity constraints in a particular market, however, there is a switch from the notional (or unconstrained) to the effective (or constrained) functional form in other markets. Assuming two markets – one for goods, the other for labour – with positive excess demand in the labour market, then the actual demand for goods is the notional unconstrained demand function; when there is excess supply of labour there is a switch to the quantity-constrained effective demand for goods, one argument of which is the quantity of labour actually sold. This switching between functional forms also applies to the supply of goods and to the supply of and demand for labour. The switching conditions are the essence of the Clower-Patinkin[3] 'dual decision hypothesis'.

Models which have been developed based on this approach recognise different equilibria regimes and this course is followed below. Fiscal policy is studied by the comparative static method which involves discrete switching between regimes. The model presented is extremely close in design to that of Muellbauer and Portes (1978)[4] (hereafter M & P) with the intention of exploiting their 'double wedge' diagram in the comparative static approach, though it does neglect an important refinement of M & P in that, to keep things as simple as possible, it ignores expectations.[5] Inelastic expectations are assumed from the outset and the two-period analysis of M & P is not elaborated here (which does not mean the model is atemporal in design).

The models produced recently have tended to neglect the role of direct taxation of labour income and usually assume fiscal policy operates solely via changes in autonomous expenditure. With this in mind the model below incorporates a tax on earned income in a fairly straightforward manner; this means that fiscal policy may operate by changes in both government spending and by manipulation of the tax rate. Moreover, little regard is usually given to the likely outcome of policy changes by making contrasting assumptions with respect to the labour market. It has been usual to assume that the substitution effect in labour supply dominates the income effect, thus ruling out a backward bending supply curve of labour. Barro and Grossman (1976), Malinvaud (1977), M & P (1978) and Dixit (1978) all make this assumption. Ehemann (1974) is an exception – he assumes a negative relation between the wage rate and labour supply, basing his assumption on empirical evidence. The following discussion attempts to analyse the consequences for fiscal policy of making different assumptions with regard to labour supply.

II THE MODEL

The assumptions of the model largely follow those of other models already referred to. It is assumed there is a 'fix-price' economy in the sense of Hicks (1965) and that there are three types of goods: commodities, labour and money, and three economic agents: the government, households and firms. It is assumed that all households are identical as are all firms, so a particular firm or household is representative of the aggregate number of firms or households.[6] Money balances are held by households and firms but there are no other financial assets in the model; this implies that stabilization policy must be in the form of fiscal policy.[7]

The rest of this section considers the notional and effective functions of the economic agents.

The government

A part of total output, y, is demanded by the government, which it finances from a proportional tax, t, on the earned income of labour and by the issue of money when a deficit occurs. The budget constraint of the government is thus:

$$gd = T + ms \tag{1}$$

where gd is the government's notional demand for commodities; T is the sum of tax revenue accruing to the government and ms is the change in the money stock required to finance any deficit. (It may of course be zero in the balanced budget case.) For the most part government behaviour is exogenously determined – it is assumed though that whenever the government can act, via fiscal policy, to bring about an 'improved' equilibrium it will choose to do so. It can be seen that the policy tools available to the government are changes in government demand (gd) and changes in the rate of taxation on earned income t. It is further assumed that the government is a preferred trading partner in that it is never rationed. This means the government is always able to purchase any amount it desires (as long as $gd \leq y$).

Households

Households are assumed to maximise utility where the utility function is of the form

$$U = U(c, \ell, m) \tag{2}$$

where c is the amount of commodities consumed, ℓ is the amount of labour supplied and m the amount of money carried forward. As Dixit (1978, p.394) points out, this is a derived utility function, where the amounts of future consumption and labour have been optimised. The parameters of this optimization, for example, expected future prices, wages, employment prospects and profit distribution should therefore be included as arguments in U. Matters are simplified by assuming this is done, and giving households and firms inelastic expectations in the sense that the established equilibrium is expected to persist at least into the next period.

To further simplify matters we take the decisions of one household as representative of all households. Labour is assumed homogeneous and each labour unit is free to determine the optimum number of hours it wishes to work when it is not rationed on the labour market. Each household faces a wage rate w, a proportional tax rate t (where the average and marginal rates of tax are the same at rate t) on earned income, and has an initial holding of money balances mo. The budget constraint is

$$pc + m = \ell w(1-t) + mo \tag{3}$$

where p is the price level. Maximisation gives the notional demand functions for commodities and money and notional supply function for labour:

$$cd = cd(p, w(1-t), mo) \tag{4}$$

$$md = md(p, w(1-t), mo) \tag{5}$$

$$\ell s = \ell s(p, w(1-t), mo) \tag{6}$$

An increase in mo will lead to a rise in cd. Changes in mo are assumed to have a pure income effect on labour supply so that increases in money holdings lead to a fall in the notional supply of labour at given wage rate w.

The response of labour supply to a change in the wage rate is more complicated. In the model it is assumed that the wage rate w is fixed, so the only way to influence the rate of earned income per period of time is by manipulating the tax rate t. It is well known that *a priori* the effect of a change in the real wage rate is indeterminate, the outcome depending on the relative strengths of the substitution effect and the income effect. Most models take one effect to be dominant, as mentioned above; here it is proposed to analyse two possible cases. If the substitution effect outweighs the income effect there will be a positivity sloped labour supply function, that is, an increase in real earnings per time period generates an increase in labour supply. The converse is the case where the income effect outweighs the substitution effect. These are the two cases that will be considered; we ignore a third possibility - a perfectly inelastic supply function with respect to the wage rate.

Firms

The objective of firms is to maximise profits, and to this end they employ labour to produce commodities. All firms are assumed to be equally efficient in production. They may hold money balances and inventories but do not pay any taxes. Output is sold to both government and households although, as indicated, the government is a preferred customer. Profit is distributed to households during the next time period.

If the firm perceives it can sell all the output it supplies and obtain all the labour which it demands at the existing wage–price vector, then profits are given by:

$$\pi = ys - w\ell d \tag{7}$$

The firms notional demand for labour is assumed to be a function of the wage rate:

$$\ell d = \ell d(w) \tag{8}$$

where

$$\ell d' < 0$$

Total output ys is assumed to be a function not only of labour input but also of government demand:

$$ys = F(\ell d(w), g) = ys(w,g) \tag{9}$$

where

$$g = gd \text{ and } ys_w < 0, ys_g > 0$$

The budget constraint of the firm is:

$$yp = w\ell + mo \tag{10}$$

III TYPES OF EQUILIBRIA

By assuming that all households are identical and that when they are rationed they are identically rationed (and analogously for firms) it is possible to aggregate the behavioural functions of individual households and firms. The complete model can then be set out algebraically as follows (a bar over a variable or function denotes effective demand or supply).

$$cd = \begin{cases} cd = cd(p, w(1-t), mo) & (4) \text{ if } \ell = \ell s \leqslant \ell d \\ \overline{cd} = \overline{cd}(p, w\ell(1-t), mo) & (11) \text{ if } \ell s > \ell d = \ell \end{cases}$$

$$cs = \begin{cases} ys = ys(w,g) & (9) \text{ if } \ell s \geqslant \ell d = \ell \\ \overline{ys} = \overline{ys}(\ell,g) & (12) \text{ if } \ell = \ell s \leqslant \ell d \end{cases}$$

$$c = \quad \min(cd,cs)$$

$$\ell d = \begin{cases} \ell d = \ell d(w) & (8) \text{ if } c = cs \leqslant cd \\ \overline{\ell d} = \overline{\ell d}(y,g) & (13) \text{ if } cs > cd = c \end{cases}$$

$$\ell s = \begin{cases} \ell s = \ell s(p,w(1-t), mo) & (6) \text{ if } cs \geqslant cd = c \\ \overline{\ell s} = \overline{\ell s}(w(1-t), mo - pc) & (14) \text{ if } c = cs < cd \end{cases}$$

$$\ell = \quad \min(\ell d, \ell s)$$

Disregarding borderline cases[8] the model allows four possible constraint regimes:

$$K = \begin{cases} c = \overline{cd} < cs \\ \ell = \overline{\ell d} < \ell s \end{cases}$$

$$R = \begin{cases} c = \overline{cs} < cd \\ \ell = \overline{\ell s} < \ell d \end{cases}$$

$$C = \begin{cases} c = cs < \overline{cd} \\ \ell = \ell d < \overline{\ell s} \end{cases}$$

$$U = \begin{cases} c = cd < \overline{cs} \\ \ell = \ell s < \overline{\ell d} \end{cases}$$

The rest of this section sets out the geometrical analysis of the model as formulated by M & P (1978). The relative slopes assumed for the households' and firms' functions in the diagrams are discussed by M & P (1978, section 5), who point out that they reflect assumptions required to get existence, uniqueness and stability of the various quantity-constrained equilibria.

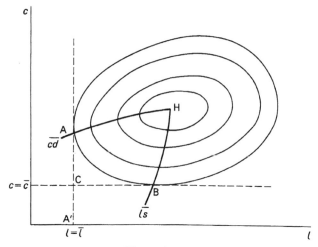

Figure 15.1

Figure 15.1 represents an example of the generalised dual-decision process for the household. The ellipses are iso-utility contours in commodity–labour space. They are obtained by substituting the budget constraint of the household into the objective function (see M & P, 1978, p. 798).[9]

The point H corresponds to the maximum value of the objective function consistent with the budget constraint, that is, it is the optimal point when no rationing is imposed and represents the highest attainable utility. The co-ordinates of H are the unrationed (notional) commodity demand and labour supply functions: (4) and (6).

Assume that labour is rationed through $\ell \leqslant \bar{\ell}$, as shown in Figure 15.1 by the dotted line tangential to an indifference curve at A. The optimal consumption level is given by AA$'$. Shifting the ℓ constraint to the right traces out the labour-rationed goods demand function (11) where $\ell < \ell s$. Similarly by shifting the goods-rationed level $c \leqslant \bar{c}$ and tracing out points of tangency such as B with the indifference curves, the commodity-rationed labour supply function (14) is obtained.

If the goods ration is $c \leqslant \bar{c}$ and the labour ration is $\ell \leqslant \bar{\ell}$, the household is at a point such as C. If both constraints are binding the household is accumulating money balances. These money balances are not without utility; if they were labour supply would be cut so that the labour ration would no longer be effective.

At point H the labour-rationed consumption function and the goods-rationed labour supply function meet. So the labour-rationed consumption function (11) coincides with the unrationed function (4) when the labour-rationed $\bar{\ell}$ is replaced by the unrationed labour supply (6). Similarly the goods-rationed labour supply function (14) coincides with the unrationed function (6) when the goods ration $\bar{c}$ is replaced by the unrationed goods demand (4).

The geometric discussion of the firm parallels that of the household. Substituting the constraint into the objective function allows the firms' profits to be expressed as a function of sales and either output or employment. In sales–labour space the iso-profit contours are shown in Figure 15.2. The point F is the optimal point when there is no rationing. The co-ordinates of F are the unrationed supply function of goods (9) and the unrationed demand function for labour (8). The locus labelled $\overline{\ell d}\,(c)$ shows the sales-rationed labour demand function of the firm (13). The locus $\overline{ys}\,(\ell)$ represents the labour-rationed supply function of the firm (12).

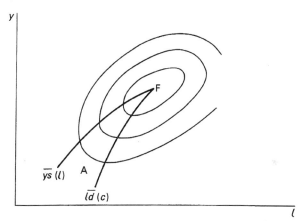

Figure 15.2

The constraint regime which arises when the firm is rationed in both markets is shown by a point such as A in Figure 15.2. This double constraint requires the assumption that current profits are used to finance inventory accumulation. This assumption is required otherwise the firm would cut production and reduce its demand for labour and so not find itself rationed in the labour market. Translating Figure 15.2 into commodity-labour space and juxtaposing it with Figure 15.1 gives the Walrasian equilibrium represented in Figure 15.3, where W is a point at

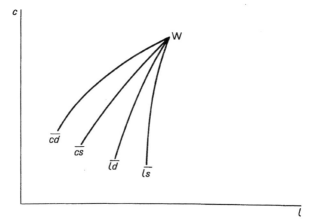

Figure 15.3

which points F and H coincide. By using this 'double wedge' diagrammatic framework it is possible to identify the alternative constraint regimes. These are considered in a discussion of comparative statics in the following section.

IV COMPARATIVE STATICS

This section considers some of the comparative static elements of the model in the context of fiscal policy. The government is able to change the level of demand for commodities g and to alter the tax rate t. The way in which the government may 'improve' a quantity-constrained equilibrium by each of these policy variables will be considered below.

Keynesian unemployment

Keynesian unemployment equilibrium with excess effective supply in both markets is realised as an intersection of the labour-constrained demand function for consumption goods and the sales-constrained demand function for labour, as shown in Figure 15.4 at point K.

The government's budget constraint is given by equation (1):

$$gd = T + ms$$

If the government wishes to increase its notional demand for commodities without altering the tax rate then an increase in g must be

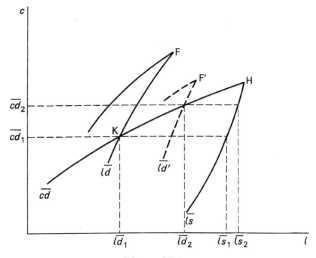

Figure 15.4

brought about by an increase in *ms*. (As stated at the beginning of
Section II, monetary policy plays no active part in this model.) An
increase in government demand will lead to an increase in the demand
for final output and so lead to a rise in the effective demand for labour
by firms. In effect, as M & P (1978, p. 812) point out, an increase in
government expenditure shifts the F-system down and the intersection
of $\overline{\ell d}$ with $\overline{cd}$ moves up and to the right along $\overline{cd}$. The usual demand
multiplier operates and the result is shown in Figure 15.4. It may be
seen from this figure that the excess effective supply of labour falls
from $\overline{\ell d}_1 - \overline{\ell s}_1$ to $\overline{\ell d}_2 - \overline{\ell s}_2$. Although the effective supply of labour
increases from $\overline{\ell s}_1$ to $\overline{\ell s}_2$ the element of involuntary unemployment is
reduced with an increase in government demand.

The alternative fiscal policy tool available to the government is to
change the proportional tax rate *t*. A change in *t* effectively changes the
wage rate facing the household. The actual wage paid by the firm is
unaltered by a change in *t*, so the F-system is unaffected by a change in
the tax rate. Assuming that the substitution effect dominates the income
effect in labour supply, a fall in *t* would cause the $\overline{\ell s}$ function to shift to
the right. For any given level of quantity constraint on the commodity
market a higher level of labour supply will now be forthcoming. The $\overline{cd}$
function will, however, shift upwards and to the left as can be seen from
equation (11), as with a fall in *t* the term $w\ell(1-t)$ increases. This will

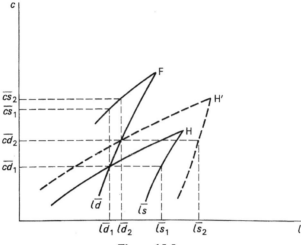

Figure 15.5

then result in an expansion of the H 'wedge' and a movement of the
point H to the right (as shown in Figure 15.5).

It may be seen that excess effective supply on the goods market is
reduced, but the result is rather more ambiguous with respect to the
labour market. The effective demand for labour has risen from $\overline{ld}_1$ to $\overline{ld}_2$
and so a greater level of employment is being experienced. At the same
time however there has been a shift in the effective labour supply

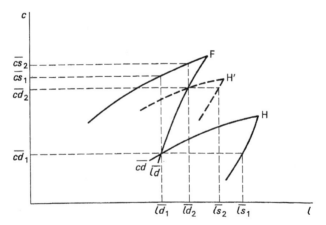

Figure 15.6

function, which results in a greater level of excess effective supply of labour. The final result is that rationing is intensified on the labour market.

Changing the assumption with regard to the labour market so that we now assume the income effect dominates the substitution effect in labour supply a different outcome is to be expected. Following a reduction in t, for the reason outlined above, the $\overline{cd}$ function will shift upwards. Given the assumption with regard to the labour market the $\overline{\ell s}$ function will also be shifted upwards and to the left, showing a fall in the amount of labour offered at each level of constrained labour supply. Consequently the H system will be displaced upwards to the left, as shown in Figure 15.6, where it may be seen that excess effective supplies in both markets are reduced.

Repressed inflation

Repressed inflation with excess effective demand in both markets is realised as an intersection of the consumption-goods-constrained supply function for labour and the labour-constrained function for consumption goods, as shown in Figure 15.7 at point R.

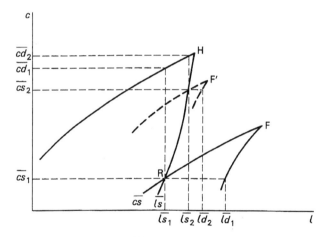

Figure 15.7

The repressed inflation regime is often considered to be the converse of Keynesian unemployment so the orthodox recommended fiscal policy would be a reduction in g and an increase in t. Analogous with the Keynesian unemployment case a fall in gd will shift the F-system upwards to the left, so that the intersection of $\overline{\ell s}$ with $\overline{cs}$ moves up along the $\bar{\ell s}$ locus. This will result in a fall in the excess effective demand for goods, as shown in Figure 15.7. The easing of the constraint on the goods market leads to an increase in the goods-constrained labour supply as shown by the move from the original equilibrium of $\bar{\ell s}_1$ to the new equilibrium of $\bar{\ell s}_2$. Following a fall in g the excess effective demand for labour declines (as does the voluntary element of unemployment).

Assuming that gd remains unchanged, a rise in t under the assumption that the substitution effect dominates the income effect in labour supply will cause a shift of the $\bar{\ell s}$ function to the left. Thus, at any given level of commodity demand less labour will be supplied. The rise in the tax rate and the fall in labour supply will tend to shift the $\bar{cd}$ locus downwards (see equation (11)). The net result is that the H 'wedge' will contract, as shown in Figure 15.8, with the H system moving downwards to the left. An increase in the tax rate causes the effective demand for goods to fall, but there is also a fall in the constrained supply of goods, In Figure 15.8 this is not as great as the fall in demand so the extent of excess effective demand is eased on the goods market. It would be possible though for the effective supply of goods to fall by a greater extent than the fall in effective demand, thereby exacerbating the position in the goods market. In the labour market, although there is a fall in the level of effective demand for labour from $\bar{\ell d}_1$ to $\bar{\ell d}_2$ there is in fact an increase in the excess effective demand for labour due to the reduction in constrained labour supply from $\bar{\ell s}_1$ to $\bar{\ell s}_2$. So, by increasing the tax rate repressed inflation is aggravated on the labour market, given the assumptions made.

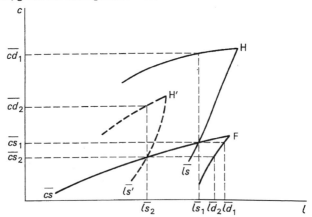

Figure 15.8

Next, assuming that the income effect dominates the substitution effect in labour supply, the $\bar{\ell s}$ locus will shift to the right as a result of a rise in the tax rate, and there will be an increase in the amount of labour offered at each level of the commodity constraint. There is also likely to be a rise in the $\overline{cd}$ locus, given the increase in labour supply, which will expand the H wedge and shift it upwards to the right. The outcome is shown in Figure 15.8 where the $\bar{\ell s}$ locus shifts from $\ell s'$ to $\bar{\ell s}$ and there is a movement along the $\bar{cs}$ locus resulting in a greater level of output and labour supply. At the new equilibrium despite the increase in effective demand on the labour market, there has been a more than compensating increase of effective supply, so that the extent of excess effective demand is reduced.

Classical unemployment
In the classical unemployment regime households are on the long side in both markets while firms do not face any quantity constraints so firms' notional demands are realized (see Figure 15.9). By manipulating the level of g the government is able to bring one of the markets into equilibrium in the sense that there will be zero excess effective demand

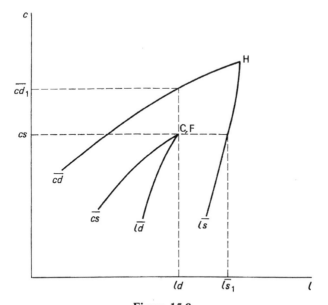

Figure 15.9

in that market. As noted, increasing g shifts the F-system down and to the right. By increasing g by just the required amount the point F would become tangential to the $\bar{\ell s}$ locus, at which point the notional demand for labour would equal the commodity-constrained supply of labour and the amount of work performed by households would increase. At the same time, however, the amount of goods available to households would decline and the constraint on the commodity market would intensify. Conversely, a reduction in g would shift the F-system upwards and to the left and the fall in g would continue until the $\bar{cd}$ locus became tangential to the point F. The goods market would be in equilibrium in that the firms' notional supply of goods matched the labour-constrained demand for goods by households. The actual consumption of households would increase, yet the amount of work carried out by the households would decline. There would actually be an increase in the degree of rationing experienced by households on the labour market.

Assuming no change in g, and considering a change in the tax parameter along with the substitution effect dominating the income effect in labour supply, a fall in t would move the $\bar{\ell s}$ locus to the right. As households are simultaneously constrained on the goods market an increase in purchasing power following a reduction in the tax rate will intensify rationing on the goods market. This will serve to diminish the absolute effect of the fall in t on the $\bar{\ell s}$ locus. Assuming that the latter effect is not strong enough to mitigate the effect of the fall in t then there will be an expansion of the H 'wedge'. There will thus be an increase in the effective supply of labour which will intensify rationing on the labour market. A reduction in the tax rate does not cause a fall in the level of unemployment in this case. Conversely, however, an increase in the tax rate will shift the $\bar{\ell s}$ locus to the left. The tax rate may be reduced until the ℓs locus just touches the point F. Now the notional demand for labour will equal the effective supply from households and the only component of unemployment in the system is voluntary.

Changing the above assumption to allow the income effect to dominate the substitution effect in labour supply causes the results of changing the tax rate to be the opposite of the case just considered. A fall in the tax rate shifts the $\bar{\ell s}$ locus to the left, whereas an increase in t shifts the $\bar{\ell s}$ locus to the right. From this it may be seen that it obviously makes a difference, in attempting to reduce effective excess supply of labour by changes in the tax rate, what assumptions are made about labour supply. In the classical unemployment case, the actual level of employment will not change, however, as a change in t does not affect firms' demand for labour.

Underconsumption

In the underconsumption case firms are on the long side in both markets while households do not experience any quantity constraints, so households' notional demands are realised, as shown in Figure 15.10. Unemploy-

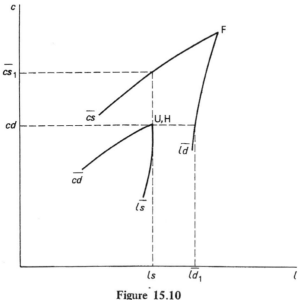

Figure 15.10

ment, as such, does not exist as a problem in this regime. Fiscal policy may be used, however, in an attempt to reduce the extent of excess effective demand and to bring one of the two markets into equilibrium in the sense that there will be zero excess effective demand in that market. Thus if the government chose to reduce g, causing the F-system to shift to the left, until point H became tangential to the $\bar{l}d$ locus, then firms' effective demand for labour would just be matched by the notional supply of labour from households. Firms would, however, be supplying commodities in excess of household's notional demand for them, and there would be a continual build-up of inventories. Firms would only be prepared to finance the accumulation of such inventories as long as they believed they would be able to sell them in future time periods; otherwise they would reduce their demand for labour. Conversely, if the government increased g by such an amount that the F-system shifted down to the right until point H became tangential to the $\bar{cs}$ locus, then firms would be supplying that amount of commodities which just matched households' notional demands for them. On the labour market, however, the rationing of firms would be intensified as the excess effective demand for labour would increase.

Analogous to the Keynesian case, a reduction in the tax rate, assuming that the substitution effect dominates the income effect in labour supply, will shift the H-system to the right and cause the 'wedge' to expand. The tax rate may be reduced until point H just touches the $\overline{\ell d}$· locus so that firms will be able to satisfy their effective demand for labour, although there will still be a build-up of inventories by firms. Assuming that the income effect dominates the substitution effect in labour supply a fall in t will shift the H-system to the left and t may be reduced by just enough to cause point H to meet the $\overline{cs}$ locus. Households would now consume all of the effective supply of goods from firms and there would be no inventory accumulation but the degree of rationing experienced by firms on the labour market would intensify.

An increase in the rate of tax will have the converse results from those indicated above for this regime.

Having considered the basic effects of changing the policy tools in each of the equilibrium regimes it is worthwhile indicating the regime the economy would move into, assuming it was initially at Walrasian equilibrium for the given levels of g and t. Starting with the Walrasian equilibrium as shown in Figure 15.3 an increase in g would move the F-system down to the right. Equilibrium would occur at the intersection of $\overline{\ell s}$ and $\overline{cs}$, so producing repressed inflation. Households would now experience both rationing on the goods market and unemployment. A fall in g, starting from a Walrasian equilibrium, would shift the F-system upwards to the left, so giving rise to Keynesian unemployment, where equilibrium would occur at the intersection of the $\overline{\ell d}$ and $\overline{cd}$ loci.

Assuming that the substitution effect dominates the income effect in labour supply, a reduction in the tax rate will lead to a movement of point H upwards and to the right, with an expansion of the H 'wedge'. This results in classical unemployment where households find themselves rationed on both markets. Alternatively, an increase in the tax rate by shifting the H-system down and to the left will produce undercon-, sumption where firms are on the long side in both markets.

Next, assuming that the income effect dominates the substitution effect in labour supply, a fall in t, starting from Walrasian equilibrium, will shift the H-system to the left, so leading to repressed inflation. An increase in the tax rate however, would shift the H-system to the right, so producing Keynesian unemployment.

V FISCAL POLICY AND MARKET EQUILIBRIUM

It has been shown that prevailing market conditions depend on the values of the parameters of the model, including the values of the fiscal policy parameters g and t. Further, it has been established that four constraint regimes are possible in this model. Keynesian unemployment (regime K); repressed inflation (regime R); classical unemployment (regime C); and underconsumption (regime U).

Ehemann (1974) has attempted to show the connection between these regimes and the fiscal policies that produce them. Allowing the set of alternative fiscal policies to be represented in the non-negative quadrant of the two dimensional space (g,t), then the four regimes can each be associated with a region in (g,t). It follows that each of these regimes will be separated by a locus along which only one good is in effective excess demand or supply and by a point corresponding to multi-market equilibrium (Walrasian equilibrium). It is required to obtain loci satisfying the market equalities $\overline{cd} = cs$, $cd = \overline{cs}$, $\overline{\ell d} = \ell s$, and $\ell d = \overline{\ell s}$ in the (g,t) plane. Along each locus, households or firms (but not both) are in equilibrium. The boundary of regime K is formed by the loci $\overline{\ell d} = \ell s$ and $\overline{cd} = cs$. Along the former loci, commodities, and along the latter, labour, are in effective excess supply. Similar conditions show that regime R is bounded by $\ell d = \overline{\ell s}$ and $cd = \overline{cs}$, regime C by $\ell d = \overline{\ell s}$ and $\overline{cd} = \overline{cs}$; and regime U by $\overline{\ell d} = \ell s$ and $cd = \overline{cs}$. With a model similar to the one developed above Ehemann (1974, p. 48, n.7) establishes that the shapes of these loci are positive in all four cases and are as shown in Figure 15.11. The assumption with respect to the labour market is that the income effect dominates the substitution effect in labour supply.

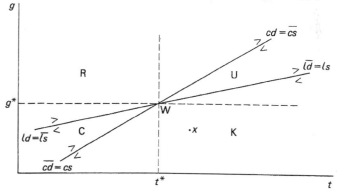

Figure 15.11

Assuming that, for the given values of the parameters in the model, fiscal policy is such that Walrasian equilibrium is achieved we may denote the level of government demand and the tax rate by g^* and t^*. In Figure 15.11 the axes g, t measure the components of fiscal policy and the point (g^*, t^*) is indicated by W. Other points in the fiscal policy space correspond to non-zero levels of effective excess demand or supply in the two markets. With a tax rate in excess of t^* and a level of government demand less than g^* both the commodity market and the labour market will exhibit excess supply. Given lower taxes and higher government demand, the commodity and labour markets will be in excess demand.

The regimes which lie to the 'north-east' and 'south-west' of W will depend on the assumptions of the model. Assuming that the income effect dominates the substitution effect in labour supply and that the initial fiscal policy combination is at point x, a small reduction in the tax rate will decrease effective excess supply in both markets (see Fig. 15.6). A tax reduction can be chosen just large enough that either (i) effective excess supply of commodities is eliminated or (ii) effective excess supply of labour is eliminated, while in the other market excess supply persists. Whether (i) or (ii) occurs depends on other parameters of the model. It is assumed in Figure 15.11 that (i) occurs so that the locus $\overline{cd} = cs$ is encountered. Using the 'wedge' diagrams introduced above, this result is shown in Figure 15.12 (adapted from Figure 15.6) and shows that the H-system has moved to the left until point F just touches the $\overline{cd}$ locus.

If the assumption made about the labour market is changed so that the substitution effect dominates the income effect in labour supply, it may be seen from Figure 15.5 that the locus $\overline{cd} = cs$ will always be encountered first if t is reduced. This assumption with respect to the labour market will be developed later.

Figure 15.11 shows that a greater tax reduction produces effective excess demand for commodities along with effective excess supply of labour, that is, we move into regime C which may be seen by envisaging a further move to the 'north-west' by the H-system in Figure 15.12.[10] A sufficiently large tax reduction may be chosen so that the excess supply of labour is just eliminated. At this point $\ell d = \overline{\ell s}$ and in Figure 15.12 the H-system would have moved so far to the left that point F would just touch the $\overline{\ell s}$ locus. It may be seen that the parameters of the model may be such that an even greater tax reduction produces effective excess demand in both markets, that is, regime R is encountered.

Again assuming the system is at point x, by holding the tax rate constant and increasing government demand the labour market will come to equilibrium first because of the assumption governing the parameters

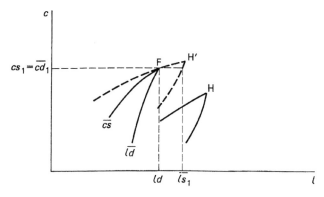

Figure 15.12

of the model that places the $\overline{cd} = cs$ locus to the 'south-west' of W, that is, we come to the $\overline{ld} = ls$ locus first with an increase in g. This is shown in Figure 15.13. A greater increase in government demand for labour jointly with excess supply of goods, that is, the F-system moves further to the right and with firms on the long side in both markets fiscal policy has produced regime U. A sufficiently large increase in government expenditure can be chosen so that effective excess supply of goods is eliminated and locus $cd = \overline{cs}$ is reached; in terms of Figure 15.13 the point H would be cut by the $\overline{cs}$ locus. A still further increase in g produces effective excess demand for both goods, that is, the system moves into regime R.

Returning to possibility (ii), that a policy of tax reduction from the initial point x first eliminates excess supply of labour, again it is noted

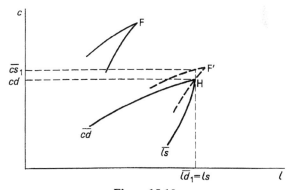

Figure 15.13

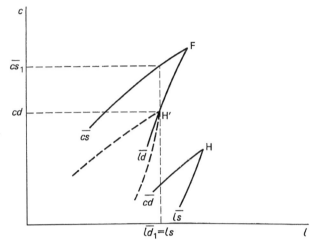

Figure 15.14

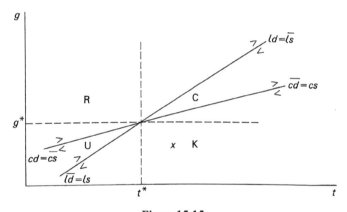

Figure 15.15

that this will not be the case where the substitution effect dominates the income effect in labour supply (see Figure 15.5). As noted, this is consistent with Ehemann's (1974) model which is based on the opposite assumption holding in terms of labour supply. So with a fall in t the locus $\overline{ld} = ls$ is encountered, a result which is shown in Figure 15.14. As the locus $\overline{ld} = ls$ is encountered first this outcome fixes the relative positions in Figure 15.15 of the three remaining loci. A further reduction

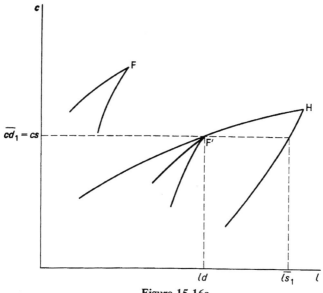

Figure 15.16a

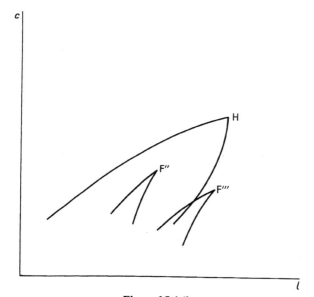

Figure 15.16b

in the tax rate (leftward movement from point x in Figure 15.15) leads to the locus $cd = \overline{cs}$, that is, in Figure 15.14 a further rightward movement of the H-system would take place until the $\overline{cs}$ locus cut the point H'. If the fall in t continues the effect will be to move into regime R, where there is effective excess demand for both goods.

Starting from point x in Figure 15.15 an increase in government demand will take the economy to the locus $\overline{cd} = cs$, then into the C regime. This may be envisaged from Figures 15.16a and 15.16b. With a continued increase in g the economy will ultimately move to the region of effective excess demand for both goods, that is, regime R.

It is apparent from Figures 15.11 and 15.15 that the geometric position of the four regimes in (g,t) space are not uniquely determined. Depending on assumptions made with regard to certain parameters of the model regimes C and U, the regions of effective excess demand in one market and effective excess supply in the other may 'switch' positions. Despite the assumptions made, however, the R and K regimes always occupy the same part of (g,t) space. A fundamental aspect of the model which influences the location of the loci of market equalities in Figures 15.11 and 15.15 is the assumption regarding the labour market. Ehemann (1974) assumed that the income effect dominated the substitution effect in labour supply. Applying that assumption to the manipulation of the 'wedge' diagrams it is not surprising that Ehemann's geometric results are upheld. It is possible though, in general terms, to consider the converse assumption of labour supply to see how (g,t) space may be partitioned. As noted above, if the substitution effect dominates the income effect in labour supply, and the economy is assumed to be in regime K, a fall in the tax rate will initially lead to commodity market equilibrium, that is, the locus $\overline{cd} = cs$ is met in the (g,t) plane. A further reduction of t would lead to regime C, that is, classical unemployment. Starting from a point in regime K and increasing t would lead to labour market equilibrium, that is, the $\overline{\ell d} = \ell s$ locus is encountered with a further increase in the tax rate, moving the economy to regime U.

If a point is chosen in regime R and the tax rate reduced by a small amount initially, the labour market will come to equilibrium along the locus, $\ell d = \overline{\ell s}$. A further fall in t will move the economy into regime C. Again, starting from a point in regime R and raising the tax rate the locus $cd = \overline{cs}$ will be encountered, so producing equilibrium in the commodity market. A further increase in t will move the economy into regime U. Those results are shown in Figure 15.17[11] where the relative positions of the regimes are shown. The slopes of the loci are assumed from a general consideration of the model involving discrete changes

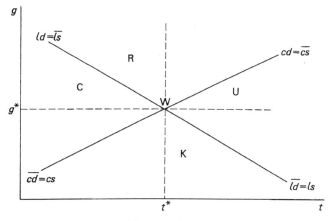

Figure 15.17

between regimes as outlined above. The relative positions of the regimes
and loci are also consistent with changes in government expenditure. If
the economy is at a point in regime C, for example, an increase in g by
shifting the F-system of the 'wedge' diagrams to the right, will first lead
to equilibrium in the labour market where the locus $\ell d = \overline{\ell s}$ is met.
Further increases in g will move the economy into regime R. Conversely,
by starting from a point in regime C and reducing government expenditure
by a small amount, the commodity market will first reach equilibrium on
the $\overline{cd} = cs$ locus. A further fall in g will move the economy into regime K.

It has been shown in Figures 15.11 and 15.15 that a switching of the
regimes C and U in the (g,t) plane is possible if it is assumed the income
effect dominates the substitution effect in labour supply, and given other
parameters of the model. If the converse assumption is made with regard
to labour supply, no such 'switching' occurs and for given changes in
g and t configuration of the regimes will be as shown in Figure 15.17.
From the diagrams drawn in the (g,t) plane, it may be observed that the
correct fiscal policy mix will depend on the assumptions made about the
parameters of the model and especially with respect to labour supply
responses to changes in the tax rate. It is apparent that Walrasian
equilibrium will not be achieved if only one of the policy tools is
used, unless the other happens to coincide with the correct level to
bring about the Walrasian equilibrium. In all the diagrams in (g,t)
space, if excess supply exists in both markets (i.e. the economy
is in regime K) the traditional anti-deflationary policy mix of increasing g and reducing t will only apply to a particular set of the parameters

of the model. In the cases where the income effect dominates the substitution effect in labour supply (Figures 15.11 and 15.15) for certain parameters of the model in regime K a fiscal policy of increasing g and t simultaneously is required, while for other parameters g should be increased while t is reduced. For the converse assumption with regard to labour supply (Figure 15.17) it is always necessary to increase g but for certain parameters it is necessary to reduce t.

Considering regime R, the orthodox policy recommendations would be a reduction in g and a rise in t. This though only applies for certain parameters of the model. Figures 15.11 and 15.15 show it may be necessary to have a policy mix of an increase in both g and t or a fall in both g and t for certain parameters of the model. With the (g,t) plane as partitioned in Figure 15.17 however, the former policy would not apply.

Where the income effect dominates the substitution effect in labour supply, as Ehemann (1974, p. 51) points out, it may be observed from Figures 15.11 and 15.15 that if excess demand exists in one market while there is effective excess supply in the other, then the policy tools must be applied in the opposite direction. So, depending on other parameters of the model, it may be necessary to raise both g and t in regime C, while for a different set of parameters for the model it may be necessary to reduce both. The same is true for regime U. If the converse assumption applies to the labour market, for regime C Figure 15.17 shows that a policy of raising the tax rate is always applicable. For certain parameters of the model an increase in g is required while for others a fall in g is necessary. For regime U in Figure 15.17 a policy of reducing t is always required, for certain parameters a fall in g is required while others necessitate an increase in government spending.

VI   A PROGRESSIVE TAX STRUCTURE

The income tax system considered in the model has been an extremely simple one of proportional taxation. It would be possible though to rework the model for a progressive tax structure. An indication of the way this would affect the model is discussed here by the introduction of the simplest type of progressive tax – that of a proportional tax with exemption. With such a tax individuals whose incomes are below the exemption level or tax threshold pay no tax at all, while those with incomes above this level pay in tax a constant proportion of the difference between their income and the exemption level. As a representative household has been assumed in the model it will make sense to introduce this form of tax system only if the earnings of the household exceed the exemption level, otherwise changes in the tax rate would have no effect. This form of tax system does allow scope, however, for consideration of the effects of changes in the exemption level.

The simple progressive tax system can be represented in the following way: Let

$$T = t(w\ell - a)$$

where

T = tax bill of the household
t = tax rate
w = gross wage rate
ℓ = total number of hours worked at wage rate w
a = exemption level

The household will then have disposable income, Y, given by

$$Y = w\ell - T$$
$$Y = w\ell(1-t) + at$$

which shows that the household's net income is just what it would have been had it been taxed at the rate t on all earned income and then been handed back the amount paid in tax on the first a units of income.

The household's notional demand function for commodities will now be of the form

$$cd = cd(p, w(1-t), mo + at) \tag{15}$$

and where the household is constrained on the labour market the effective demand function for commodities will be of the form:

$$\overline{cd} = \overline{cd}(p, w\ell(1-t), mo + at)$$

Both the unconstrained and the constrained demand functions indicate that the term at will have a pure income effect on commodity demand. The household's notional labour supply function will now include the exemption level as one of its arguments (as will the goods constrained labour supply function):

$$\ell s = \ell s(p, w(1-t), mo + at) \tag{16}$$

The labour supply response to a change in the wage rate is:

$$\frac{\delta \ell s}{\delta w} = \left(\frac{\delta \ell s}{\delta w}\right)_s - \frac{\ell s \delta \ell s}{\delta y} \tag{17}$$

where

$$\omega = w(1-t)$$
$$y = mo + at$$

The sign of (17) may be positive or negative depending on the relative sizes of the substitution and income effects and *a priori* it is indeterminate.

The response of labour supply to a change in the tax rate is:

$$\frac{\delta \ell s}{\delta t} = -w\frac{\delta \ell s}{\delta \omega} + a\frac{\delta \ell s}{\delta y}$$

$$= -w\left(\frac{\delta \ell s}{\delta \omega}\right)_s + (w\ell s + a)\frac{\delta \ell s}{\delta y} \tag{18}$$

Again *a priori* the sign of (18) is indeterminate, but, given the presence of the exemption level in the second term on the right-hand side of (18), it may be argued that the income effect is likely to predominate. Thus with a progressive tax system it is plausible to argue that the income effect will dominate labour supply responses for given changes in the tax rate. As mentioned at the beginning of this chapter this runs against the assumptions of most disequilibrium models so far produced. It does lend support, however, to Ehemann's model in which the income effect dominates the substitution effect. It would appear, then, that the most appropriate analysis of changes in fiscal policy where there is a progressive tax system is given in those parts of Sections IV and V where the income effect dominates.

VII   CONCLUSIONS

It may be argued from the results of Section V that in a model where prices are rigid a reliable qualitative guide to fiscal policy cannot merely rely on qualitative information about the state of effective excess demand in various markets. As Ehemann (1974, p.51) concludes:

'Determining the proper direction of change in fiscal policy, and not just the proper magnitude of change, requires detailed empirical assessment of the aggregate demand and supply functions of market participants.'

It has been one of the objectives of this chapter to show that an important piece of information is that of the labour supply responses of households. Not only is this information necessary to indicate the appropriate fiscal policy but a neglect of such information may exacerbate a situation if a particular fiscal mix is implemented. Comparing regime C in Figures 15.15 and 15.17 for example, given other parameters of the model, where the substitution effect dominates the income effect in labour supply (Figure 15.17), the appropriate policy may be an increase in both g and t. Such a policy mix would only aggravate the situation where the converse assumption holds for the labour market (as in Figure 15.15).

It is obvious that much more work is required in this area. The model presented here is very simple as are the assumptions concerning behaviour in the labour market. As M & P (1978, p. 818) point out, a basic problem arises in aggregating, especially over labour markets where different sub-markets may be in different regimes. A more sophisticated approach would entail the introduction of skill differentials for households. Also the behaviour of the government may be developed to include benefit payments for those experiencing unemployment.

NOTES: CHAPTER 15

1 No 'classical model' as such existed. What is usually meant by this is the prevailing orthodoxy before the publication of the 'General Theory'. Keynes took Pigou's *'The Theory of Unemployment'* (1933) as representative of the classical view.
2 Most of this section is based on Leijonhufvud (1968, Ch. 2)
3 Patinkin (1956).
4 Although the model does owe much to Barro and Grossman (1976).
5 This may constitute a fundamental weakness in the comparative static approach (see M & P, 1978, p. 813).
6 This avoids uniqueness problems (see Hare, 1978) although, as Hildenbrand and Hildenbrand (1978, p. 256) point out, the 'representative' economic agent may not simplify but complicate the analysis.
7 Monetary policy would require another market – that for bonds – and another price – the rate of interest.
8 When, for example, it is assumed that price or wage adjustment clears one of the two markets.
9 For a similar type of diagram used in a slightly different context see Grossman (1971).
10 From the discussion in Section IV, if households are on the long side in both

markets an increase in g will lead to the locus $\ell_d = \overline{\ell_s}$, as shown in Figure 15.13.

11 The discrete changes between regimes which generate Figure 15.17 are not shown in terms of the 'double wedge' diagrams in the text but may be easily constructed by the reader.

Chapter 16

Inflation, Taxation and Income Distribution

This chapter analyzes the effects of unindexed tax systems on the incentive to work and the distribution of income. In a period of rapid inflation real tax rates rise rapidly if nominal taxes are unaltered. Little attention has been paid to the effects of these changes in real tax rates on the supply of labour. Two exceptions are Prest (1973) and Allan and Savage (1974)[1]. This chapter provides both a framework for analysing these changes and an application of the analysis to the British and Australian income tax systems. It is argued that the complexity of the expected effects on labour supply, coupled with the inability to forecast the rate of inflation, means that there are likely to be unforeseen (and unforseeable) effects on both the size and distribution of national income.

We assume throughout that:

(1)   Labour supply decisions are made on an individual rather than say a household basis.

(2)   Income and leisure are both normal goods. (This is consistent with our provisional findings for weekly-paid workers in Great Britain. See Section II.)

(3)   Individuals are free to work as much or as little as they wish.

(4)   All employment income is in the form of an hourly wage.

(5)   The gross hourly wage is the same for each hour worked (i.e. there is no overtime premium).

(6)   Gross hourly wage rates rise at the same rate as prices.

We ignore any secondary impact on labour supply or income distribution arising from the extra tax revenue (due to fiscal drag), except briefly in Section IV.

An earlier draft of this chapter was submitted to the United Kingdom Royal Commission on Income Distribution. Since the chapter was first written steps have been taken to index the UK and Australian income tax systems. Clearly the analysis will no longer apply to these particular countries but it will apply to countries whose tax systems have not been indexed.

The admitted unrealism of some of these assumptions does not weaken our main thesis. We show that complex predictions follow even with these simple assumptions. If the complexity is too great for legislators to foresee when the assumptions are simple, *a fortiori* the same conclusion would follow from a more complex model.

We have restricted our analysis to the effects of totally unindexed tax systems. Recent studies (Tanzi, 1980; OECD, 1975) have shown considerable variation in the extent to which tax systems are adjusted in the light of inflation. (For more detailed calculations of the British case see Allan and Savage (1974) and Paish (1975).)

Where tax systems are fully indexed the present analysis is clearly inapplicable. However the present analysis can readily be extended to include partial adjustments for inflation and we indicate briefly how this can be done at the end of Section II.

In Section I we review the familiar individual labour supply model and in Section II we extend the argument to deal with unindexed tax systems. We show that the predicted effects on labour supply depend both on the shape of the tax schedule and on the rate of inflation. In Section III we illustrate these arguments for the British and Australian tax systems and in Section IV we consider the implications of the analysis for the size and distribution of national income.

I THEORY ASSUMING NO INFLATION

The analysis in this chapter is based on a familiar model of labour supply adapted to deal with the complex budget situations that arise with non-proportional tax. In this section the model is explained assuming constant prices and in the next section it is extended to an inflationary situation.

We assume an independent individual and two homogenous commodities: leisure, which is measured in time, and a consumption good called income. That part of an individual's time not spent in leisure is called work. The individual has an endowment of AN units of non-employment income which may be positive, zero or negative (if, for example, he has net debts or faces a pool tax). The individual is also assumed to have a preference ordering over these commodities which obeys the usual conditions. The individual maximises his utility subject to his budget constraint and so generates a supply of labour function. If the wage rate (W) is constant the budget constraint depends only on AN and W as is illustrated in Figure 16.1. Note that the budget constraint has an intercept (in this case non-employment income) AN and a slope (the net marginal wage rate W). Equilibrium will be at ϵ_1. The effect on hours

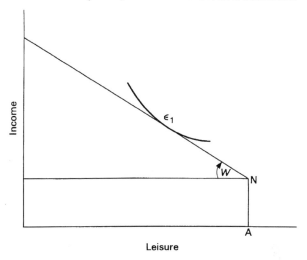

Figure 16.1

of work of a unit change in the wage rate is a price effect (P) and of a
unit change in the intercept is an income effect (Y), and the substitution
effect (S) is found in the usual way ($S = P - YH$ where H is hours
worked).

The introduction of a proportional tax that exempted precisely AN
units of income would thus have a pure price effect. Typically all hours
are not paid at the same net marginal wage rate so the effect of a tax
change will comprise price and income effects, because both the net wage
and the intercept will change. A simple example is given by a proportional tax with an exemption[2]. In Figure 16.2 we assume: non-employment income is zero, income up to Y_1 is exempted from tax and income
above Y_1 is taxed at t_1, the actual budget constraint is CBA and
equilibrium is at ϵ_1. Note that ϵ_1 would also be the equilibrium position if
the budget constraint had been CI. Thus if the individual had non-
employment income of AI and a net wage of W_{N1} he would be in
equilibrium at ϵ_1. If the tax rate were increased from t_1 to t_2 (leaving
the exemption level unchanged at Y_1) the new budget constraint would
be C'BA and the new equilibrium ϵ_2 (ϵ_2 is of course the equilibrium that
would have been chosen if non-employment had been AI' and the net
wage rate had been W_{N2}). The movement from ϵ_1 to ϵ_2 can be thought of
as the sum of two moves. First, there is the move from ϵ_1 to ϵ_3, which is

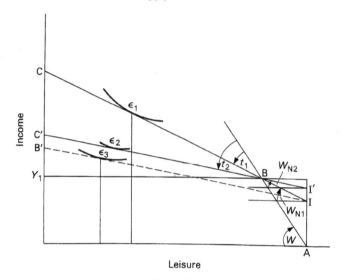

Leisure

Figure 16.2

a price effect caused by the change in the net marginal wage rate with the intercept unchanged. The sign of this effect on hours of work is of course unknown *a priori*. Secondly, there is the move from ϵ_3 to ϵ_2. This move is associated with the change in the intercept from AI to AI'.[3]

The second move is thus equivalent to an increase in non-employment income from AI to AI'. This second move is clearly an income effect and must on its own reduce hours of work (i.e. ϵ_2 must lie to right of ϵ_3). The total effect depends on the sum of the two moves. If the price effect is positive or zero, hours worked will fall. If the price effect is negative, hours worked will rise if the negative price effect more than offsets the positive income effect.

When there are a number of tax brackets with different marginal rates there are a large number of possible tax changes. The tax rates and/or width of brackets in some or all tax brackets can be changed. While there are many possibilities any such changes will alter both the actual and the linearized budget constraints,[4] and will thus have both price and income effects.[5]

II THEORY WITH INFLATION

Inflation has two effects on real tax rates. First, it reduces the real value of tax allowances thus raising the average tax rate and secondly it *may* cause the individual to move into a higher marginal tax rate bracket. The predicted effects on labour supply differ depending on whether or not the second effect is present.

It is convenient to begin with the case where the individual remains in the same tax bracket (i.e. where there is no change in the marginal tax rate). This will occur if he is already in the highest bracket or if his income is sufficiently far below the top of his current band. In Britain the great majority of tax payers are in the first ('basic rate') tax bracket and many will remain in that bracket for several years even with current rates of inflation so this case is of particular interest for Britain. Figure 16.3 aids the exposition. The diagram has *real* income on the vertical axis (thus *W* represents a constant gross real wage). Suppose that in year 1

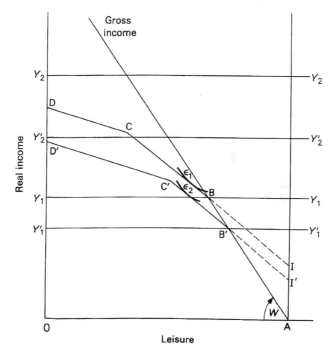

Figure 16.3

the tax system exempts income up to Y_1, taxes income between Y_1 and Y_2 at a tax rate of t_1 and taxes (gross) income of Y_2 or more at a rate of t_2. (t_2 is levied on *gross* incomes above Y_2. Note, however, that the corresponding net income is lower. Thus the *net* income at point C corresponds to a gross income of Y_2.) In this circumstance the budget constraint will be ABCD in year 1. If prices rise by r per cent in year 2 the effect of inflation is to reduce the (gross) income starting point for each band by $1/(1 + r)$. Thus Y_1 becomes $Y_1' (= Y_1/1 + r)$ and Y_2 becomes $Y_2' (= Y_2/1 + r)$ so that in year 2 the budget constraint is AB' C' D'. In year 1 equilibrium is ϵ_1 on the linearized budget constraint CI and in year 2 equilibrium is at ϵ_2 on the linearized budget constraint C' I'. There is by assumption no change in tax band so that the effect is a pure income effect caused by the change in the intercept. The intercept is lower in year 2 because less real income is going untaxed. The effect is the same as the effect of a fall in real non-employment income and

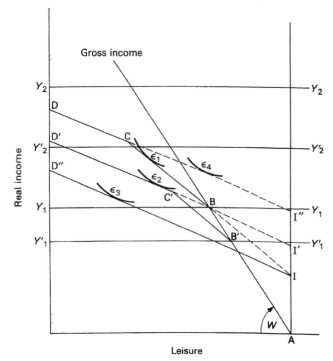

Figure 16.4

should cause the individual to reduce his consumption of both leisure and income (i.e. the individual will work longer hours) given our assumption that leisure and income are both normal goods.

We have established then, that if after labour supply adjustment someone remains in the same bracket he will work harder. This argument has two corollaries. The first is that everyone who in year 1 had a gross income between Y_1 and Y_2 will necessarily work harder in year 2. (If he did not, he would still stay in the same tax bracket, but then our argument guarantees that he will work harder - a contradiction). The second corollary is that everyone with gross income in year 1 between Y_2' and Y_2 will move into a higher tax bracket (i.e. if income in year 1 is in the range between Y_2' and Y_2); there will be both an income effect and a price effect as illustrated in Figure 16.4. Once again the budget constraint changes from ABCD in year 1 to AB' C' D' in year 2 and equilibrium changes from ϵ_1 on the linearized budget constraint CI to ϵ_2 on D' I'. The move from ϵ_1 to ϵ_2 can be thought of as the sum of two moves:

(1) ϵ_1 to ϵ_3, a price effect reflecting the fall in the net marginal wage rate arising from the shift into the higher tax bracket,
(2) an income effect ϵ_3 to ϵ_2.

As shown in the diagram, the intercept I' lies above I. This need not always be the case, for there are two offsetting influences on the intercept. The first influence (I to I') arises from the shift into the higher tax bracket, and just as argued in note 3 (p.268) must raise the intercept. The second influence (I'' to I') arises from the effect of inflation in pulling down the real exemption level of this higher tax bracket. Because the first influence depends on the nature of the tax schedule and the second depends on the rate of inflation it is necessary to calculate these changes for specified tax schedules and specified rates of inflation to find out if the intercept will rise or fall. This is done for British and Australian tax schedules in the next section.

These arguments can be readily extended to more realistic cases where tax bands are changed to partially offset the effects of inflation. For example, if the exemption level were indexed but higher tax bands were not the incentive to those in the lowest tax bracket to work harder would be removed. The starting point for the next bracket would be $Y_2' = Y_2 - (Y_1 - Y_1')$ (not shown in the diagram) rather than $Y_2' = Y_2/(1 + r)$. The partial indexing would mean that everyone would have a higher intercept and this would tend to reduce work relative to the case of no allowance for inflation. While we continue our analysis of the non-indexed case we hope it is clear in principle that the analysis can be readily extended to partial indexation.

III APPLICATION TO BRITISH AND AUSTRALIAN TAX SYSTEMS

The analysis of the previous section is now applied to the 1975 British and Australian tax systems (assuming no allowance for inflation). These two systems were chosen for illustrative purposes because both have relatively high current rates of inflation and because they have quite different tax schedules. The marginal rates schedules (for a married man with one child under 11) for the two countries are plotted on Figure 16.5 (converting Australian \$ into £ at \$1.68 = £1.00). The British schedule has a very wide first (or basic rate) tax band of 35 per cent which includes the great majority of all tax payers. Tax rates then rise by steps to a maximum (for earned income) of 83 per cent. The Australian rates start very much lower, but the tax bands are narrow and rates exceed British rates for middle incomes (if the exchange rate is used for conversion) and fall below British rates at high incomes.

In the last section it was argued that a person will work harder in year

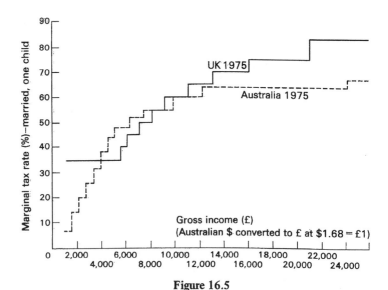

Figure 16.5

2 if his gross income in year 1 is less than the top of the year 1 tax bracket after that tax bracket has been deflated. Whether someone's income remains in the same band depends not only on the width of the bands but also on the rate of inflation and whether the individual is near

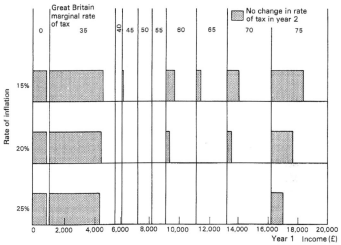

Figure 16.6

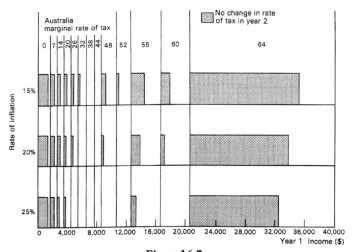

Figure 16.7

the top of the band. Calculations have been made of income levels where work will definitely increase for assumed rates of inflation of 15 per cent, 20 per cent and 25 per cent and are shown in Figure 16.6 for Britain and Figure 16.7 for Australia. In these diagrams the hatched areas show income levels in year 1 such that work will increase in year 2. It can be readily seen that when tax bands are wide and when the rate of inflation is relatively low people are more likely to remain in this hatched area. In Britain this is most likely at relatively low income levels. Neither diagram shows the highest bands (starting at about £21,000 and $40,000) where of course anyone already in the band will remain in the band.

The position is more complex for people who move into higher tax brackets (the unhatched parts of Figures 16.6 and 16.7). It has already been argued that these people will have both price and income effects. While we do not know *a priori* if the price effect will increase or decrease work, the predicted direction of the income effect components is straightforward once we know the sign of the change in the intercept. Calculations of the change in intercept for selected income levels for the two countries are given in Tables 16.1 and 16.2 (using the formula given in note 5) again for a married man with one child. Except when indicated to the contrary all of the selected income levels involve a change in tax bracket.

The pattern of the intercept changes is somewhat different in the two countries. In Britain all but two of the changes are positive and the changes are quite large (up to 11 per cent of net income in year 1). The

Table 16.1   *Change in intercept Great Britain selected income levels[a]*

Year 1 Income £		Year 1 Intercept £	Change in intercept in year 2					
			15% inflation		20% inflation		25% inflation	
			£	%[b]	£	%[b]	£	%[b]
1	5,000	418	+194	+5.3	+168	+4.6	+393	+10.7
2	6,000	703	+178	+4.1	+441	+10.2	+396	+9.2
3	7,000	1,013	+181	+3.7	+472	+9.7	+414	+8.5
4	8,000	1,373	+577	+10.7	+495	+9.2	+422	+7.9
5	9,000	1,783	+167	+2.9	+85	+1.5	+460	+7.9
6	10,000	2,243	+194	+3.1	+91	+1.5	0	0
7	11,000	2,243	+194	+3.4	+641	+11.4	+528	+9.4
8	12,000	2,803	+208	+3.0	+81	+1.2	-32	-0.5
9	15,000	3,463	+252	+3.2	+96	+1.2	-44	-0.6
10	20,000	4,273	+916	+9.9	+699	+7.5	+502	+5.4

[a] Married, one child under 11.

[b] Of *net* income in year one.

Table 16.2 *Change in intercept Australia selected income levels[a]*

Year 1 Gross income $	Year 1 Intercept $	Change in intercept in year 2					
		15% inflation		20% inflation		25% inflation	
		$	%[b]	$	%[b]	$	%[b]
3,000	300	−39[c]	−1.4	−50[c]	−1.7	+114	+4.0
5,000	794	+189	+4.2	+148	+3.3	+111	+2.5
6,000	1,131	+199	+3.8	+143	+2.8	+93	+1.8
9,000	2,330	−302[c]	−4.3	−34	−0.5	−124	−1.8
10,000	2,330	+68	+0.9	−34	−0.5	−124	−1.6
12,000	2,755	−28	−0.3	−143	−1.7	−246	−2.9
15,000	3,134	+316	+3.2	+171	+1.7	+40	+0.4
18,000	3,965	+202	+1.8	+27	+0.2	−131	−1.2
20,000	3,965	+202	+1.7	+27	+0.2	−131	−1.1
30,000	4,790	−623	−4.0	−798	−5.1	−956	−6.1

[a] Married one child under 16
[b] Of *net* income in year one.
[c] No change in tax bracket.

proportion of negative intercept changes (even disregarding the ones due to the person remaining in the same bracket) is larger in Australia and the intercept changes tend to be a smaller proportion of net income. It is also worth noting that while the change in intercept as a proportion of net income tends to be higher at relatively low incomes in both countries this effect is more pronounced in the Australian case.

This somewhat different pattern of intercept changes in the two countries depends on the characteristics of the tax schedules, the initial level of income and the rate of inflation. With a stepped (i.e. discontinuous) tax function it is not easy to characterise the precise way in which these factors cause the intercept to rise or fall.[6]

Nevertheless it is possible to describe in general terms the factors that cause the intercept to change. Narrow tax bands will tend to cause the intercept to rise because it is more likely that the individual will move up one or more tax brackets. If income in any year is near the top of a tax band the intercept is more likely to rise. The intercept will also tend to rise if there is a sharp rise in marginal rate between one bracket and the next. If the rate of inflation is high an individual is more likely to move into a higher bracket (thus raising the intercept) but high rates of inflation also reduce the value of the tax allowances (thus reducing the intercept). These factors explain at least roughly the pattern of intercept changes between the two countries. The sharply rising marginal rates appear to account for the increases in the intercept at low income levels in Australia while the greater proportion of falls in the intercept at higher income levels is associated with the flattening tax schedule. Similarly the positive intercept changes in the British case are associated with the steep schedule of marginal rates (see Figure 16.5 for incomes above about £6,000).

For a given price effect an increase in the intercept will reduce work while a decrease in the intercept will increase work. It has been argued that if inflation carries an individual into a section of the tax schedule with steeply rising marginal rates and narrow bands his intercept will tend to rise, and in these circumstances the income effect can be expected to reduce work, but of course the total effect depends on the price effect as well.

This section has tended to concentrate on the income effect because it is possible to make a statement about it without a detailed empirical knowledge of labour supply. However even the sign of the price effect requires empirical study, which means that it is conceivable that the total effect (price plus income effect) will differ in sign from the income effect alone if the price effect is both of opposite sign and of larger absolute size than the income effect.

A growing body of empirical evidence is now becoming available. See Brown (1980) and Godfrey (1975) for two recent surveys. Our own work on weekly-paid workers in Britain (reported in Part Two of this volume) shows provisional evidence of negative income and price effects. Negative price effects are also consistent with the long-term downward trend in the length of the working week. Most of this evidence relates to low income people. Exceptions are in Break (1957), Fields and Stanbury (1971), Barlow, Brazer and Morgan (1966).

IV IMPLICATIONS FOR INCOME DISTRIBUTION

The analysis of labour supply effects is now extended to the size and distribution of national income.

The *gross* incomes of all those who work longer will rise. Thus all those who remain in the same tax bracket will have higher gross incomes. Those who move into higher tax brackets may have higher or lower gross incomes. While it is possible to identify whether an individual will move into a higher tax bracket and to discover if his intercept will rise or fall, it is not possible without a detailed knowledge of labour supply to predict if he will work more or less. Total gross income may thus rise or fall. It seems likely that there will be complex changes in the distribution of gross incomes between those that move into higher brackets and those that remain in the same bracket.

Total *net* income will clearly fall as average tax rates rise. If there were no labour supply adjustments it is almost certain that the distribution of net income would become more equal but it is not possible to be categorical about this given labour supply adjustments.

When discussing net incomes it is important to remember that the effects of changes in government revenue are ignored. Clearly there are a variety of ways the extra revenue might be used; for example, if the money were paid out in the form of a uniform lump-sum handout the total change in net income would equal the total change in gross income and the distribution of income would be more equal. The handout would of course cause everyone to work less so that total income might well fall.

While there is a popular preoccupation with the distribution of income, as economists we are also interested in the distribution of welfare and would wish to include leisure in our measure of welfare which implies some kind of weighting system between income and leisure.

V CONCLUSIONS

The analysis in this chapter has been conducted with a whole range of restrictive assumptions. Some of these assumptions (e.g. no extra payment for overtime hours) could be readily relaxed within the present framework. Others are more difficult and would require a full general equilibrium analysis to incorporate. For example, it was assumed at the outset that wages increased at the same rate as prices. It was then argued that it is likely that labour supply will alter. If the wage rate is at all responsive to labour supply this calls into question the initial assumption.

This means that the conclusions are at best highly simplified. That would be a serious drawback if the intention were to make confident predictions about the detailed effects of an unindexed system. However, the intention is in fact very different. We all know that real tax rates will rise rapidly with an unindexed system in an inflationary period. It is suggested here that these real tax changes will have complex effects depending not only on the characteristics of the tax system but also on the rate of inflation, which probably could not be accurately predicted even if all the other problems could be solved. Even if it were possible to accurately predict the effects of an unindexed system there would be ample scope for disagreement about whether the predicted changes were desirable or otherwise. We believe the arguments in this chapter strengthen the case for indexing the tax system so that changes in real tax rates come about not through failure to control inflation but because a case has been made for change.

NOTES: CHAPTER 16

1 Prest is brief: 'A prolonged period of inflation must be expected to raise nominal incomes and shift people into higher income tax brackets thus raising both average and marginal tax rates, with the usual conflict between income and substitution effects on work incentives.'

2 Except for a small minority of tax payers who pay higher rates of tax, the British income tax is such a tax so the example is not unrealistic.

3 The argument behind this rise in the intercept is as follows. In treating the individual as if he had the linear budget constraint CI, we are effectively taxing all of his income at the rate t_1 but giving back to him in a lump-sum handout the tax he now has to pay on the first Y_1 units of income. The higher the tax rate the greater the amount of money that has to be handed back.

4 Unlike the case discussed in the previous paragraph the intercept may either rise or fall depending on the parameters of the old and new tax schedules.

5 The price effect is $\partial H/\partial MW$ where H is hours worked and MW the marginal wage. The income effect is $\partial H/\partial I$ where I is the intercept. I can be calculated from the formula:

$$I^i = I^{i-1} + (t^{i'} - t^{i-1})\, Y^{i-1}$$

where I^i is the intercept associated with the ith tax bracket and Y^i is the gross income at the top of the ith tax bracket.

6 A formal characterization of the position for a continuous tax function is as follows: Let real gross income be Y, r the rate of inflation and $T(pY)$ the tax paid when the price level is p. Then the real intercept is

$$I(Y,p) = Y - \frac{T(pY)}{p} - Y\,[1 - T'(pY)]$$

where $T'(pY)$ is the marginal rate of tax.

If the price level is rising at the rate of r per cent then the rate of change of the real intercept is given by

$$\dot{I} = (Y, p, r) = \frac{dI}{dt}(Y,p) = \frac{T(pY)}{p}\, r - T'(pY)\, Yr + Y^2\, T''(pY)\, pr$$

that is,

$$\dot{I}(YrT'(pY))\left(\eta - 1 + \frac{A}{M}\right),$$

where η is the elasticity of the marginal rate of tax with respect to (money) income, A is the average rate of tax and M is the marginal rate of tax.

It can be seen that in this continuous case the change in the intercept depends on the rate of inflation, the average and marginal tax rates and the rate of change of the marginal tax rate.

Bibliography

Allen, R. I. G. and Savage, D. (1974), 'Inflation and the personal income tax', *National Institute Economic Review* (November), pp. 61–71.

Allingham, M. G. (1972), 'The measurement of inequality', *Journal of Economic Theory*, vol. 5, pp. 163–96.

Ashworth, J. and Ulph, D. T. (1977a), 'Estimating labour supply with piecewise linear budget constraints', University of Stirling, mimeo. (revised version now Chapter 6).

Ashworth, J. and Ulph, D. T. (1977b), 'On the structure of family labour supply decisions', University of Stirling, mimeo. (revised version now Chapter 9).

Aspin, A. A. (1949), *Biometrika*, vol. 36, p. 290.

Barlow, R., Brazer, H. E. and Morgan, J. N. (1966) *Economic Behaviour of the Affluent* (Washington, D.C: Brookings Institution).

Bowen, W. G. and Finegan, T. A. (1969), *The Economics of Labour Force Participation* (Princeton, NJ: Princeton University Press).

Branson, W. H. (1972), *Macroeconomic Theory and Policy* (New York: Harper and Row).

Break, G. F. (1957), 'Income taxes and incentives to work: an empirical study', *American Economic Review*, vol. 47, pp. 529–49.

Brown, C. V. (1968), Misconceptions about income tax and incentives, *Scottish Journal of Political Economy*, vol. XV, pp. 1–21.

Brown, C. V. (1980), *Taxation and the Incentive to Work* (Oxford: Oxford University Press).

Brown, C. V. and Jackson, P. M. (1978), *Public Sector Economics* (Oxford: Martin Robertson).

Brown, C. V. and Levin, E. (1972), 'Misconceptions about taxation and the tax credit scheme', Mimeo.

Brown, C. V. and Levin, E. (1974), 'The effects of income taxation on overtime: the results of a national survey', *Economic Journal*, vol. 34 (December) (revised version now Chapter 4).

Brown, C. V., Levin, E. and Ulph, D. T. (1974), 'On taxation and labour supply', University of Stirling Discussion Paper No. 30.

Brown, C. V., Levin, E. and Ulph, D. T. (1976), 'Estimates of labour hours supplied by married male workers in Great Britain', *Scottish Journal of Political Economy*, vol. 23 (November) (revised version now Chapter 5).

Brown, C. V., Levin, E. and Ulph, D. T. (1977), 'Inflation, taxation and income distribution', in V. Halberstadt and A. Culyer (eds.), *Public Economics and Human Resources* (Paris: editions Cujas), (revised version now Chapter 16).

Burtless, G. and Hausman, J. (1978), 'The effect of taxation and labour supply – evaluating the Gary negative income tax experiment', *Journal of Political Economy*, vol. 86, pp. 1103–30.

Cain, G. C. and Watts, H. (eds.) (1973), *Income Maintenance and Labor Supply* (Chicago, Ill: Markham Press).

Chow, G. C. (1960), 'Tests of equality between sets of coefficients in two linear regressions', *Econometrica,* vol. 28, pp. 591–605.

Christenson, L. R., Jorgenson, D. W. and Lau, L. J. (1973), 'Transcendental logarithmic utility functions', Technical Report No. 94, Institute for Mathematical Studies in Social Sciences, University of Stanford.

Clower, R. (1965), 'The Keynesian Counter-Revolution. A theoretical appraisal' in F. Hahn and F. Brechling (eds), *The Theory of Interest Rates* (London: Macmillan), pp. 103–25.

Cohen, M. S., Rea, S. A., Jr. and Lerman R. I. (1970), 'A micro-model of labour supply', BLS Staff paper no. 4, US Department of Labor, Washington, DC.

De Vanzo, J. and Greenberg, D. H. (1973), *Suggestions for assessing Economic and Demographic Effects of Income Maintenance Programs,* Rand (R-1211-EDA), Santa Monica, California.

Dixit, A. (1978), 'The balance of trade in a model of temporary equilibrium with rationing', *Review of Economic Studies,* vol. XLV (3), no. 141.

Ehemann, C. (1974), 'General disequilibrium, fiscal policy and a wage-price freeze', *Economic Inquiry* (March), pp. 35–52.

Feldstein, M. (1973), 'On the optimal progressivity of the income tax', *Journal of Public Economics,* vol. 2 (November), pp. 357–76.

Fields, D. B. and Stanbury, W. T. (1971), 'Income taxes and incentives to work: some additional empirical evidence', *American Economic Review,* vol. 61, pp. 435–43.

Fleisher, B. M., Parsons, D. O. and Porter, R. D. (1973), 'Asset adjustments and labor supply of older workers', in G. G. Cain and H. W. Watts (eds), *Income Maintenance and Labor Supply* (Chicago, Ill.: Markham Press).

Gill, P. E. and Murray, W. (1973), 'Safeguarded steplength algorithms for optimisation using descent methods', National Physical Laboratory Report NAC 37.

Glaister, K. W., McGlone, A. and Ulph, D. T. (1979) 'Labour supply responses to tax changes: a simulation exercise for the UK', paper presented to the SSRC/NBER Conference on Econometric Studies in Public Finance, Cambridge, (revised version now Chapter 12).

Glaister, K. W. and Ruffell, R. J. (1979a), 'Single workers: labour supply and preferences', University of Stirling, Department of Economics, Discussion Paper No. 66, (revised version now in Chapter 7).

Glaister, K. W. and Ruffell, R. J. (1979b), 'On preferences and the labour supply of single workers: a further investigation', University of Stirling, Department of Economics, mimeo. (revised version now in Chapter 7).

Godfrey, L. (1975), 'Theoretical and empirical aspects of taxation and the labour supply' (Paris: OECD).

Goldfield, S. M. and Quandt, R. E. (1972), *Nonlinear Methods in Econometrics* (Amsterdam: North Holland).

Greenberg, D. H. (1972), 'Problem of model specification and measurement', in *The Labor Supply Function,* Report R1085 EDA.

Greenhalgh, C. R. (1976), 'Estimating labour supply functions with progressive taxation of earnings', Centre for the Economics of Education.

Greenhalgh, C. (1977), 'A labour supply function for married women in Great Britain', *Economica*, vol. 44.

Greenhalgh, C. R. (1979), 'Participation and hours of work for married women in Great Britain', University of Southampton Discussion Paper No. 7905.

Grossman, H. (1971), 'Money, interest and prices in market disequilibrium' *Journal of Political Economy*, vol. 79, pp. 943–61.

Hall, R. E. (1973), 'Wages, incomes and hours of work in the US labor force', in G. C. Cain and H. Watts (eds.), *Income Maintenance and Labor Supply* (Chicago, Ill. : Markham Press).

Hanoch, G. (1976) *Hours and Weeks in the Theory of Labour Supply*, Rand, Santa Monica, California.

Hare, P. G. (1978), 'Non-uniqueness of constrained demand equilibrium', University of Stirling, Department of Economics, Discussion Paper No. 63.

Hare, P. G. and Ulph, D. T. (1980), 'The welfare economics of private and public education', in D. A. Currie and W. Peters (eds.), *Contemporary Economic Analysis*, vol. 2 (London: Croom Helm).

Heckman, J. J. and Killingsworth, M. R. (1979), 'Recent theoretical and empirical studies of labour supply: a partial survey', HM Treasury Conference, Magdalen College, Oxford, mimeo.

Hicks, J. (1965), *Capital and Growth* (London: Oxford University Press).

Hildebrand, K. and Hildebrand, W. (1978), 'On Keynesian equilibria with unemployment and quantity rationing', *Journal of Economic Theory*, vol. 18, pp. 255–77.

Hill, C. R. (1973), 'The determinants of labor supply for the working urban poor', in G. C. Cain and H. W. Watts (eds), *Income Maintenance and Labor Supply* (Chicago, Ill. : Markham Press).

Holland, D. H. (1977), 'The effect of taxation on incentives in higher income groups', in *Fiscal Policy and Labour Supply* (London: Institute for Fiscal Studies).

Kendall, S. (1967), *The Advanced Theory of Statistics*, Vol. 2, 2nd edn, pp. 139–48.

Keynes, J. M. (1936), *General Theory of Employment, Interest and Money* (London: Macmillan).

Killingsworth, M. R. (1973), 'Neo-classical labour supply models: a survey of recent literature on determinants of labour supply at the micro level', Fisk University, Nashville, Tenn., mimeo.

Kolm, S. CH. (1969), 'The optimal production of social justice', in G. Margolis and H. Gruitton (eds), *Public Economics* (New York/ London: Macmillan).

Kosters, M. (1969), 'Effects of an income tax on labor supply', in A. C. Harberger and M. J. Bailey (eds), *The Taxation of Income from Capital* (Washington, DC: Brookings Institution).

Layard, P. R. G. and Zabalza, A. (1979), 'Family income distribution: explanation and policy evaluation', *Journal of Political Economy*, vol. 87, pp. 5133–5161.

Layard, R., Greenhalgh, C. and Zabalza, A. (1977) 'Married women's participation and hours', Centre for Labour Economics, LSE Discussion Paper No. 29.

Leijonhufvud, A. (1968), *On Keynesian economics and the Economics of Keynes* (London: Oxford University Press).

Leuthold, J. H. (1968), 'An empirical study of formula income transfers and the work decision of the poor', *Journal of Human Resources,* vol. 3 pp. 312–23.

Mahoney, T. A. (1961), 'Factors determining the labour force participation of married women', *Industrial and Labour Relations Review,* vol. 14.

Malinvaud, E. (1966), *Statistical Methods of Econometrics,* 1st edn (Amsterdam' North Holland).

Malinvaud, E. (1977), *The Theory of Unemployment Reconsidered* (Oxford: Blackwell).

McGlone, A. and Ruffell, R. J. (1978a), 'Preferences and the labour supply of married women', University of Stirling, Department of Economics, Discussion Paper No. 62 (revised version in Chapter 7).

McGlone, A. and Ruffell, R. J. (1978b), 'Preferences and the labour supply of married women', *Economic Letters,* vol. 1, pp. 167–8 (revised version in Chapter 7).

McGlone, A. and Ruffell, R. J. (1979), 'Preferences and the labour supply of married men', University of Stirling, Department of Economics, Discussion Paper No. 65 (revised version in Chapter 7).

Mirrlees, J. A. (1971), 'An exploration in the theory of optimum income taxation', *Review of Economic Studies,* vol. 38, pp. 175–208.

Mirrlees, J. A. (1977), 'Labour supply behaviour and optimal taxes', in *Fiscal Policy and Labour Supply* (London: Institute for Fiscal Studies).

Mirrlees, J. A. (1978), 'Arguments for Government expenditure' in M. Artis and A. R. Nobay, *Contemporary Contributions to Economic Analysis'* (Oxford: Basil Blackwell 1978).

Muellbauer, J. and Portes, R. (1978), 'Macroeconomic models with quantity rationing', *The Economic Journal,* vol. 88, pp. 788–821.

OECD (1975), 'The adjustment of personal income tax systems for inflation' (Paris: OECD).

Paish, F. W. (1975), 'Inflation, personal incomes and taxation', *Lloyds Bank Review* (April), pp. 1–20.

Patinkin, D. (1956), *Money, Interest and Prices* (New York: Harper and Row).

Peckham, G. (1970), 'A new method for minimising a sum of squares without calculating gradients', *The Computer Journal,* vol. 13, no. 4, pp. 418–20.

Pigou, A. C. (1933), *The Theory of Unemployment* (London: MacMillan).

Powell, M. J. D. (1964), 'An efficient method for finding the minimum of a function of several variables without calculating derivatives, *The Computer Journal,* vol. 7, pp. 155–62.

Prest, A. R. (1973), 'Inflation and the public finances', *The Three Banks Review* (March), pp. 3–29.

Robinson, P., Athanasious and Head, B. (1969), 'Measures of occupational attitudes and occupational attitudes', Institute for Social Research, University of Michigan, Michigan.

Rosen, H. P. (1976), 'Taxes in a labour supply model with joint wage-hours determination', *Econometrica*, vol. 44, pp. 485–507.

Smith, C. *et al.* (1965), 'Cornell studies of job satisfaction: I, II, III, IV, V, VI', Cornell University, mimeo.

Stern, N. H. (1976), 'On the specification of models of optimum income taxation', *Journal of Public Economics*, vol. 6, pp. 123–62.

Tanzi, V. (1980), *Inflation and the Personal Income Tax: An International Perspective* (Cambridge: Cambridge University Press).

Theil, H. (1971), *Principles of Econometrics* (London: Wiley).

Tobin, J. (1972), Inflation and unemployment', *American Economic Review* (March).

Ulph, D. T. (1978b), 'Labour supply, taxation and measures of in-equality', University College, London, mimeo (revised version now Chapter 11).

Ulph, D. T. (1978a), 'On labour supply and the measurement of in-equality', *Journal of Economic Theory*, vol. 19, no. 2.

Wales, T. J. and Woodland, A. D. (1979), 'Labour supply and progressive taxes', *Review of Economic Studies*, vol. 46, pp. 83–95.

Watts, H. W. and Rees, A. (1977), *The New Jersey Income Maintenance Experiment*, Vol. 2 (New York: Academic Press).

Whalley, J. (1975), 'A general equilibrium assessment of the 1973 United Kingdom tax reform', *Economica*, vol. 42, pp. 139–61.

Wolberg, J. R. (1967), *Prediction Analysis* (Princeton NJ: Van Nostrand).

Index

hours, and effect of income taxation on, 22, 23, *24,* 25, 26, 28, 29, 34; and piecewise linear budget constraints (endogeneity II) 106, *107,* 108, 115, *138, 140;* and effects of preferences variables 86-91, 100, 141-2; tax changes, and labour supply response to, *see* tax changes results

men, single 97-9; overtime hours, and effect of income taxation on 22, 23, *24,* 26, 28; *see also* single people

minimand *107,* 109, 110

minimum distance estimation 110-11, 112, 116

model, basic, of labour supply 35-52; constraints 49-50, *see also* piecewise linear budget constraints; definitions of variables in 40-6, 48; econometric objections to 38-40; and elementary theory of labour supply 35-7; and lowered elasticity of substitution 55; and non-hourly payment systems 48; and preferences, *see* preferences; and restrictive functional form 54, 55; and working wives 49

NCH, *see* dependants

need; and applicability of basic model 50-1; and labour supply responses to tax changes 185

neoclassical model, of family labour supply decisions 117, 118, 130-2, 183; endogeneity bias 131; results of 125-30; specification of 121, 123; utility function of 121-2; *see also* macroeconomic model

n-good case, and measurement of inequality 151-4

non-commodity model 145-51; the *n*-good case 152-4; the one-good case 146-51

non-employment income: in basic model 38-9, 40, 43, *44;* in household models 118, 124-5, 127, 131; in piecewise linear budget constraints model (endogenity I) 55, 60, 67; in preferences model 71; *see also* intercept

non-hourly payment systems, and applicability of basic model 48

non-proportional taxes, and macroeconomic implications 218-20

non-response bias 12, *14*-15, 20, 45; and unemployment 16

non-working time, *see* leisure

occupation of population sample, and comparison with 1971 Census *18*

OCH, *see* dependants one-good case, and measurement of inequality 146-51

one-good case, and measurement of inequality 146-51

optimal income taxation, implications for **189-212**; and Feldstein's model of government expenditure benefit 190-1, 194-6; full optimum analysis 202-11; general treatment of government expenditure 196-202; optimal linear tax rates 192-*3*; simple model of 191-4

origins, of project 1

'other income': in basic model 44-6, *47,* 60, *136;* measurement of, difficulties arising 45; in piecewise linear budget constraints model 60, *138* overtime hours for men, and effect of income taxation on 21-34; constraints *24,* 28-9, *32-3,* 50, 52; and household models 124; limitations of results 30-1; plausibility of claims *24,* 26-8, *32-3;* net effect 29-30; and piecewise linear budget constraints model (endogeneity I) 59, 60; taxation claims 23-6

utility functions: and Feldstein's model of government expenditure benefit, *see* Feldstein's model; of household models 118, 120, 121-4; and the one-good case 146-51; and optimal income taxation, *see* optimal income taxation; and the *n*-good case 151-4; *see also* direct utility function, indirect utility function

virtual income, *see* intercept

wage rate: definition of in basic model 42-3; and elementary theory of labour supply 36, 37, 40; in piecewise linear budget constraints model (endogeneity I) 55, 57; *see also* marginal wage rate

Walra's Law 225-6, 243

wealth (COMY, WLTH); as a preference variable: for married men *89-91*, 108; for married women 77-9, 81, *83-5;* for single people 94, *95-7*

WLTH, *see* wealth

women: low hours worked and truncation bias *19*, 20; overtime hours worked 21; population sample, and comparison with 1971 Census *16-18; see also* women, married; single people

women, married: and results with basic model *47*, 49, 114-15; and

household models, *see* household models; and outside work 9, 114-15, 185; and piecewise linear budget constraints model (endogeneity I) 60, 61, *63*, 64, 65; and piecewise linear budget constraints model (endogeneity II) 106, *107*, 108, 112, 116, *138;* preferences of, *see* women, married, preferences of

women, married, preferences of **72-86**, 100; age 81-2, *83-5;* demands on leisure time (TASS, TIME) 77, *83-5;* dependants (YINF, XINF) 75-7, *83-5*, 86; education (EDUC) 80-1, *83-5*, 86; energy (ENER) 80, *83-5;* job satisfaction (SAT) 80, 81, *83-5;* results of 82-6, 141-2; selection of sample 72-4; unemployment of one main earner (UME) 79, *83-5;* wealth (COMY, WLTH) 77-9, 81, *83-5*

women, single 97-9; *see also* single people

work constraints: and applicability of basic model 49-50, 52; and number of hours overtime worked 28, *32-3*, 34

workers: definition of 5-6; and small cell bias 11; *see also* men, women

XINF, *see* dependants

YINF, *see* dependants

Printed in Great Britain
by Amazon